"*Anxiety, Psychoanalysis and Law: Confronting Chaos*, edited by Ronald Doctor, Adrianne Harris and Plinio Montagna is a remarkable second book produced by the IPA Psychoanalysis and Law Committee. It is published at a dramatic moment of the world, full of anxiety, wars, uncertainty, generalized fear of the future, environmental disasters strongly connected with human attacks to nature, and the increasing presence of totalitarian leaders who threaten the law and the global geopolitics established and maintained after the end of the Second World War. What has psychoanalysis to say about the world we live in and which are the áreas in which it is contributing with analytic listening, thinking and intervening? I strongly recommend this ensemble of contributions from some of our most distinguished authors who bring their thoughts and experience and show the vitality and strong presence of our discipline in order to face current challenges and confront the prevailing chaos."

Cláudio Laks Eizirik, *Professor Emeritus of Psychiatry,*
Federal University of Rio Grande do Sul, Former IPA President,
Training and Supervising Analyst, Porto Alegre Psychoanalytic Society

"With a new Dark Ages descending on us, no book is more crucially needed than this for confronting the chaos of a world in which unbridled power, greed and hatred have been unleashed. Psychoanalysis has no greater contribution to make these days than such an incisive and brilliantly thoughtful inquiry and approach as is in this remarkable and desperately needed work. Deeply thoughtful and wise, it is eminently readable, not merely to be recommended, but to be prescribed. It is clear, it is profound, and it is *essential*."

Warren Poland, *author of* Intimacy and Separateness in Psychoanalysis

Anxiety, Psychoanalysis and Law

Anxiety, Psychoanalysis and Law examines the challenges of maintaining a psychoanalytic stance when working in chaotic times, with international contributors reflecting not only on their work with severely disturbed patients, but also during times of massive disturbances in society.

Presented in five parts, the book considers war, violence, society, pandemics and the family, with chapters reflecting on environmental destruction, new technologies, women's healthcare, digital media and racial injustices. This cutting-edge collection also considers whether it is possible to make sense of these ambiguous and confusing times by looking at the issues from individual clinical work with patients who have had contact with the judicial process – from the bottom up.

Anxiety, Psychoanalysis and Law will be essential reading for psychoanalysts in practice and in training, as well as psychiatrists, psychologists and social and political scientists interested in global anxiety and the challenges facing society.

Ronald Doctor is a fellow and a training analyst of the British Psychoanalytical Society and the Association of Child Psychotherapy. He was a past consultant psychiatrist in psychotherapy at the West London NHS Trust, UK. He is Chair of the IPA Psychoanalysis and Law Committee.

Adrienne Harris was a past faculty and supervisor at both New York University and the Psychoanalytic Institute of Northern California as well as being an editor of Psychoanalytic Dialogues, and Studies in Gender and Sexuality.

Plinio Montagna, MD, is a psychoanalyst, training analyst and past president of the Brazilian Society of Psychoanalysis of São Paulo and the Brazilian Federation of Psychoanalysis. He was the past chair of the Committee of Psychoanalysis and Law for the International Psychoanalytical Association and former member of its Board of Representatives. He also works as a psychiatric and psychoanalytic expert in family courts in São Paulo, Brazil.

IPA in the Community

Series Editor: Harvey Schwartz

For more information about this series, please visit: www.routledge.com/
IPA-in-the-Community/book-series/IPAC

Anxiety, Psychoanalysis and Law

Confronting Chaos

Edited by
Ronald Doctor, Adrienne Harris and Plinio Montagna

Routledge
Taylor & Francis Group

LONDON AND NEW YORK

Designed cover image: Avril Doctor: 'Hanging on'.

First published 2026
by Routledge
4 Park Square, Milton Park, Abingdon, Oxon OX14 4RN

and by Routledge
605 Third Avenue, New York, NY 10158

Routledge is an imprint of the Taylor & Francis Group, an informa business

British Library Cataloguing in Publication Data
A catalogue record for this book is available from the British Library

Library of Congress Cataloging-in-Publication Data
A catalog record has been requested for this book

ISBN: 9781041086147 (hbk)
ISBN: 9781041086130 (pbk)
ISBN: 9781003646266 (ebk)

DOI: 10.4324/9781003646266

Typeset in Palatino
by Taylor & Francis Books

Contents

Contributors

Jurenice Picado Alvares is an effective member of the Brazilian Psycho-analytic Society of São Paulo and of the IPA; Professor at Instituto Durval Marcondes of the Sociedade Brasileira de Psicanálise de São Paulo (SBPSP) and Co-coordinator of a project to combat domestic violence at the SBPSP Community Service Directorate. He is the founding member and current President of the Center for Psycho-analysis of Santos and Region/NPSR. He is also an author of several articles in journals, including journals of psychoanalysis on the feminine, adolescence, gender and sexualities.

Alejandro Luis Bègue, MD, is a psychiatrist and psychogerontologist. He is a training candidate of the Ángel Garma Institute (APA).

Claudia Borensztejn, MD, is a psychoanalyst. She is a former President of the Argentine Psychoanalytical Association (APA) (2016–20), Latin American representative of the IPA Board (2021–23) and editor of the *Dictionary of Argentine Psychoanalysis*.

Louis Brunet is a psychologist, training analyst and Director of the Canadian Institute of Psychoanalysis QE. He was Professor and Director of the Psychology Department, Université du Québec à Mon-tréal, 1996–2023 and is an ex-President of the Canadian Psychoanalytic Society. He holds the Citation of Merit from the Canadian Psycho-analytic Society and is editor of the *Canadian Journal of Psychoanalysis*. He is a member of the International Psychoanalytic Association, and of the IPA Board (2019–23), and the author of more than 180 publications, including seven books. He is an Invited Professor at the Université Lyon 2 (France), Université Paris-Descartes (France) and the Université Paris-Nanterre (France). His main research fields are functions of the analyst for narcissistic identity suffering patients, destructivity in the psychoanalytic process and in social violence (terrorism and radicali-sation) and projective identification and containing function in the psychoanalytic process.

Olga Cartañá is a psychologist, UBA psychoanalyst, full IPA member.

Gley P. Costa is a doctor, psychiatrist and psychoanalyst. He is a founding, full and training member of the Brazilian Psychoanalytic Society of Porto Alegre and Professor at the Mário Martins University Foundation. He is also the author of several books on psychoanalysis, including *Dynamics of Marital Relationships* (1992), *Conflicts of Real Life* (2005), *The Conjugal Scene* (2000) and *Love and Its Labyrinths* (2007).

Ronald Doctor is a past Consultant Psychiatrist in Medical Psychotherapy, West London NHS Trust, and has a private psychoanalytical practice. He is a fellow and training analyst of the British Psychoanalytical Society, senior member of the British Psychotherapy Foundation, Chair of the IPA Committee of Psychoanalysis and Law and past board member of the International Association for Forensic Psychotherapy. He is Visiting Professor of the University of Ngoya (2024) and Co-ordinator of the Klein Module of the master's degree in psychoanalysis at University College London (UCL). He has edited two books, *Dangerous Patients: A Psychodynamic Approach to Risk Assessment and Management* (2003) and *Murder; a Psychotherapeutic Investigation* (2008), contributed chapters to numerous books, including *Psychoanalysis, Law and Society* (2019) and published papers, including 'History, Murder and the Fear of Death' (2015).

María Cristina Fernández is a psychologist (UBA), APA psychoanalyst, APA group committee coordinator and an IPA member.

Adrienne Harris, PhD, is on the faculty, and is supervisor of, the New York University (NYU) Postdoctoral Program in Psychotherapy and Psychoanalysis, also known as the NYU Postdoc. She is also a professor at the New School for Social Research, where she teaches, and where she founded (with Lewis Aron and Jeremy Safran), the Sandor Ferenczi Centre. She is on the faculty, and is supervisor of, the Psychoanalytic Institute of Northern California (PINC). She is an editor of *Psychoanalytic Dialogues* and *Studies in Gender and Sexuality*.

Cândida Sé Holovko is a member of the Brazilian Psychoanalytic Society of São Paulo and of the IPA; Professor at the Instituto Durval Marcondes of SBPSP; Co-chair of the Committee on Women and Psychoanalysis, COWAP-IPA for Latin America (2014 to August 2017) and member of the Pierre Marty-IPSO-Paris Institute of Psychosomatics. She is also Coordinator of the Psychoanalytic Psychosomatics Study Group at the School of Paris at SBPSP, and Co-coordinator of a project to combat domestic violence at the SBPSP Community Service Directorate. She is the author of national and international articles on femininities, masculinities, gender, sexual violence and psychoanalytic psychosomatics.

Osamu Kitayama, MD, after his medical studies, started psychoanalytic training in London and qualified at the Japanese Psychoanalytic Institute in 1984. He is a professor at Kyushu University, President of the Japan Psychoanalytic Society (2016–19) and now President of Hakuoh University, while also working with patients in private practice. He is the author of articles in the *International Journal of Psychoanalysis*, and books such as *Prohibition of Don't Look* (2011).

Shimpei Kudo is a candidate of the Japan Psychoanalytic Society, a boarding member of the Japanese Association of Criminal Psychology and a member of the International Association for Forensic Psychotherapy. He is Associate Professor at the Student Service, Nagoya University. He also conducts psychotherapy in private practice, providing psychotherapy services to people suffering from delinquency and criminal problems. In addition to working in psychiatric hospitals and clinics, he has also offered weekly individual psychotherapy sessions in prisons (2007–14). Since 2013, he has taken on the role of Supervisor in Japan for the sex offender program in prisons. In Japan, clinicians in the forensic field are isolated in various locations; in 2022, he established a network for clinicians working with delinquency and crime to connect them, serving as its representative.

Arthur Leonoff is a supervising and training analyst with the Canadian Psychoanalytic Society, a recipient of the Citation of Merit and an honorary member of the American Psychoanalytic Association. His contributions include the book *When Divorces Fail, Disillusionment, Destructiveness and High-Conflict Divorce* (2021), and his most recent publication is 'Mourning, Melancholia and War' (2024). He is the current Chair of International New Groups in the IPA and an active teacher, supervisor and clinical analyst.

Massimo De Mari works as a consultant psychiatrist in the prison system in Padua and in the Law Court in Padua. He is a member of the Psychoanalysis and Law Committee of the Italian Psychoanalytic Society (SPI) and of the IPA Committee on Psychoanalysis and Law. He is a member of the board of the International Association for Forensic Psychotherapy (IAFP) and teaches 'Forensic Psychiatry' (with a psychoanalytic approach) and 'Psychoanalytic Issues in Prison' at the IUSVE University in Venice (School of Forensic Psychology and Master on Criminology). He has edited a book in Italian, *L'io Criminale. La Psichiatria Forense Nella Prospettiva Psicoanalitica* [The criminal ego. Forensic psychiatry from a psychoanalytic perspective] (2018).

Maria Eliana de Rezende Barbosa Mello is a full member of the IPA, and a training psychoanalyst of the Psychoanalytic Society of Rio de Janeiro. She is Director of the SPRC Social Clinic, with two ongoing projects assisting Brazilians volunteering from the BrazUkra project, which offers help to refugees from the war in Ukraine. She is also Coordinator of the Community Project in the Maré neighborhood, Rio de Janeiro. She is ex-President of the Psychoanalytic Society of Rio de Janeiro, ex-member of the House of Delegates IPA, Coordinator of the Jacques Lacan Seminars in the Analytic Training and a member of the IPA Committee on Psychoanalysis and Law.

Carine Minne is a psychoanalyst with the BPAS and Consultant Psychiatrist in Forensic Psychotherapy at Broadmoor Hospital and the Portman Clinic (NHS, Public Health Service, UK). She chairs the IPA Violence Committee in the Community and World and is editor-in-chief of the *International Journal of Forensic Psychotherapy* (IJFP) Carine was President of the International Association for Forensic Psychotherapy until May 2022. In her work, she brings together the disciplines of forensic psychiatry and psychoanalysis to work directly with offender patients in different settings, and indirectly via teaching, training and lecturing to professionals from various disciplines, nationally and internationally.

Plinio Montagna, MD, is a training analyst and former President of the Brazilian Society of Psychoanalysis of Sao Paulo. He is a Master of Psychiatry, former Assistant Professor of the Faculdade de Medicina da Universidade de São Paulo and Consultant to the Psychoanalysis and Law Committee, and former Chair. He is former President of the Brazilian Federation of Psychoanalysis and former editor of the Revista Brasileira de Psicanalise. Plinio is author of the book *Alma Migrante* (2019); co-editor and co-author of *Dimensões: Psicanálise* (2012); editor and co-author of *Psychoanalysis, Law and Society* (2019) and *Album de Familia, Ed Casa do Psicólogo* (1994). Plinio is also the author of several prefaces and chapters in books of colleagues, and an expert witness for judicial courts in São Paulo.

Kai Ogimoto, PhD, is a psychologist and a candidate of the Psychoanalytic Training Institute of the Contemporary Freudian Society. He is an International Psychoanalytical Studies Organization (IPSO) member of the IPA in the Humanitarian Field Committee and Associate Professor at Sagami Women's University, Kanagawa, Japan. He is the author of several books and an article, 'The Inability to Mourn and Nationalism in Japan after 1945' (2024).

Laura Orsi, MD, is a psychoanalyst, former Coordinator of the APA Psychoanalysis and Society Department, APA Press and Diffusion, Chair of the IPA Social Media Subcommittee, Past Director of Fepal Publications and co-author of a chapter in *Psychoanalysis, Law and Society* (2019).

Ruth Axelrod Praes, PhD, obtained her doctorate at the Faculty of Psychology at UNAM. She is a didactic psychoanalyst for children, adolescents and adults of the Mexican Psychoanalytic Association (APM), affiliated with the IPA and the Federation of Psychoanalytic Societies of Latin America (FEPAL). She was President of the APM (2014–16), Director of the Institute of Psychoanalysis of the APM (2016–18) and Director of the Center for Graduate Studies of the APM (2018–20). She was the Latin American representative before the Board of the IPA and for two consecutive terms (2015–17) and Co-chair of the Committee for Women and Psychoanalysis (COWAP) of the Northern Zone of Latin America (2015–17). She is Director of the radio programme 'Dialogue with My Psychoanalysts', Mexican Heraldo (2019–24), Member of International Affairs Committee APM (2022–26) and is on the editorial committee of the *Caliban Magazine* – FEPAL.

Igor Romanov is a psychologist, philosopher and a psychoanalyst. He is a training and supervising analyst of the Ukrainian Psychoanalytic Society (IPA study-group). Associate Professor of the J. B. Shadt Department of Theoretical and Practical Philosophy of the Educational and Research Institute of Philosophy, Culture Studies, and Political Studies of the V. N. Karazin Kharkiv National University. He is the author of works on psychoanalytic theory, technique, history, philosophy of psychoanalysis and applied psychoanalysis. His publications include 'Collective Traumas, Personal Overcoming' (2023), 'Equation, Moralisation and Denial' (2025) and 'Contemporary Propaganda and Propagandistic States of Mind' (2023; in Swedish and Ukrainian). He is Head of the Ukrainian programme of Kleinian seminars (from 2003 to date) and the programme 'Help for Helpers' (from 2022 to 2023), both supported by the Melanie Klein Trust. Since 2022, he has been an organiser of the Ukrainian Psychoanalytic Society Friends' Meetings.

Sonia Sandleris is an Ángel Garma Institute (APA) psychoanalyst and APA specialist in family, couples and groups. She is also Coordinator of the APA Group Commission and an IPA member.

Vivian Secco is a psychologist and a training candidate of the Ángel Garma Institute (APA).

Rakesh Shukla has a deep engagement with law, constitutional jurisprudence, human rights and justice, melded with training and clinical practice in psychodynamic psychotherapy, contributing to insights into law, society and the psyche. He is a member of the Indian Psychoanalytical Society, a member of the International Psychoanalytical Association and the Indian Association of Family Therapy. He is a consultant to the IPA Committee of Psychoanalysis and Law, a member of the Supreme Court Bar Association and a member of the International Council of Jurists.

Alex Winter is a psychoanalyst and a member of the British Psycho-analytical Society. He works in private practice and is on the staff at Camden Psychotherapy Unit, a community mental health charity, where he is a psychotherapist and a clinical supervisor. He also sits as a trustee of the Listening Place, a charity for people who are struggling with suicidal thoughts and feelings. Before qualifying as a psycho-analyst, he worked as a barrister in Lincoln's Inn, London, specialising in civil litigation.

Introduction

*Ronald Doctor, Adrienne Harris and
Plinio Montagna*

Following the publication of the first book by the International Psychoanalytical Association (IPA) Psychoanalysis and Law Committee, entitled
Psychoanalysis, Law and Society (2019), we felt that new reflections about
the world we live in today from a psychoanalytical perspective would
help with facing issues of global uncertainty and anxiety that confront
each one of us. Anxiety is a pervasive emotion that shapes human behaviour and thought across various domains, including psychology, law
and social interaction. Its impact can be profound, influencing individual
decisions, actions and perceptions. Understanding anxiety through psychoanalysis provides valuable insights into its underlying mechanisms;
while considering its effects on law and legal practice opens avenues for
improving the legal system's responsiveness to human vulnerability. This
book explores the intersections of anxiety, psychoanalysis and law,
emphasising how psychoanalytical theory can shed light on the emotional and psychological dimensions of legal decision making and the
broader implications for justice. In this endeavour, our aim is to try to
examine the challenges of maintaining a psychoanalytical stance when
working in these chaotic times, not only when working with severely
disturbed patients but also during a time when there are massive
disturbances in society, including wars, pandemics, environmental
destruction, new technologies and racial injustices.

In these uncertain times, the world is facing rule breakdown in many
institutions, both political and societal, with a profound impact on individual subjectivity, leading to anxiety and eventually helplessness. Politics, law and morals are becoming increasingly hard to grasp, with law
enforcement either being questioned or becoming increasingly oppressive. This book is a collection of 17 chapters by a diverse group of eminent and international psychoanalysts from all regions of the world,
including North America, Canada, South America, Europe, Ukraine,
India and Japan, involved both in the practice of psychoanalysis and the
law, on and off the couch. The book offers a unique strength, in that the
subject of each chapter is a testament to the ability of psychoanalysis to
think and recognise the wide range of both personal challenges and

DOI: 10.4324/9781003646266-1

societal ills, with its emphasis on the legal implications of the personal and societal encounters.

If law could be defined as a system of rules and guidelines which are enforced through social institutions to govern behaviour, then all the chapters are about social issues, including wars, violence, society, the pandemic, and family and relationships. Law is a rational ordering of things that concern the common good. This is particularly relevant to both personal and societal issues in which the law and the individual meet. From a broad perspective, the law also responds to societal anxieties, often reflecting collective fears and prejudices. Legal systems tend to reflect the anxieties of the time, whether related to issues of national security, racial injustice or economic inequality. Similarly, legal systems may become punitive in times of societal instability, reflecting the anxiety of populations anxious about crime or perceived moral decline.

We have divided the book into five Parts. In the first Part, 'War and Its Impact', crime and activism have become ambiguous; for example, Russians claim to believe they are ridding Ukraine of Nazis and Ukrainians claim Russians have become war criminals. In any conflict or war, each side believes that truth and law are on their side, and with the deepening irrationality and anxiety of the times, we are beset by delusional ideas, fake news and conspiracy theories. In periods of great cultural stress, some people try to explain the terrifyingly inexplicable by creating a narrative that seems to make sense of it all and creates groups of others.

We will attempt to examine the many *societal issues* that have plagued us all in the last few years, including the COVID pandemic, which has impacted on the rule of law in some countries. For example, in India, where the imposed and harsh lockdown, established to try to ameliorate the misery of the virus, had a major impact on people's lives and mental health; while in Brazil, negligence regarding the recommendations of science led to an extremely high number of deaths.

We will examine *violence and the law,* and within this turbulent context the book will explore the challenges of maintaining a psychoanalytic stance working with violent people in a clinical setting. This includes patients within our normal clinical setting as well as those suffering from severe personality disorder who have committed serious offences and are considered high risk. Also, a focus of discussion will be refugees in Italian prisons, as well as refugees because of the Ukrainian–Russian war. We will refer to the Brazuca project, i.e. Brazilians living in Ukraine, who have now become refugees arriving in Poland.

Treatment cannot happen solely within the dyad of patient and therapist, but is located within the triad of patient, therapist and the law. The task of helping patients face the damage done to others and self is a complex process, which requires the capacity to not condemn or dismiss, yet also not to excuse.

We want to pose the question as to whether it is possible to make sense of these ambiguous and confusing times by looking at the issues from individual clinical work with patients, who have had contact with the judicial process – from the bottom up.

We will examine the impact on the professional, with all the anguish and apprehension of working in the line of fire. It may not only be the patient, but the psychoanalyst as well, who may barricade themselves behind causal theories of what happens in analysis, leading to a belief that they possess the truth, which they like to impose on the patient. In other words, there may be too much emphasis on the epistemic side of representation, i.e. the desire for subjective certainty that appears to provide broad, internally consistent explanations, which allow people to preserve beliefs in the face of uncertainty and contradiction. Some rules may thus need to be broken to preserve meaningful treatment. Similarly, judges, lawyers and jurors are not immune to the effects of anxiety, and these emotional states can shape the legal outcomes that may not always be rational or just.

In conclusion, the book centres on the relationship between psychoanalysis and law, within the context of the present time, with particular emphasis on social and psychological challenges. Law and its interactions with everyday social issues, producing anxiety and uncertainty, mediated by psychoanalytical insights, lies at the centre of all the chapters in the book. This embraces a predominantly psychoanalytical perspective of psychological distress and anxiety caused by social upheaval, war, violence, pandemics, family matters and individual suffering. Psychoanalysis provides profound insights into the unconscious forces that drive human actions, and understanding anxiety from this perspective can enhance the legal system's capacity for fairness and justice.

All topics have as their backdrop the law and its vicissitudes, which must be addressed and used in understanding the component cases of the chapters. The essential focus of the book is the peculiar relationship between the law and a psychoanalytical approach, which may appear to be incompatible, though in fact both are inherently intertwined with societal mores through the nature of anti-social and aberrant behaviour.

This may disconcert some people, which can be a good sign, inasmuch as the chapters have been written from within the situations described; for example, sessions of psychoanalysis within the Ukrainian war, help for people within the context of COVID, personal experiences within a context of an illegal action, etc. We believe this perspective will invite readers to come along and join the authors' experiences.

In the event that our purpose is not clear to some people, this Introduction, as well as those at the beginning of each Part, will help the reader dive into the core purpose of the book: to bring essential contributions of psychanalysis under the protection of law, and describe when psychoanalysis sometimes defies the law and converses with its boundaries.

Part 1

War and its impact

Introduction

In this Part on war and its impact, there is invariably a violation of the law in terms of border violations, crimes against humanity and war crimes. Psychoanalysis has long been concerned with understanding the unconscious forces that shape human behaviour and the emotional conflicts that often lie beneath the surface of human consciousness.

In Chapter 1, 'The Malaise of the Twenty-first Century: The Return of the Wars', Maria Eliana de Rezende Barbosa Mello considers questions regarding the uncertainty and anguish of present times. In recent years, we have found ourselves facing situations that have put our existence under constant threat, such as the pandemic that began in 2020 and Russia's war with Ukraine. Can psychoanalysis find a place in confronting and understanding the reality of wars and pandemics and the need for changes in analytical technique? The author uses as illustration a clinical case with an analysand residing in Germany who created the Brazucra project to help refugees from Ukraine; and a case from her private clinic of someone who developed panic syndrome after the pandemic.

Igor Romanov's chapter, 'Psychoanalysis in the Time of War: Continuity of Mental Life and Oedipal Situation' (Chapter 2), relates the possibilities and difficulties of psychoanalytic work during war, and discusses the continuity of mental life and its ongoing interactions with external reality. It also examines the specific experiences that are actualised in the circumstances of war connected with Oedipal conflicts and revenge. The author attempts to demonstrate that revenge, often regarded as an elementary reaction to a traumatic 'wound', is unconsciously connected with the Oedipal situation.

Chapter 3, 'The Mind of the Psychoanalyst on the Frontline: Limits, Frontiers and Beyond', is a particularly interesting collaboration by Alejandro Luis Bègue, Claudia Borensztejn, Olga Cartañá, María Cristina Fernández, Laura Orsi, Sonia Sandleris and Vivian Secco. It came about when they were summoned to attend a prestigious rehabilitation and

DOI: 10.4324/9781003646266-2

geriatric institution. Group psychoanalytic assistance was provided to health workers, since they were abruptly subjected to a severe disruptive situation in their workplaces, due to the occurrence of COVID-19, similar to working on the frontline, as in a war. Nine reflection groups were created and coordinated by Argentine Psychoanalytic Association (APA) professionals with experience in groups. The objective was to accompany and contain the group members in their fears, anguish, feelings of vulnerability and exhaustion, in order to prevent burnout. They thus generated and created a space of trust and hope, recovering the deteriorated integrity of the affective bonds between co-workers, who had been devastated in different ways by this humanitarian catastrophe.

1 The malaise of the twenty-first century
The return of the wars

Maria Eliana de Rezende Barbosa Mello

In his exchange of letters with Freud in 1932, Einstein, who was somewhat perplexed by human evil, addressed Freud with this question: 'Is there any way to free humanity from the threat of war?' (Freud & Einstein, 1933).

Einstein himself suggested several paths, but at the same time he realised that they would be ineffective: 'It speaks of the possibility of an international agreement that would be a legislative and a judicial body to arbitrate any conflict that arises between nations' (Freud & Einstein, 1933). He continued:

> A court is a human institution which, in relation to the power it has, is inadequate to enforce its verdicts. Law and power inevitably go hand in hand, and juridical decisions come closer to the ideal justice demanded by the community. However, we are far from having any supranational organisation competent to issue judgments of incontestable authority and to guarantee absolute compliance with their verdicts.
>
> The intense lust for power which characterises the ruling class in every nation is hostile to any limitation of its national sovereignty.
>
> Represented by a small but powerful group that exists in every nation that are indifferent to conditions and social controls.
>
> On the contrary, they regard war, the manufacture and sale of weapons simply as an opportunity to expand their personal interests.
>
> The current ruling class has the schools, the press, and generally the church in its power. And this makes it possible to organise and control the emotions of the masses and make them the instrument of the same minority.
>
> (Einstein, 1932 in Freud & Einstein, 1933)

He ends his letter to Freud by speaking of the desire for hatred and destruction that exists within men. He addresses a question to Freud about whether it is possible to solve the question in search of world peace.

DOI: 10.4324/9781003646266-3

Freud replied to Einstein:

> You began by talking about the relationship between right and power. I completely agree, but I would like to replace the word power with the word violence.
>
> At first it seems that one is the antithesis of the other. However, we have to remember that the law was originally brute force and that even today it cannot do without support for violence.
>
> (Freud, 1932 in Freud & Einstein, 1933)

Freud talks about his theory of Eros and Thanatos (1920) and how it drives and highlights everything he has written in *Group Psychology and the Analysis of the Ego* (1921).

Einstein says, 'Why do you, I, and so many others revolt so violently against the war?' And Freud answers:

> We react to war in this way, it is because every person has the right to his own life, because war puts an end to a life full of hope, because it leads men to humiliating situations, etc., etc.
>
> And a future war could involve the extermination of one of the antagonists or perhaps both.
>
> All this is so true that one cannot but feel perplexed at the fact that war has not yet been unanimously repudiated.
>
> (Freud, 1932 in Freud & Einstein, 1933)

In 2022, after a pandemic that started in 2020, and when we were still recovering from all the traumas and losses of this deadly virus, we woke up to a war started by Russia against Ukraine. And in the face of these events, it is up to a psychoanalyst to think as Freud did and once again repudiate war. Against a virus, we can only protect ourselves with the use of masks, vaccines, confinements, etc. However, in a war, where the protagonists are visible, we have more weapons to be able to think of faster and more possible exits. Because, as Freud tells us, with the improvement of weapons – and it is worth remembering that in 1932 there were no nuclear or chemical weapons – the world would end. Therefore, this paper raises some questions of our time.

Regarding Russia's war against Ukraine, let's think about the effects it has on the Ukrainian and Russian peoples and also on the entire planet.

That's why I decided to participate in the Brazucra project, to serve Brazilians, refugees from Ukraine. My first psychotherapy consultation was with one of the founders of the project, whom I will call X, who asked for help because she was having problems with insomnia and a lot of anguish.

In my initial contact with X, she began to tell me about her work: she and her colleagues receive Brazilian refugees from Ukraine in their city in

Germany. Their task is to find temporary shelter for the refugees and provide them with food. Then, to look for cities where they can work and start their lives over.

In this process, X began to identify with the refugees, and her personal story began to blend in with the living conditions of the refugees. X had been living in Germany for three years and was married to a musician who lived in another country in Europe. She had a young son. She also felt like a refugee who left Brazil, among other reasons, due to difficulties with her family.

When she tells her family she is a volunteer in the project none of them show any concern about the local proximity to Ukraine. In the first session, it was about the family attack, she felt down and almost lost her humanitarian objectives. In further sessions, X was already feeling more self-possessed, and her initial idea of leaving the project was forgotten.

X went back to working with the refugees until a certain point when, during a speech by a minister in Vladimir Putin's government, Russia claimed that if Ukraine did not give in to NATO, a third world war would be declared. She stated:

> At that moment, the war, which seemed very distant from me and my country, was very close in the face of this threat, which made me re-read the correspondence between Einstein and Freud. How to prevent a new threat of war, since, as Einstein said to Freud, the Planet would not resist in the face of today's sophisticated weapons.

What I am saying is what kind of real-time care arouses in the psychoanalyst the anxieties of the real? In other words, X, in the face of war, returns to her internal and external wars. The psychoanalyst also finds him- or herself 'at the front', having to separate what is the order of fantasy and what is the order of the real.

Another analysand of mine from my private practice decided to go to the front to document the war. Once again, I found myself overcome with anguish! Communications between the two of us were infrequent, and I heard from him through his wife. This was the therapy of a couple who were going through a 'marriage war' when they came to me. We were in the middle of the couple's conflict when he decided to go to Ukraine to document the war.

At first, I thought it was because of his fascination with dangerous situations and an escape from the war with his wife. Gradually, I came to understand that going to document the war was to get closer to his European origins and to his father, who also participated in the Algerian war.

However, in the midst of these consultations, the situation of X, who lived in Poland, was threatened with a possible attack at the border; now it was the issues of her escape and that of her family which became a priority.

The one who is there to help refugees found herself in the same situation of having to look for an escape route. In other words, what is present in these consultations is uncertainty and insecurity. The helplessness that is the condition that marks human life is naked and raw in those moments where the real is present without any mask of the imaginary.

In these last three years, it seems that the wheel of time has returned to the past: Spanish fever reappears dressed as a pandemic that haunted us all on planet Earth for two and a half years and left indelible traumas in all of us.

We are living in very dark times: the pandemic, the Russia–Ukraine War and, in 2023, the terrorist attack from Gaza against the population of Israel.

There are several types of war: in my country we have daily violence caused by drug traffickers and militias that lead to bandits on the road. What I'm saying is that we are living under the aegis of the death drive that is spreading around the world.

Jacques Lacan (2006, 2007), in the 1970s, named capitalist discourse as that discourse which breaks with social bonds, where the subject becomes an object to better manipulate and dominate; remembering Freud, in his text *Group Psychology and the Analysis of the Ego*, he says that the human being is not fit to belong to a group, it belongs to a horde (Freud, 1921, 1913). It refers to the father of the horde as the mythical father of totem and taboo; one who does not accept castration. And what we see is that these 'fathers of the horde' re-emerge from time to time, causing disintegration, segregation that culminates in wars and the violence of our daily lives.

And Freud catches our attention with a phrase that gives us goosebumps: 'The individual in the mass thirsts for obedience, this thirst creates the leader who loves no one.'

Today, we are under the aegis of a new discourse: cybernetic. At the same time that we live and see a real-time image of any event in the world, we also have an invisibility in the scope of cybernetics. It means that through satellites, many visible and named and other unnamed strangers appear in the universe without being accountable to anyone. In the same way that via satellite we can communicate simultaneously with any place in the world, we have what Spielberg pointed out to us with his *Star Wars* movies – the threat arises 'in the stars'.

As Shakespeare says, between heaven and earth there is much more than our vain philosophy supposes.

Why didn't Israel, which has one of the best security and early warning systems on the planet, receive the signal that it was being invaded by Hamas? In the age of the algorithm, where we are driven by what the 'algorithm' supposes about us, our desires are being driven by this 'new leader'.

The 'father of the horde' today holds a mass of data, stolen or taken from the public by some kind of force through the Internet. This discourse is permeated by capitalist discourse, but we see that it has become more and more a new discourse. In this one, the leader is commanded by the algorithm where ideas are pulverised by fake news, images and words that are reproduced insistently, directing no longer to the masses but to the individual, with phrases such as 'This is for you'.

The intention is to reach the masses, but the one-by-one operation of each individual is to create a mass of individuals thinking or disagreeing in the same way. It is this new discourse that creates false leaders supported by slogans made by robots that transmit their messages in the interest of those who want to manipulate the data. This is how the Bolsonaro phenomenon occurred in Brazil, and in the United States, the Trump phenomenon.

We know all the good that technology brings us, but if we don't focus on the fact that behind this world there are some humans who use cybernetics to take down financial systems, who invade our privacy, and become entrenched in everything that is most important for life, we will be immersed in an invisible war with unimaginable risks for our planet. In other words, this discourse unfolds in cyber acts leading to mass attacks!

I have many Jewish analysands with family in Israel who are absolutely traumatised by these latest events. We know that it is a very complex war, but this work does not propose to scrutinise the relations between Israel, Palestine and Hamas. But to think with Freud, as long as the weapons of war are visible, we are better able to fight them. When these weapons become chemical and nuclear, what is at risk is life on planet Earth.

The malaise is the product of the dominant discourse in our current culture: the capitalist discourse and the cybernetic discourse. These are the most averse to civilisation because they aim to abolish individual desire, doing everything to destroy it. We have seen the growth of fascism, authoritarianism and religions all over the world. We are under the aegis of psychic and real terrorism!

In times of the banalisation of evil (Arendt, 1994), the death drive becomes like a crawling snake, swallowing singularities and subjectivities. The serpent's egg is born there: the forcible symbolic, the imaginary chained to the image and the performance, and the real, the helplessness, takes advantage of it to create 'figures of protection', and perversion makes the party totemic.

As Freud tells us, the masses do not think, they want to be thought for and guided by those who know what is best for them, diluting themselves in objects of use. On the other hand, the counterpart to this discourse is also growing; decolonisation is a priority. But there are those who still love to be colonised without realising that it is in this place that they are being dispossessed of themselves.

And the analyst's discourse is the possibility where listening to the other is possible, allowing the analysand the possibility of subjective change and thus appropriating him- or herself, not allowing him- or herself to be seduced by alienating discourses.

Conclusion

Psychoanalysis must continue to be the plague because it does not make herds, but individuals responsible for their choices, where its proper name will be signed, and not the name of the hordes that want to co-opt it in order to better dominate.

References

Arendt, H. (1994). *Eichmann in Jerusalem: A Report on the Banality of Evil* (Rev. ed.). New York: Penguin Books.

Freud, S. (1913). *Totem and Taboo* (Trans. by A. A. Brill). London: Routledge & Kegan Paul.

Freud, S. (1920). *Beyond the Pleasure Principle* (Trans. by C. J. M. Hubback). London: The Hogarth Press.

Freud, S. (1921). *Group Psychology and the Analysis of the Ego* (Trans. by J. Strachey). London: The Hogarth Press.

Freud, S., & Einstein, A. (1933). *Why War?* Paris: International Institute of Intellectual Cooperation.

Lacan, J. (2006). *Écrits: The First Complete Edition in English* (Trans. by Bruce Fink). New York: W. W. Norton & Company.

Lacan, J. (2007). *The Seminar of Jacques Lacan, Book XVII: The Other Side of Psychoanalysis* (Trans. by R. Grigg). New York: W. W. Norton & Company.

2 Psychoanalysis in the time of war
Continuity of mental life and Oedipal situation[1]

Igor Romanov

In this chapter, I would like to think about the possibilities and difficulties of psychoanalytic work during war, the continuity of mental life and its ongoing interactions with external reality, as well as the specific experiences that are actualised in the circumstances of war, connected with Oedipal conflicts and revenge. I will attempt to demonstrate that revenge – often regarded as an elementary reaction to a traumatic 'wound' and unconsciously connected with Oedipal situation – is more or less primitive. I use examples from the organisational dynamic of the Ukrainian Psychoanalytic Society, from cinema and clinical examples to illustrate these points; the 'unfreezing' of the mental life after severe traumas and the revival of the Oedipal scenarios within individuals and groups. The complex interaction between external and internal realities in these examples are very illustrative too.

War in Ukraine and the Ukraine Psychoanalytic Society

The outbreak of a full-scale war between Russia and Ukraine, although somewhat expected, caused a shock reaction among the vast majority of Ukrainians, including my psychoanalyst colleagues. Naturally, the first question for each of us was that of our safety and the safety of our loved ones. I remember how, having left Kharkiv with my family in the early morning of 24 February, I received a call from a colleague asking me to take her daughter with me. To do this, it was necessary to return to the city, which was almost impossible due to the traffic jams stretching for many kilometres. Most importantly, however, I was not at all sure that the direction we had chosen was safe. It seemed impossible for me to take responsibility for someone else's child in this situation, and my colleague agreed with me. In general, I turned out to be right, because very soon we found ourselves in a city surrounded by Russian troops where we hid in the basement from repeated shelling and anticipated a seemingly inevitable occupation – although our situation was better than in my native Kharkiv. Being in relative safety, I was still tormented by guilt for several days, especially while receiving photos and videos of the

DOI: 10.4324/9781003646266-4

devastation in Kharkiv and hearing from my colleague about the suffering of her family. This burden fell from my shoulders only after I learned about her and her family's successful evacuation to Europe. At that time, we were still in the surrounded city and were looking for ways to escape.

Fortunately, the vast majority of the members and candidates of the Ukrainian Psychoanalytic Society (UPS) were able to avoid the threats of war. Approximately half were able to emigrate to safe countries in Europe, where they received significant assistance from the International Psychoanalytic Association (IPA), national psychoanalytic organisations and personally from many foreign colleagues. The other members of the Society remained in Ukraine for various reasons. Men of military service age were not allowed to leave the country due to possible mobilisation (although to date only one of our members is serving in the ranks of the Armed Forces of Ukraine and one is undergoing military training). Some of the men evacuated their families abroad, while they themselves remained in Ukraine. There were those who, on principle, did not want to leave their homes, and others who moved to safer places of the country. Over time, some of those who left the country or moved to safer regions began to return to their native areas.

In the very first days of the war, the Headquarters for Assistance to UPS Members and Candidates was created, which coordinated financial assistance, accommodation abroad and established contacts with the IPA and those colleagues who offered aid. It is difficult to overestimate the importance of the work conducted by the Headquarters, as well as the help of the IPA and colleagues abroad. I heard many words of gratitude and admiration from our members and candidates for such complex care and there was solidarity from the entire international psychoanalytic community (Mirza & Romanov, 2022).

As issues of safety were relatively resolved, the question arose of the restoration of professional activities. Most UPS analysts and candidates continued to maintain contact with their patients even during the most acute periods of hostilities, and most began to restore their practice a month or two after the start of the war. Generally, this was with online work, to which many had managed to adapt during the pandemic, although some of our colleagues from relatively safe regions of the country managed to return to work in their consulting rooms.

In addition, almost all members of the Society and most of the candidates participated in one way or another in various forms of volunteer work: helping refugees and displaced persons, consulting the military and victims of violence, etc. Over time, several international programmes were launched in the same vein: The Melanie Klein Trust's programme for counselling psychologists, 'Help for Helpers', groups for the UPS with members of the Psychoanalytic Assistance in Crises and Emergencies Committee IPA (PACE), short-term therapeutic groups of Israeli analysts for UPS members and candidates, groups for analysts and candidates working with children and many initiatives by international colleagues who sought to help us in such difficult circumstances. Individual members of the Society used their contacts with international organisations to develop psychiatric services, psychological services in the army, child psychotherapy, assistance for victims of violence and other projects.

After approximately three months, we raised the question of restoring the work of the psychoanalytic Society itself. On my initiative, we organised a series of online meetings, 'Meetings of the Ukrainian Psychoanalytic Society's Friends', which brought together about 150 participants from around the world. Usually, we made two or three short presentations on relevant clinical or applied topics and then had a long discussion with the audience. The first five meetings were held monthly, then the intervals became longer. Discussions with international colleagues at this stage and in this format were extremely valuable. They performed a containing function, not only in the sense of support in living through sometimes unbearable conditions but also with help in the beginning of thinking about the war and its harsh consequences in the current situation. It was important for us to convey our experience to international colleagues and be met with their more detached, albeit sympathetic, view of the situation. Questions and problems that arose at these meetings were further developed in discussions, communication with colleagues, articles and conferences. How could psychoanalysts work in wartime when more pressing needs prevail and the basic safety of both the analyst and the patient is questioned? Are we, Ukrainian psychoanalysts, able to communicate now with colleagues from Russia, a country whose army is destroying our homes and fellow citizens? How to understand the power of propaganda in the current war, and how to counteract it? Is psychoanalysis, as a general human science, able to contribute to the understanding of the social processes taking place now? This is an outline of the main issues raised at the meetings (see, for example, Romanov (2023a)). I think in themselves they became a kind of diary of our experiences and first attempts to 'think under fire' in Bion's wide sense (Brown, 2012). The importance of the psychoanalyst's function as an 'annalist' was underlined at one of the meetings by Michael O'Loughlin (O'Loughlin, 2022).

International psychoanalytic conferences and seminars dedicated to the war in Ukraine were also important events. Of course, we did not always find the strength to participate in them, and we generally learned about some by chance and after the fact, but, in particular, the Centro Veneto di Psicoanalisi conference, 'Psychoanalytic Thinking and Experience of War' (KnotGarden, 2023; Romanov, 2023b), was an extraordinarily important event, both emotionally and intellectually. To exchange experiences with colleagues who have experienced similar situations (as in former Yugoslavia), with those who have studied them from a psychoanalytic point of view, to discuss their experiences and issues related to the trauma of war, the opportunities and difficulties of working in emergency circumstances – the value of such professional communication cannot be overestimated. Some of such possibilities were limited because of Russian attacks on Ukrainian infrastructure during the winter of 2022–23, but in spite of this it is still continuing. In November 2023, we again organised a UPS annual conference online after its omission in 2022, and in December 2023 our candidates held an IPSO conference in a combined format; of course, both events were full of war topic discussions – the military psychological service, psychotherapeutic work with children during war time, general psychoanalytic understanding of causes and consequences of war … these activities involved many foreign colleagues and have an important continuation – in writing papers and books, the creation of international teams (see Thinking Labs: IPA, n.d.) and so on.

Over time, we have felt the readiness to restore psychoanalytic training in the UPS. We, the members of the Training Committee, as well as the members of our Sponsorship Committee – Ingo Focke, Sølvi Kristiansen and Alexander Janssen – doubted for a long time that this was possible. However, after the first meetings with UPS candidates, our doubts were dispelled. With rare, objectively and subjectively understandable exceptions, the candidates wanted to continue their training and felt its structure was an important factor of stability in this unstable situation. We are grateful to the IPA International New Groups Committee and our sponsoring committee for the attention to the needs of our candidates, for the balance of flexibility and rigour in following the psychoanalytic rules of training that have been achieved. The fact that during the war period new candidates, analysts and training analysts appeared in the UPS, I find extremely promising.

At one of the first meetings, Patrick Miller from Paris raised a question that remains relevant to us to this day: is psychoanalysis possible in times of war? He used as a metaphor the words of our colleague, serving in the ranks of the Armed Forces of Ukraine, about useless bulletproof vests that hurt soldiers more than bullets and shrapnel. 'Isn't psychoanalysis during war a defective and therefore dangerous form of body armor?' asked Patrick (unpublished discussion). Like many other psychoanalytic questions, I think this one does not have an unambiguous and simple answer. Of course, all of us in Ukraine now have to do a lot of work that is not psychoanalysis proper: crisis counseling, psychotherapy, working with groups and organisations, etc. I hope that we do all this as psychoanalysts, that is, with the use of psychoanalytic thinking and methods. However, I believe that even in these traumatic circumstances there is room for psychoanalysis as such. Moreover, this is where it is often needed and, as I will try to show with some examples, effective; of course, provided there are conditions for psychoanalytic work, the most important of which is the internal state of the analyst.

Continuity of mental life

I would like to start this section with a discussion of the brilliant film *Twenty Days Without War* (1976) by the Soviet director Aleksey German (Wikipedia, n.d.a). It seems important in connection with two topics of my interest here: the continuation of the 'ordinary' mental life, with its conflicts, unconscious desires, anxieties, phantasies and relational patterns in the extreme circumstances of war, and the endurance of impulses and effects of revenge and forgiveness in the complex dynamics of external and internal factors.

The film tells the story of the brief vacation of the protagonist, writer and war correspondent Vasily Lopatin (actor Yuri Nikulin), who takes a trip 'for personal reasons and on business' from the frontlines back to Tashkent (the events take place during World War II and the plot is based on a story by Konstantin Simonov). The beginning of the story is preceded by scenes of Lopatin's war memories. Further on, there is a scene of his conversation with a fellow traveller in his train compartment, pilot Yuri Stroganov, returning from vacation (actor Alexei Petrenko). Having learned about Lopatin's profession, Yuri tells him his story – a long monologue follows, filmed in a single shot and played with incredible talent by Petrenko. The story is relatively banal, but from the category of universal human experience: the wife's betrayal during her husband's time at the frontlines, his torment when confronted with this fact, a soldier overwhelmed with resentment and rage arriving home, his fluctuation between the desire for revenge and love for his wife, asking for forgiveness. This story ends with Yuri's request addressed to Lopatin to write a letter to his wife on his behalf. 'But how can I write this?' asks Lopatin. 'You yourself don't really know how to live on.' 'No, I don't know,' Yuri answers: 'I must forgive, of course. I believe that she doesn't live with that bastard anymore, people say so …. But it's very difficult for me.' Then, repeating his request again, he says: 'I did not go just because of the children. Because of her, too …. So that she feels what she did to me.' It becomes clear that this is exactly what he expects from Lopatin's description of his feelings.

The scene seems to play no role in the story that unfolds further. It serves rather as an epigraph and a kind of counterpoint to the story of the protagonist. One of the goals of Lopatin's trip also turns out to be a meeting with his wife, or rather his ex-wife at that point, living happily with another man. In the first few minutes of meeting them, he says: 'Come on, guys. I am not a victim, you are not defendants. And on this we shall stand, sit, and drink vodka, if you have it.' He signs the divorce papers. In parallel with this personal story, another one unfolds – a discussion of a theatrical production about the war based on Lopatin's play.

The film *Twenty Days Without War*, like most German's works, is multi-layered. It intertwines various storylines, and often the 'texture' of the film or individual scenes is more important than the plot. The central part of the film is the story of a brief love affair between Lopatin and Nina

Nikolaevna (actress Lyudmila Gurchenko), a theatre costume designer. This brief romance is a respite in the inferno of war. We can't know if it will continue or how it will end. But we feel the sincerity and strength of human love, unexpectedly breaking through in seemingly completely inappropriate circumstances.

One of the leitmotifs of the film is the hero's protest against the false portrayal of the war in the theatre. A real war, he insists, is more terrible, but also more humane than theatrical. And we see it. The film begins with Lopatin's recollection of the death of a soldier during a bombing – Lopatin himself could well have been in his place. In the final scene of the return to the front, a young lieutenant miraculously survives during the shelling. 'And I thought that was it, the end,' he says. 'Is this really the end?' the soldier replies with a laugh. 'This is just the beginning.' A minute before, Lopatin, hiding from the explosions, thinks: 'If there are three more shells and then silence then everything will be fine with us.' There are three explosions – and silence.

In Soviet realities, the topic of personal relationships, and even more so against the backdrop of the heroic Great Patriotic War of the Soviet People, was not very welcome. If it were not for the intercession of Konstantin Simonov, six-time Stalin laureate and winner of one Lenin Prize, the film would most likely have met the sad fate of being kept 'on the shelf' until better times (Wikipedia, n.d.b). It is sufficient to recall what kind of persecution Andrei Platonov was subjected to for the story with a similar plot: 'The Return' (author's title 'Ivanov's Family'). 'Vulgarity', 'the most vile slander against Soviet people, the Soviet family, the victorious soldiers returning home' – these are just a few examples of criticism directed at one of the greatest Russian prose writers of the twentieth century. Interestingly, in his case, the intercession of Konstantin Simonov also came in handy (Wikipedia, n.d.c).

I will continue my reflections with a clinical example.

Clinical example A

Patient A is a woman in her mid-thirties who is under analysis four times a week, which currently takes place online. She has stayed in Ukraine, and although she planned to leave several times, she returned after each attempt. Her parents are in the occupied territory. One of the problems that troubles her is loneliness, in particular the inability to build a satisfying relationship with a man. Traumatic experiences from the past gravitate over her: binge drinking and the aggressive behaviour of her father, the hysterical behaviour of her mother with suicidal threats and also periodic alcohol abuse, poverty, and having to take care of her younger siblings. Her character and lifestyle are largely determined by defensive decisions in the form of narcissistic pseudo-maturity, hysterical dramatisation and perverse sadomasochistic relationships with men.

I will describe the first session of the week during her third year of analysis, which was quite productive. She started by saying that she could hardly wait for our appointment after the weekend, although before the session even began she felt that everything that worried her no longer seemed so important. She also warned me that she would not be able to attend her session on the following day due to a scheduled doctor's appointment, which she regretted. Overcoming her sudden indifference, she told me what she was going to say initially: about her acute feeling of loneliness over the weekend, bitter tears when looking in the mirror, awareness of age-related changes, despair, and disbelief in her ability to overcome loneliness. Both at the weekend and during the session itself, the patient's mood changed quite quickly – from acutely painful to relatively calm consideration of the situation, and then even to a certain elation. She is dealing with her problems, which means she will definitely solve them with my help, and so on. At some moments, A clearly realised that the feeling of loneliness was connected not only with the absence of a partner and family, but also with the almost complete absence of any truly close friends and with a strange indifference to the fate of her parents. She could not forgive her psychopathic, aggressive father for the childhood trauma he had inflicted, although she expressed sympathy for him in the current situation. She accused her mother of lying: condemning her father again and again, even exposing him as a monster in front of the children, but nonetheless going back to him.

The war and all the anxiety associated with it increased the patient's fear that she had no one to rely on and no one to turn to for help in difficult times. She then spoke about the situation that caused her outburst of rage – she saw her ex-boyfriend's expensive car parked in the street. At first, she rejoiced at her 'indifference'. But then a friend sent her a link to pictures of this guy from the gym, which brought A back to feelings of jealousy and anger that she seemed to have already overcome. She began to tell me stories (repetitive by now) about her ex's terrible behaviour, his sexual perversity, and at the same time about her anger when other women claimed his body and car. At that moment, I said that I heard, as if it were, the voice of her mother who vilifies her father but returns to him again and again, for reasons which are incomprehensible to their children. It seemed to me that this interpretation shocked A, but was accepted as an important insight. She painfully began to talk about the identity of these situations, although it was unpleasant for her. She seemed ready to delve further into the subject of her continued attachment to her ex-boyfriend. But the end of the session was approaching, and A expressed regret about missing the next day's appointment, which sounded quite sincere.

Two days later, I met a completely different patient. She was estranged, sat in upset silence for a long time, then said that she had not slept well and she had no thoughts in her head. All A remembered from the previous session was that I said she was faking and exaggerating just like her mother. In this regard, she could not believe her feelings, just as she did not believe her mother. What is the truth: that her father is a monster, or that her mother passionately loves him? And what is the truth in her feelings? Apparently nothing and therefore she did not know what to talk about now. In fact, she didn't even know if she had real problems or if she had made it all up. I tried to tell her about the image of me as an object that did not believe her, with whom there was 'nothing to talk about', especially when I looked indifferent to her absence yesterday, but my efforts were not very successful. The session ended with a rather long and painful silence.

The next session, which was the last one for this week, was productive again. The patient immediately notified me that she had slept well and intended to work during the session; she was sorry that she had 'lost two sessions this week' when she actually really appreciated them. She had had some dreams, but remembered only fragments – something about her old school and either her mother or a teacher in worn clothes. The atmosphere in the dream changed when she met her beloved grand-mother. Then she reflected on the previous session and expressed sur-prise at why everything happened the way it did. I told her about my understanding of the situation: about her indignation at what she con-sidered my 'disbelief' (which I considered her own dissociation), her resentment and doubts about whether our decrepit analytical house and I could withstand all the pressure of her indignation. After that, she began to talk quite energetically about her understanding of her parents' situa-tion, its influence on her, and why it was so painful for her to hear that she was like her mother. From time to time, she inserted rather caustic attacks on me in the form of comments like 'you, of course, will say this and that, but I don't think about it that way'; however, I did not feel them to be really destructive or disruptive for our contact.

She spoke about the terrible behaviour of her drunken father and how she had to calm him down by doing errands for her mother. She had to say that she loved her father, although she felt nothing but disgust for him – the smell of alcohol emanating from him, for her own pretence. 'Of course, you will say that unconsciously I was pleased to feel like his chosen one!' she commented sarcastically. It was unbearable for her to feel like her mother in all this – it's like becoming as fat as she became after the birth of her next child.

At this moment, I drew A's attention to her sarcasm about my 'Oedipal interpretations' and said that I completely understood her distaste for her drunken father, as well as for the perverted boyfriend she mentioned in passing. But I also noticed how this picture changed in her mind when her father or boyfriend looked attractive to other women. 'Not really,' she replied. 'It's embarrassing for me to admit it, but most of all I feel sorry for losing his money. He owes me. I spent so much effort on him. Thanks to me he achieved a lot, and now another woman will get it all?! I want the car that he promised me.' This was followed by a series of childhood memories, accompanied by feelings of shame: she took bottles to a bottle bank to get money, everyone looked at her as a child from an alcoholic's family, she did not have beautiful notebooks at school and beautiful clothes in her teens. She was jealous of other children and learned to pretend that she was 'above it all'. In the end, she independently achieved success in life, which she still couldn't fully believe. She and her work were worth something! And so, as soon as she relaxed and believed that she could rely on someone, everything went to someone else. She couldn't just let it go!

I must say, I was stunned by this torrent: the unexpected concreteness of her claims (Shakespeare's 'pound of flesh' from *The Merchant of Venice*), the volume of shame and helplessness revealed behind this, a frank recognition of the impossibility of forgiving and letting go. Strikingly, thoughts of resentment and 'righteous indignation' flashed through my mind a few minutes before the patient spoke about it. They were related to the ongoing war and the behaviour of some of my foreign colleagues, which looked to me as if it was betrayal. These thoughts seemed completely unrelated to what the patient was talking about (although I now wonder if they were provoked by her causticity?). When A's story came to the same point of its own accord, I was struck by the coincidence.

The session was almost over, and I didn't feel the need to say much in this situation of understanding at some deeper unconscious level. I only confirmed that I heard in her words the pain of injustice and humiliation that she had to endure, and the desire to somehow compensate for this.

Discussion of the clinical example

The example of A seems important to me from several points of view. In her case, how do vengeful impulses resulting from the collapse of 'Oedipal illusions' (Steiner, 1993, 1996; Britton, 1989) combine with attempts to 're-play' the objectively traumatic circumstances of her childhood? Do her vindictive phantasies serve some therapeutic function for her (Akhtar, 2014) or do they serve only 'pleasure' of 'passing on the bad treatment' (Pick, 2018), circling back to 'repetition compulsions' (Freud, 1920)? How does the situation of war, the knowledge that she herself, her parents and partner, her analyst, are in a situation of real danger, affect her experience of basic anxieties and the actualisation of traumatic memories? All these issues require detailed consideration, which is beyond the scope of this chapter. In my opinion, the case of A confirms two of Freud's theories of hysteria: the preliminary idea that hysterics suffer from (traumatic) memories, and the later idea that they suffer from their unconscious (Oedipal) phantasies.[2]

The boundary-breaking, sometimes seductive, sometimes frightening actions of her parents looked like very concrete realisations of childhood phantasies, making them omnipotent. The current situation of the war added to this. In this regard, some kind of enactment or acting out and acting in of these scenarios of seduction, disappointment and humiliation, revenge and fear of retaliation in a relatively safe analytic situation was healing when they touched us both without destroying the basic analytic frame and trust (Rosenfeld, 1964; Joseph, 2003). In these moments, the image of an adult – perhaps her grandmother from her dream – who could be asked simple questions (to which, of course, there are not always simple answers) arose in the analytic space, and this form of relationship trans-formed the defensive and volatile scene. This kind of adult was perceived as able to forgive the child's vindictive impulses, who could then forgive herself without engaging in masochistic revenge-through-self-punishment. I believe that this process also opened up the possibility for some forgive-ness of her objects and reconciliation, but at this stage of analysis it would be premature to make a judgement about this.

Conclusions about the Oedipal dynamic

It is remarkable that both in this cinematic example and in the clinical one, the continuity of mental life is associated with a certain unfreezing of Oedipal conflicts, awareness and the beginning of overcoming Oedipal illusions. Authors such as Jacob Arlow (1980), John Steiner (1993, 1996), Michael Feldman (2008), Ronald Britton (1989, 1998) and many other psychoanalytic writers emphasise the connection of resentment, grievance and vindictiveness with the reaction to Oedipal exclusion.

I recall the classic case of Richard, with whom Melanie Klein (Klein, 1945, 1961) worked during World War II, and in which primitive Oedipal material was carefully examined. In her published work, she did not explore in detail the interplay of individual Oedipal dynamics with the social catastrophe of war, although it is now known how much attention she paid to the perception of Hitler as an omnipotent destructive figure, a participant in the most primitive versions of the primary scene and Oedipal conflict (Frank, 2020).

In his book *Psychoanalysis of War*, Franco Fornari wrote:

> The wonderful description of Richard's case which Melanie Klein has given us in her 'Narrative of a Child Analysis', may be regarded as the best preparatory reading for the psychoanalytic theory of the war phenomenon. If Hitler is seen not only as a real historical entity, but also as Richard's bad father and at the same time as Richard's pro-jected sadism, the problem that confronts us is how to know what we are supposed to make of these psychoanalytic discoveries. We find here all that is essential for tracing the war phenomenon to the unconscious.
>
> (Fornari & Pfeifer, 1974, p. 243)

Freud revealed the connection of our experience of war with mourning and the death drive (Freud, 1915, 1917, 1933), but perhaps it is Klein who gives us a hint of his connection with primitive Oedipal anxieties. An all-powerful, Hitler-like father and a traitorous mother, as in the case of A, exclusion experienced as betrayal and humiliation and therefore crying out for revenge – we owe much of our understanding of all of these phenomena to the concept of the early Oedipus complex developed by Klein and her followers (Segal, 1973; Britton et al., 1989; Rusbridger, 2004).

In the cases that were presented, we can see that a kind of 'unfreezing' and restoration of mental life occurs as a result of an increasing ability to distinguish between internal and external reality. This is a long-known feature of working through traumatic experiences (Weiss, 2020; Bohleber, 2007). For me, it was rather surprising to find that in many cases this process of psychic life restoration started from the revival of Oedipal. This indicates their basic structural function in human mind and society, what Freud never tired of repeating. I suppose that in the organisational dynamic of the UPS, we could find the same triangular structure – the finding of collaborators, the struggle with enemies and the task of creating new generations by the training process.[3] We should remember Klein's discoveries in the area of the most primitive forms of Oedipal configurations – the involvement of the splitting process in the creation of Oedipal phantasies, the projection of destructiveness in one or both figures of the Oedipal pair, the consequences of these processes in the impossibility to struggle for good objects and fear to be identified with such a destructive figure. I see both the extreme hatred and attempts of false reconciliation as the attempt to resolve these primitive Oedipal conflicts. But the main obstacle of this way is a traumatic coincidence of internal phantasies with external reality impact (Romanov, 2022).

Notes

1 Translated by Breanna Vizlakh.
2 It is worth remembering that Freud himself tried to combine these perspectives into a unified theory (Freud, 1895, 1908; Wisdom, 1961).
3 How the war distorts the real family ties in Russia can be seen in a documentary film by Andrey Loshak (Loshak, 2022).

References

Akhtar, S. (2014). Revenge: An overview. In Akhtar, S., Parens, & H. (eds), *Revenge: Narcissistic Injury, Rage, and Retaliation*. Lanham, MD: Jason Aronson, pp. 1–18.

Arlow, J. A. (1980). The revenge motive in the primal scene. *Journal of the American Psychoanalytic Association*, 28: 512–541.

Bohleber, W. (2007). Remembrance, trauma and collective memory: The battle for memory in psychoanalysis. *International Journal of Psychoanalysis*, 88: 329–352.

Britton, R. (1989). The missing link: Parental sexuality in the Oedipus complex. In Steiner, J. (ed.), *The Oedipus Complex Today*. London: Karnac Books, pp. 83–102.

Britton, R. (1998). Oedipus in the depressive position. In Britton, R., *Belief and Imagination: Explorations in Psychoanalysis*. London: Routledge, pp. 29–40.

Britton, R., Feldman, M., O'Shaughnessy, E., & Steiner, J. (eds) (1989). *The Oedipal Complex Today: Clinical Implications*. London: Routledge.

Brown, L. J. (2012). Bion's discovery of alpha function: Thinking under fire on the battlefield and in the consulting room. *International Journal of Psychoanalysis*, 93: 1191–1214.

Feldman, M. (2008). Grievance: The underlying Oedipal configuration. *International Journal of Psychoanalysis*, 89: 743–758.

Fornari, F. & Pfeifer, A. (1974). *The Psychoanalysis of War*. New York: Anchor Books.

Frank, C. (2020). On Melanie Klein's contemporaneous references to Hitler and Second World War in her therapeutic sessions. In Milton, J. (ed.), *Essential Readings from the Melanie Klein Archives: Original Papers and Critical Reflections*. London and New York: Routledge, pp. 84–104.

Freud, S. (1895). Studies on hysteria (with J. Breuer). In Strachey, J. (Ed.), *The Standard Edition of the Complete Psychological Works of Sigmund Freud*, Vol. 2. London: Hogarth Press, pp. 1–323.

Freud, S. (1908). Hysterical phantasies and their relation to bisexuality. In Strachey, J. (Ed.), *The Standard Edition of the Complete Psychological Works of Sigmund Freud*, Vol. 9. London: Hogarth Press, pp. 155–166.

Freud, S. (1915). Thoughts for the times on war and death. In Strachey, J. (Ed.), *The Standard Edition of the Complete Psychological Works of Sigmund Freud*, Vol. 14. London: Hogarth Press, pp. 273–300.

Freud, S. (1917). Mourning and melancholia. In Strachey, J. (Ed.), *The Standard Edition of the Complete Psychological Works of Sigmund Freud*, Vol. 14. London: Hogarth Press, pp. 237–258.

Freud, S. (1920). Beyond the pleasure principle. In Strachey, J. (Ed.), *The Standard Edition of the Complete Psychological Works of Sigmund Freud*, Vol. 18. London: Hogarth Press, pp. 1–64.

Freud, S. ([1932]1933). Why war? (Einstein and Freud). In Strachey, J. (Ed.), *The Standard Edition of the Complete Psychological Works of Sigmund Freud*, Vol. 22. London: Hogarth Press, pp. 197–219.

International Psychoanalytical Association (IPA). (n.d.). Thinking labs. https://www.ipa.world/ipa/IPADev/Events/Thinking_Labs/Dev/Events/Thinking_Labs/Thinking_Labs_5.aspx?hkey=98afc81d-7f65-46ba-ade9-346472fbeee6

Joseph, B. (2003). Ethics and enactment. *European Journal of Psychoanalysis*, 57: 147–153.

Klein, M. (1945). The Oedipus complex in the light of early anxieties. *International Journal of Psychoanalysis*, 26: 11–33.

Klein, M. (1961). *Narrative of a Child Analysis*. London: Hogarth Press.

KnotGarden: Idee, intrecci e snodi della Psicoanalisi (2023). 2. War [conference]. https://www.centrovenetodipsicoanalisi.it/knotg-2023-2-war/

Loshak, A. (2022). *Broken Ties* [film]. https://www.youtube.com/watch?v=5qmQs2LbnaE

Mirza, O. & Romanov, I. (2022). Letter from the Ukrainian Psychoanalytic Society. *International Journal of Psychoanalysis*, 103: 427–430.

O'Loughlin, M. (2022). Kriget I Ukraina. *Divan*, 2022, 3–4: 4–13. [In Swedish. The paper originally presented via Zoom as 'The war in Ukraine, the obscenity of understanding and the obligation to remember' at the 'Meeting of UPS Friends'.]

Pick, I. B. (2018). Лики травмы: между личностным и социальным. «Удовльствие» передавать плохое обращение [Faces of trauma: between the personal and the social. The 'pleasure' of passing on the bad treatment] [Paper presentation]. Kyiv seminar. http://psychoanalysiskharkov.com/лики-травмы-между-личностным-и-социал/#_ednref1

Romanov, I. (2022). Collective traumas, personal overcoming: In memory of Tatyana Nikolaevna Pushkareva. *Psychoanalysis, Culture & Society*, 28: 376–392. doi:10.1057/s41282-022-00363-4

Romanov, I. (2023a). Equation, moralization and denial. *Journal for the Psychoanalysis of Culture and Society*, 28: 109–115. doi:10.1057/s41282-022-00339-4

Romanov, I. (2023b). The wars inside and outside: Experience of war in a patient, a psychoanalyst, and a society in Ukraine.. *KnotGarden: Idee, intrecci e snodi della Psicoanalisi*, 2: 67–101.

Rosenfeld, H. (1964). On the psychopathology of narcissism: A clinical approach. *The International Journal of Psychoanalysis*, 45(2–3): 332–337.

Rusbridger, R. (2004). Elements of the Oedipus complex: A Kleinian account. *International Journal of Psychoanalysis*, 85: 731–747.

Segal, H. (1973). The early stages of the Oedipus complex. In Segal, H. *Introduction to the Work of Melanie Klein*. London: The Hogarth Press.

Steiner, J. (1993). Revenge, resentment, remorse and reparation. In Steiner, J., *Psychic Retreats: Pathological Organizations in Psychotic, Neurotic and Borderline Patients*. London and New York: Routledge, pp. 74–87.

Steiner, J. (1996). Revenge and resentment in the 'Oedipus Situation'. *International Journal of Psychoanalysis*, 77: 433–443.

Weiss, H. (2020). *Trauma, Guilt and Reparation*. London: Routledge.

Wisdom, J. (1961). A methodological approach to the problem of hysteria. *International Journal of Psychoanalysis*, 42: 224–237.

Wikipedia (n.d.a). German, Aleksei Yuryevich. *Wikipedia*. https://en.wikipedia.org/wiki/Aleksei_Yuryevich_German

Wikipedia (n.d.b). Twenty days without war. *Wikipedia*. https://en.wikipedia.org/wiki/Twenty_Days_Without_War

Wikipedia (n.d.c). Platonov, Andrey Platonovich. *Wikipedia*. https://en.wikipedia.org/wiki/Andrei_Platonov

3 The mind of the psychoanalyst on the frontline

Limits, frontiers and beyond

*Alejandro Bègue, Claudia Borensztejn,
Olga Cartañá, María Cristina Fernández,
Laura Orsi, Sonia Sandleris and Vivian Secco*

Within the framework of a reflection on what happened during the COVID-19 pandemic and its consequences, we present our work that could be a model to be replicated not only in emergency situations but in any situation that requires an intervention and response to alleviate social suffering.

During the lockdowns, many groups implemented a type of assistance that lasted beyond them and remains a landmark of our recent past and a challenge for the present and the future. Because of COVID and the feeling of vulnerability, due to the threat of dying, virtual work spread a tool that came to stay and is still very much used in addition to the traditional framework of psychoanalysis.

Group psychoanalysis has a long tradition. It is worth considering the work of Bion (e.g. 1963) during World War II, also as a result of a need and an urgency. Group psychoanalysis has had an important development in Argentina with the theories of pioneers such as Enrique Pichon Rivière (e. g. 1977), José Bleger, Janine Puget (e.g. Puget & Wender, 1982) and Isidoro Berenstein (e.g. Puget & Berenstein, 1987). Other authors in the psychoanalytic world then developed more complex theories, and the practice of group therapy has matured to the current time, with many different lines of thought.

In the 1960s, family therapy also boomed in Argentina, with the emergence of Dr García Badaracco as the head of a new dispositive and theory of illness. His model of multifamily therapy is today studied and applied in different parts of the world. The development of family, couple and group therapies led to the creation of a degree of specialisation in this area at the Argentine Psychoanalytic Association (APA). Due to the quantity and quality of psychoanalysts who are experts in group practice at our institution, it was possible to assemble a team that, in spite of their different experiences and theoretical frameworks, joined together in starting a social solidarity action plan. In this way, a model was built during the emergency. Virtuality was the only possible tool in the conditions imposed by the pandemic: isolation.

DOI: 10.4324/9781003646266-5

The following is a narrative synthesis of the experience written in 2021, 'Caring for Those Who Care in Times of COVID-19'. It is the experience of our group work in a geriatric institution, with an important section on rehabilitation. In March 2020, when the pandemic reached Argentina, the APA created a new space in the service of the community: APA SOLIDARIA. Its purpose was to provide psychoanalytic assistance to the population at risk. In this context, the APA president was contacted to assist a prestigious institution with more than 800 health, maintenance and administrative workers and 200 hospitalised patients. The purpose of this chapter is to give an account of the project designed and carried out by the APA between April and August of that year.

Context

The new virus, the pandemic, the lockdowns, the virtualisation of our practice and the fear of uncertainty were fundamental elements that affected us all. In Argentina, the most populated district, known as AMBA (Buenos Aires metropolitan area) suffered a long, compulsory lockdown, reinforced by the phrase repeated everywhere: 'Stay at home, don't go out, take care of yourself'. The order to protect ourselves from the virus had a paradoxical effect on health workers who, unable to isolate themselves, had to resort to very strict safety and hygiene protocols in order to carry out their indispensable work, while being permanently exposed to contagion and the consequent risk of death. Assistance for health workers was essential. They were suddenly subjected to a disruptive situation, which generated enormous fears and anxieties. The emotional atmosphere in their work and lives changed dramatically, and the difficulties in human relations became more acute. If the disruptive life is coming from the social world (Benyakar, 2002), it is necessary that what heals and repairs also comes from the social environment.

We suggested accompanying and containing the anguish that had arisen, generating a

space based on solidarity, trust and hope, in order to create and/or recover the deteriorated integrity of the affective bonds between co-workers, devastated in different ways by this humanitarian catastrophe. We thus thought of the potential of the group space to generate new views, observations and reflections that would allow the alleviation of this present, and to invest and structure a possible future.

Group therapy generates a space, a transitional intermediate space, which promotes the metabolisation of potentially traumatic experiences by reflecting on them. We understand reflection as the psychic work that refers to one's own subjectivity and to the group as a place where others function as supporters and offer the possibility of exchange.

The APA's response was immediate. A group of professionals: Dr Alejandro Bègue; Lic, Gabriel Finquelievich; Dr Florencia Fernández; Dr

Laura Orsi; Lic Rosalia Álvarez; Lic, Sonia Sandleris; Lic María Cristina Fernández; Lic Olga Cartañá and Lic Vivian Secco, were summoned and coordinated by the president of the institution, Dr Claudia Borensztejn.

Methodology

We decided on various levels of organisation:

A) Reflection groups coordinated by psychoanalysts

The groups were open to all professionals who wanted to, and could, attend at the required time. The groups were heterogeneous not only in terms of the different disciplines (nurses, occupational therapists, kinesiologists, physicians, psychologists, social workers, members of the human resources department) but also in terms of the hierarchical position they held in the institution (coordinators, collaborators, medical directors). The meetings were held on a weekly basis and lasted one hour. The number of members in each group ranged from four to eight.

B) Group of coordinators (APA Team)

The coordinators established a space for reflection, together with the president of the APA, on a weekly basis of two and a half hours.

C) Periodic communications between directors

The president of the APA and the directors of the institution that required our help were in close contact, to comment on the issues that came up in the groups and in the management.

D) Meetings of the APA team with the directors

The directors joined the Sunday meeting of the APA team and they exchanged mutual feedback.

Objective: 'Caring for those who care'

A) Our purpose in the groups was to generate a trustworthy space where members could share what was happening to them, listen and be listened to. We proposed the group space as a model of containment so that in the future members would be able to promote their own communication network in their daily work, avoiding emotional isolation. We consider that the support and maintenance of bonds is a necessary resource to have psychic immunity and for the prevention of burnout.

B) In the APA psychoanalysts group, the purpose was to share experiences and unify work criteria. In this way, we became a network of communication and support. This helped us to bear the difficult task of thinking about what was happening in each group and at the different levels of the institution. By not working in isolation, we were also providing ourselves with the necessary immunity to face the dangerous situation. In this supportive network, it is important to highlight the role of the president of the institution, who did not participate in the groups but at the same time was the link between the two institutions. This avoided the risk of being trapped in the net, since we were simultaneously protagonists and spectators of these new realities that involved us all (Puget & Berenstein, 1987).

Narrative of the experience

Often, 'the richness that is woven together goes unnoticed at the time it happens' (Jeanette Dryzun, 2020).

We organised nine groups. At the beginning, there were differences among the groups in relation to how each of them experienced the changes in their place of work. On one extreme, there were those who felt protected by the institution, saying, 'This will never happen to us, COVID will not enter, the institution takes care of us,' and, on the

other, those who felt overwhelmed by the changes they had to incorporate: 'I get home and I keep receiving WhatsApps with the new protocols. I can't get used to one, and another one is coming.' It seemed to be understood that there was a double discourse from the higher levels from where, in order to take care of them, they were exigent and demanding. In these higher levels, some of those who participated in the groups also had complaints.

It should be noted that although we are all specialists in groups, it was the first time we had worked with a group virtually. There were some added problems because the members shared the physical space and therefore were all wearing masks and sometimes even safety glasses. It was a great effort for us to be able to understand what they were saying, to be attentive to all the other forms of expression: looks, gestures, postures. Sometimes, it was difficult to recognise them, to put names and faces together, to identify who was speaking. What seemed to be uniform at the beginning was differentiated by virtue of the greater knowledge of each one, and the process that was taking place in each group. In this way, singularities were highlighted as well as, at the same time, group productions.

The initial theme had to do with the fear of infecting themselves or infecting their elderly patients, especially those who, being in rehabilitation, were extremely vulnerable. They also feared infecting their families. Working with a high-risk population, the professionals felt a high level of anxiety to which was added discrimination, which at one time was evident in some social groups because of their work.

At the beginning, feelings of vulnerability, helplessness and uncertainty appeared in the groups. We worked on how to accept, understand, tolerate and metabolise all the unprecedented situations that arose on a daily basis. The anguish of the hospitalised patients also increased due to the uncertainty of the lockdowns. They lost closeness with their relatives and contact through their senses with the professionals who attended to them, due to the social and sensory distance imposed by the protective barriers. How do you replace the usual language with an uncovered face? The possibility of seeing gestures, listening well, approaching, touching, kissing, had disappeared between professionals and patients. When this contact was lost, patients began to greet each other with a kiss. It was then also necessary to put face masks on the patients.

The work of the professionals became overloaded. The constant organisation and reorganisation was not only related to the tasks to be performed, but also to the complexity of the protocols. This implied a high degree of meticulousness in the new procedures, resulting in an enormous threat, since any error in them would ruin so much effort. At one point, the virus entered the institution and the feared scene became a fact.

Psychological considerations

The intertwining of three types of issues began to emerge clearly for us:

a   The coronavirus with all that it demanded;
b   Pre-existing institutional problems;
c   Personal problems, which emerged in a veiled manner in the last meetings.

These issues were the subject of an inter-institutional meeting and a reflection on the scope of our work. We realised that the temporality of the framework would not be given by the times of the pandemic, but by the times of its elaboration. We could not address the other two levels detected: the intra-institutional and the personal. The time frame was important for us to anchor an axis in the midst of the loss of habitual rhythms in lockdown.

At the institutional level, we heard that the level of demands, control, limitations, failures in communication due to the absence of information and the way it was transmitted increased, and with it the tensions, the lack of time to comply with all the demands imposed by the work, and the pressures staff felt from their superiors. The staff felt exhaustion, insomnia, feelings of guilt and physical discomfort, which became more and more acute. Some had fantasies of becoming ill. Some said they did not feel recognised by their superiors for the hard work they were doing.

The more difficult the work situation became, the more they felt the need to take advantage of the group space, which they saw as a respite in the midst of an overwhelming situation. One of the groups started to call the weekly meetings 'el campito' (the countryside) as a representation of an open and relaxing place.

The group work began to show results. Communication started to circulate more fluently among the co-workers, who experienced that in this way they were taking care of each other: supporting each other, sharing experiences, suggesting possible ways out. A speech therapist who on her day off had prepared a training session on sign language for her colleagues, as they had to attend to a deaf patient who was unable to read lips because of his mask, gave an account of this situation.

We worked on the possibility that their discomfort could be expressed beyond the group space. As the pandemic had increased pre-existing conflicts, especially communication conflicts, not only between them but also with their superiors, we worked on how to convey, either verbally or in writing, their discomfort or situations that they felt were unfair. This was also discussed with the managers in one of the meetings; the communication went in one direction only and it was important to listen to them more.

What they expressed as pressures and demands received (here you have to work 100 per cent; there can be no mistakes) gave rise to thinking about how each one's own demands, which had always been present, were at play, because they felt they belonged to a prestigious institution, almost a model institution. The persecutory aspect alternated with gratitude for being cared for, so that the atmosphere gradually changed, becoming calmer and more reflective, as reflected in the following comment: 'I have a lot of work behind me, stories I have to complete, but I didn't want to stop coming. I'm calm, I really didn't have time, I'll do it tomorrow or when I can.'

We started thinking that the time had come to bring our intervention to a close – the the objective for which we had been convened was being fulfilled. The members of the groups had already found enough tools to work with during the rest of the pandemic. We agreed with the directors to end the task, despite their wish that we would continue until the peak of the virus had subsided. In Argentina, that time was uncertain. We considered and we conveyed that certain issues that were not in our proposed approach continued to persist, but we were not there for an institutional analysis or to make therapeutic groups. Instead we were there to provide support and help to the health team in the face of COVID. What we had worked on already had effects that would continue to act on everyone, and on the institution, whether the virus was circulating or not. A closing was agreed with time to prepare the farewell. The end of the task included evaluations of the changes that had taken place throughout the process with a high emotional commitment. The last meeting was a scene, in all groups, of immense appreciation in an intensely affective atmosphere. Also, in a letter, the managers thanked the APA professionals for their commitment and high professionalism.

Effects of the task

- Group members were able to stop thinking 'this only happens to me'. Talking and thinking with their peers in the workplace was an apprenticeship in managing common anxieties, strengthening networks and increasing solidarity.
- The group experience brought about fluidity in communication. Members were able to convey their discomfort to their coordinators. Communication began to circulate differently throughout the institution.
- Members expressed the desire to continue with the space, in the manner of a self-management group.
- There was a change in us as we went through the experience. We had to rework our way of being and being with each other in the pandemic. Far and near, behind the line of fire. To value intensely what health workers do and to be able to care for those they care for. At the same time, we believe that solidarity works in common and should be a path to be consolidated beyond the pandemic, incorporating community work into the institutional functions of training analysts and disseminating psychoanalysis.

We reconsider the three levels of conflict that we described in our work:

1   The pandemic, for which we were summoned.
2   The personal conflicts that COVID deepened: We believe that one of the effects was the awareness, in some cases, of personal conflicts that were also revealed in the group work. Some of the members of the groups, as a result of this experience, sought individual therapy.
3   Intra-institutional: It became clear to us how difficult, demanding and conflictive it is to sustain such a large institution. With so many years of prestige and with the firm intention of maintaining a level of excellence, in the midst of the pandemic in which so many nursing homes were evicted and closed, it resulted in a high mortality rate of elderly people. We have helped the institution continue to operate within controlled risk to the institution and its workers.

Towards the end of our intervention, the hypothesis we are working with emerged, which is that of an interplay between an 'institution threatened by COVID', a 'possible institution' and an 'ideal institution'. We think of the phantasmatic presence of an 'ideal institution', where everything functions perfectly in the manner of an ideal self, exempt from all criticism. We work in an 'institution threatened by COVID' and we strive for the acceptance at all levels of a 'possible institution'. Faced with the demands of the institutional ideal, communication failures were understandable. As it circulated between corridors, it concealed and distorted what was really happening, in order to continue to sustain the imaginary utopia of the ideal institution. What happened during the pandemic functioned as a magnifying lens to what was happening before the pandemic in that 'possible institution'. 'Possible institution' and 'ideal institution' were the tension that sustained our work and reverberated in the anxieties that circulated between paranoia and gratitude.

In synthesis, we could say that although the coronavirus determined a new context, it added to the pre-existing context of the institution, and both, in the groups, were revealed to us as text.

We are interested in underlining group work, thought psychoanalytically, as a privileged place that brings into play the healthy resources of the psyche and refers to the creative and healing potentialities existing in each subject. So far, this is the story of the work done. It emerged at a time when we were dominated by the force of COVID-19, a producer of illness and death that traumatically fractured the relationship with the other, revealing the feeling of helplessness. At the same time, it was an opportunity to look for new ways of strengthening and creating bonds with others, a task that implied an impulsive commitment, a mobilisation of desire, of eros, which is openness towards and with the other. The virtual group work opened up these possibilities. A model of psychoanalytic work was generated that prioritised caring for those who care, stimulating solidarity in emergency situations in an effective and replicable way. 'Sharing experiences and narrating them is as necessary for the soul as eating and drinking is for the carnal body' (Benjamin, 2020).

References

Benjamin, W. (2020, 30 April). Cited in Vinar, M., Yo y la humanidad ante lo inesperado [Humanity and me in the face of the unexpected]. *Brecha*. https://brecha.com.uy/yo-y-la-humanidad-ante-lo-inesperado/

Benyakar, M. (2002). El encuadre y el campo psicoanalítico ante catástrofes sociales, la guerra y el terrorismo [The psychoanalytic framework and field in the face of social catastrophes, war and terrorism]. Paper presented at the International Meeting between the APA and SPP, 2002.

Bion, W. R. (1963). *Experiencias en grupo*, Editorial Paidós, Buenos Aires.

Dryzun, J. (2020). Una condición de excepción en los tiempos del COVID 19: los profesionales y trabajadores de salud no pueden aislarse [An exceptional condition in the times of COVID-19: health professionals and workers cannot isolate themselves]. *Acta Psiquiátrica América Latina*, 66(1): 70–74.

Puget, J. & Berenstein, I. (1987). *La perspectiva vincular en psicoanálisis* [The linking perspective in psychoanalysis]. Revista de la Asociación Argentina de Psicología y Psicoterapia de Grupo.

Puget, J. & Wender, L. (1982). *Analista y paciente en mundos superpuestos* [Analyst and patient in overlapping worlds]. Revista psicoanálisis APDEBA.
Rivière P. (1977). *El proceso grupal del psicoanálisis a la psicología social* [The group process from psychoanalysis to social psychology]. Nueva Visión, Buenos Aires.

Further reading

Anzieu, D. (1971). *La dinámica de los grupos pequeños*. Kapelusz, Buenos Aires.
Anzieu, D. (1986). Del método psicoanalítico y sus reglas en las situaciones de grupo, in *El grupo y el Inconsciente*. Biblioteca Nueva, Madrid.
Aulagnier, P. (1984). *Condenado a investir*, in *Revista de Psicoanálisis*, XLI (2/3).
Aulagnier, P. (1986). *El aprendiz de historiador y el maestro-brujo*. Amorrortu, Buenos Aires.
Aulagnier, P. (1998). *Los destinos del placer*. Paidós, Buenos Aires.
Benyakar, M. (2003). Capítulo I: 'El impacto del entorno en el psiquismo', y Capítulo II: 'Entornos disruptivos', in *Lo disruptive*. Editorial Biblos, Buenos Aires.
Dellarosa A. (1979). *Grupos de Reflexión*. Paidós, Buenos Aires.
Fernández, A. (1989). *El campo grupal*. Nueva Visión, Buenos Aires.
Fernández, C. & Sandleris, S. (2004). El grupo de reflexión: texto articulador en la formación, XXXI Congreso Interno. XLI Symposium APA.
Fernández, C. & Sandleris, S. (2016). Sumando miradas, X Argentine Congress of Psychoanalysis.
Freud, S. (1914). Remembering, repeating and elaborating. *A.E.*, XII.
Freud, S. (1913). Totem and taboo. *A.E.*, XIII.
Freud, S. (1921). Mass psychology and analysis of the ego. *A.E.*, XVIII.
Freud, S. (1923). The ego and the id. *A.E.*, XIX.
Freud, S. (1926). Inhibition, symptom and distress, *A.E.*, XX.
Lapassade, G. (1999). *Grupos, organizaciones e instituciones*. Gedisa S.A., Barcelona.
Orsi, L. (2018). *Grupos Balint*. Un dispositivo útil para prevenir el desgaste. Burn out en los profesionales que realizan mediación en ámbitos penitenciarios. Congreso Mundial de mediación y cultura de la paz, Buenos Aires.
Sandleris, S. (1994). Fantasías en historietas, historia de la fantasía, recreación de la fantasía en el espacio grupal. XL Congreso Latinoamericano de Psicoterapia Analítica de Grupo, Buenos Aires.
Sandleris, S. (2005). El grupo como facilitador del cambio terapéutico: una experiencia con pacientes HIV positive. *Revista Aperturas* 20.
Winnicott, D. (1971). *Realidad y juego*. Gedisa, Buenos Aires.

Part 2

Violence and the law

Introduction

Louis Brunet's chapter, 'The Work of Desymbolisation and Disidentification in Some Forms of Individual and Group Violence' (Chapter 4), looks at symbolisation from the angle of process; a process that is normally progressive but which can become regressive under some conditions. This position does not see the concept of symbolisation as a manifest result but as a process and, in this sense, it is not categorically and systematically opposed to violent action as has been postulated in some classic theories of the criminal mind. Symbolisation is an ability that can be lost in certain circumstances. This chapter aims to offer a reflection on individual and group violence and its links to desymbolisation and disidentification, which allow extreme violence to manifest.

Plinio Montagna's chapter, 'Mind, Psychoanalysis and Law in the Line of Fire' (Chapter 5), deals with disruptive and traumatic elements to the ego, linked to aggressive interpersonal relationships and authoritarian political systems; trauma occurs on the one hand as the failure of an organisation and, on the other, as a defensive operation of the ego, with the function of preserving its own existence. He states that psychoanalysis is in the line of fire in situations of high stress, crisis or intense risk, which may be of social origin. Elements of power defy the law or use it in a perverse way, as occurred during the COVID-19 pandemic in countries like Brazil, when denialism and a model of destructive narcissism came to the fore.

Carine Minne's chapter, 'Radicalisation and Delusions of Sanity?' (Chapter 6), illustrates the similarity in the background histories of young men who have carried out atrocities and who have been diagnosed with psychotic illnesses; many of whom have also been diagnosed with personality disorders and a few labelled as radicalised terrorists. She describes what she believes to be a blurred boundary between what is considered psychiatrically psychotic and psychoanalytically psychotic; how the general public tends to hate the term 'mad' in cases of terrorist atrocities and prefer 'bad';

DOI: 10.4324/9781003646266-6

and what, if anything, can be done about this to contribute to understanding and, especially, to prevention.

Ronald Doctor's chapter, 'Oedipal Complex: Collective Conspiracy Theories and Individual Delusional Beliefs' (Chapter 7), describes the urgency of a need for relief from apparently intolerable mental states involving intense but diffuse anxiety, which seems to be critical in the development of individual psychotic states and collective conspiracy theories. Bearing the anxiety and confusion involved seems to be impossible. A psychotic organisation or a conspiracy theory involves omnipotent certainty, delusional meaning and violent murderous forms of action. It seems to be the only means available to the individual or group that offers a sense of order that can bring an immediate relief to what is otherwise an unbearable form of anxiety. It operates on the principle that within the delusional world there could be complete freedom from pain and a licence to indulge in sadistic activities.

4 The work of desymbolisation and disidentification in some forms of individual and group violence

Louis Brunet

All therapists and clinicians working with murderers may testify to the difficulties of symbolisation or the peculiarities of the symbolisation of some of these people. However, it is simplistic to dichotomise such a complex phenomenon and to claim that one symbolises and the other does not symbolise, be it a criminal or a murderer. We are all familiar with the classic positions that oppose action and symbolisation. These positions are historically important in psychoanalytical models of the functioning of the violent being. My purpose is not situated in this dichotomous vision of symbolisation seen from the angle of its apparent manifestations.

What struck me, both in my work with young psychotics, with criminals and murderers, is that it was not useful to conceive of symbolisation in a dichotomous way: presence or absence. Moreover, it seemed erroneous to study symbolisation from the sole angle of the manifest representational result of it. To judge the symbolisation capacity of an individual from the quality of the representation seems a trap, just as one cannot judge the sublimatory capacities of someone from the quality of a drawing or painting he has created. The conception that guides my reflection rather examines symbolisation from the angle of process; a process that is normally progressive, but which can become regressive under some conditions. I therefore do not want to use the term symbolisation as a manifest result but as a process and, in this sense, it is not categorically and systematically opposed to violent action as it has been postulated in some classic theories of the criminal mind. Moreover, the capacity of the psyche to bind, to transform and to symbolise is not a capacity acquired once and for all. It is an ability that can be lost in certain circumstances. Not only can one lose it when the psychic apparatus is overwhelmed, but it is possible to exercise defensive processes giving rise to an erosion of the symbolisation processes.

This chapter aims to offer a reflection on individual and group violence and its links to desymbolisation and disidentification, which allow extreme violence to manifest.

My proposal will be directly influenced by my research with murderers, with former child soldiers in the Democratic Republic of Congo

DOI: 10.4324/9781003646266-7

and by the analysis of interviews with members of violent groups and terrorist groups. But it will be nourished by my analytical practice with what I have called the problematics of the archaic and which are probably quite close to what René Roussillon calls the extreme situations of subjectivity (Roussillon, 1999, 2001). In these cases, and in cases of extreme violence, what seems interesting to me is not so much an absence of symbolisation as the presence of desymbolising processes. As part of this research, my colleagues and I conducted interviews with murderers, more than 20 interviews per subject (Gabrion & Brunet, 2014). In another study, we interviewed former child soldiers who had not only witnessed massive violence but who killed and raped, sometimes people from their own village and even from their own family (Daxhelet & Brunet, 2013, 2014).

From these and other studies, two models of the dynamic conditions of extreme violence have emerged: a model of individual violence, found in a certain number of criminals and murderers (Casoni & Brunet, 2007a), and a model of group violence, found particularly in sectarian groups and terrorist groups (Brunet, 2019; Casoni & Brunet, 2007b), and in the phenomena of group regressions giving rise to acts of genocide (as in the conflict between Huttus and Tutsis). I will not describe these two models here, but rather content myself with drawing a common line concerning the desymbolisation and disidentification that we have been able to study both in the individual violent being and in those involved in a movement of extreme group violence.

A few words about symbolisation

When I first became interested in symbolisation it was during my clinical work and my psychotherapies with psychotic children, and notably through the work of Wilfred Bion. But it must be remembered that from 1920 the question of representation was no longer self-evident based on Freud's new contributions. Since Freud's turning point (Freud, 1923), all that is unconscious is not necessarily represented and consequently the psyche must carry out work so that representations may occur. For my part, I began working with the Bionnian concepts of projective identification and containing function, and a phenomenon that appeared to me clearly in the young psychotics I saw was the need to evacuate feelings, in search of symbolisation. What Bion's model helped me to see, to understand with these young psychotics, was that in some cases one could have the impression of a simple evacuation, of a simple discharge aiming at an economic equilibrium, but that it was possible, quite often, to perceive that it was not a simple evacuation but the tentative use of an object, so that this could fulfil certain psychic functions for them.

Symbol, symbolisation, symbolic equation, symbolic function, presentation and representation – all these words maybe bring confusion, but what is truly useful to understand are the processes and the unconscious motivations underlying them. It is obvious that some people have difficulty in carrying out such a process of psychic transformation. But what quickly seemed useful to understand was the direction of the process and above all the underlying motivations, considering the continuum going from the discharge process to the unconscious call to the object to fulfil psychic functions that the person (psychotic or murderer) is unable to fulfil. And this point seems to me important both for theoretical and clinical reasons if we want to help these people.

Bion (1958) proposed the concept of 'attack on linking' to account for problems of symbolisation in psychotic functioning. My way of using these various concepts related to symbolisation difficulties is that on one side of the continuum we would have:

1   Attacks on linking, destroying and preventing the process of symbolisation, secondarily followed by expulsion.
2   And on the other side of the continuum we would have activities of desymbolisation but at the same time the presence of a relational process, in which the subject is awaiting the response of an object, of a function that this object will perform. From this response will depend the possible re-establishment of the symbolisation process or, on the contrary, it will result in a regressive movement of desymbolisation.

In other words, the violent act is not always a meaningful gesture, but it can become a significative sign depending on the symbolising response of an object. Symbolisation is therefore a dynamic process and not a static and stable one, which can take a progressive path as well as a regressive path according to different hazards. This will depend on whether the psychic apparatus must protect itself from a trauma, according to the response of the object and the psychic functions that this object will be able to perform (Delisle & Brunet, 2011). Some acts of violence may have more of an evacuating aim, but others may have a symbolising potential.

Symbolisation and violence

So far as the links between symbolisation and violence are concerned, everything and its opposite have been written. But an obvious theoretical trend opposes violent action and symbolisation processes. According to this trend, the less an individual can use symbolisation the more he risks acting his violence to externalise poorly represented states, which are barely contained by a deficient symbolisation. Most authors would agree with this sentence from Roussillon that symbolisation is an internalised motor activity, which is accompanied by the restraint of external motor activity.

Where the disagreement begins is in the understanding of the nature and causes of these symbolisation failures in violent people. Is it enough to think in terms of 'lack of symbolisation?' Are we not in doing so pointing to what would only be an observable consequence that would tell us very little about the underlying process itself? We know the important works of Bouchard and Lecours (2004) or those from Luquet (2002), who describes several modes of mental elaboration and symbolisation. One of these modes describes how the affect, the quantity, can be expressed through the body, whether through somatic manifestations or through behaviours and actions, thus favouring the body route. This route of discharging a quantity through the body pathway has been recognised since the first psychoanalytical works on the criminal and on juvenile delinquents. I am thinking here of the work of North Americans like Kurt Eissler (1950), Redl and Wineman (1951), Mailloux (1971) and others who, without explicitly using the notion of symbolisation, described how action comes *instead* of feelings and thoughts. What it then described is an incapacity or a weakness of the ego in the face of excitement, of anxiety or frustration, which favours the use of the body as a means of discharge. Balier writes 'under these conditions, the act completely replaces the thought, the contents of which are particularly poor' (my translation from Balier, 1988, p. 192).

But taking up the continuum that I am proposing, which goes from pure discharge to a discharge including an appeal to the object, we must ask ourselves: in a gesture of extreme violence like murder, who is the other, and is the subject really asking him to fulfil a function? This is a first line of questioning. But a second line of questioning is necessary, which is the one in which my work of the last 30 years fits: could we rather see in it a process of desymbolisation which would then make it possible to remove the inhibition to kill?

As mentioned earlier, I have published two models, one dealing with individual violence and the other with group violence (Brunet, 2019; Casoni & Brunet, 2007a, 2007b). In each case I try to present the role of a certain number of factors such as the inversion of the importance on the superego and of the ideal ego, the identification with the aggressor, the defences against the need for an object. I will take up here a portion of these models which describes how some people come to an identificatory disengagement, a disidentification, allowing the removal of the usual inhibition towards aggression.

Some aspects of these models may explain how, in order to succeed in killing, in torturing, the one who yesterday was your colleague (as in the Huttus-Tutsi genocide), your brother or your sister (as for the child soldiers of the Democratic Republic of Congo), to kill your roommate in a non-passionate way; to kill a stranger only to prove you can do it, like André (see below); the human being must often put in place a psychic process which ensures that the other is no longer an other 'like myself being', in certain cases to ensure that the other is no longer a human being at all; in such a way that normal anxiety and guilt are deprived of their usual psychic effect.

Of course, we can repeat the cliché that everyone has the potential to be a criminal or a murderer. But the murderer in everyone does not make everyone a murderer. Some will never act on their unconscious murderous drives; others will do so under some circumstances. These circumstances can be of several kinds, among which are group dynamics (like in terrorist acts or genocide (Brunet, 2019)). But how do the group dynamics act on the usual inhibition to kill? I had previously proposed a model of group violence quite close to the work of René Kaës (1976). For psychoanalysis, it is oversimplistic to say, 'He is a criminal, for him the law has no meaning', or 'The superego is lacking', or 'He has not reached the relational mode allowing him to have empathy for the other which would inhibit his violence'. Psychoanalysis must determine if there are common factors between the Huttu university professor who beheaded his colleague and the criminal who killed a drug dealer who owed him $500.

In the book *Une saison de machetes* [A season of machetes], Jean Hatzfeld (2003) describes an implacable process of dehumanisation targeting the Tutsis. He gives voice to many Huttus involved in the massacres. Their discourse is quite similar to that of former child soldiers and on several points of murderers that we interviewed in my research group.

On the one hand, they describe within themselves a process of dehumanisation, and of contempt, such that the Tutsis gradually came to no longer have the status of human beings. At one point, the use of the word 'inyenzi' became widespread to designate them, a word that can be translated as cockroach. What do you do if you see a cockroach? First, we have a feeling of disgust and then we try to crush it. What is the effect of collectively sharing the representation of another as a non-human, as a cockroach? Psychologically speaking, it is a form of desymbolisation supported by the group, a desymbolisation that we could also analyse using the concepts of splitting and projection and which allows a degradation of the object as a human being and therefore a degradation of the relational link to the object. We are in the presence of a collective work of desymbolisation and disidentification which allows them to experience and say this:

> F says: 'I broke a mother's head with a club. I did not feel death at the end of my arm. I went home in the evening without even thinking about it.'
>
> (My translation)

Those who did massacre explain they had the same feeling as going to work in the fields. They would leave in the morning, pick up a friend and go to work (which was to massacre a village) and come back from work in the evening to eat with their family.

In contrast, some Huttus report a more troubling feeling.

> P says: 'However, I remember the first person who looked at me, at the time of the bloody blow. That was something. The eyes of the one killed are immortal if they face you at the fatal moment. The eyes of the killed, for the killer, are his calamity if he looks at them. They are the blame of whoever he kills.'

If the eyes meet, there is therefore the possibility of the return of the 'other as human'; to see oneself in the other, therefore to identify with him, to re-humanise him.

H says: 'I had killed chickens but never an animal of the corpulence of a man.' He also says: 'It was a recognition without the knowledge ... Her features were very similar to those of a person I knew.'

He also describes how the Tutsis reacted, frightened, freezing: 'They stood motionless or huddled together.' He adds, 'It's more tempting to kill a bleating, shaking goat than a feisty, jumping goat.'

In the case of the child soldiers, we did not see a group phenomenon of dehumanisation but the children nevertheless showed desymbolisation processes, a disidentification and a desubjectivation process. As we know, child soldiers are often forced to commit murder or mutilation on a member of their village or even of their family as a process of initiation. One would think that once demobilised, the former child soldiers would have found a way to conceal this period of intense violence and killings that they experienced in the army, but this was not the case. Almost systematically, the children described to us that during their life as soldiers, they had lost the 'memories' of their village, their friends and their family. They only lived in the present moment. Strangely, it is not the armed period that they concealed to themselves but the period before the army. Why? Because it was impossible for them to kill and rape while maintaining a strong relationship with their family, their friends, their past. During their life in the army, they were living in the present, cutting themselves off not only from the past but from relational ties with the past. Thus, they could live in a dehumanised and desymbolised world in which there were few links to the 'similar-other'. The people they were killing might have been fighters but not humans like them. Here, desymbolisation, disidentification and desubjectivation are intertwined in a significant way.

Not only was the enemy not experienced as a 'like-myself' object (both another but similar because of identification with him), but their connection to their past was broken. In terms of desubjectivation or subjective disappropriation, an interesting phenomenon has developed in most of these children. They came to believe that the violence they enacted did not belong to them but was the act of a spirit which inhabited them, and which protected them at the same time. This phenomenon of subjective disappropriation played an important role in the fact that they could kill without too much emotion, inhibition or remorse, being the spectators of their own violence. But these children, to be able to avoid guilt and remorse, trapped themselves, because this desubjectivation survived their demobilisation for a large number of them. Consequently, they could attack another person (even in the demobilisation centre) without any restraint since this violence did not belong to them. If the violence did not belong to them, then they could not control it by the usual psychic means and inhibitions.

One of the child soldiers explained how from the moment he got his weapon, he began to act differently. He had seen other soldiers carrying out tortures but from the moment he received his weapon he said he was influenced by it. He said, 'To have become someone else ... bigger, stronger' and to have also had 'the idea of torturing'. The idea of torturing was the consequence of a kind of possession of his psyche by the spirit of the weapon he said. A double-edged sword because by, relying on this entity, other than himself for his protection, he gained a reduction in anxiety and guilt but also a dehumanisation process, a disidentification with the 'similar other', and finally he gave up the possibility of controlling himself.

M says: 'My head wasn't really there, I wasn't present.' Another said: 'Before I wasn't like that, I didn't like fights, it's after I got into this habit and now when I hear that noise I really feel compelled to going to fight and at the same time I feel the spirit coming and forcing me to get my knife or my razor blade.'

Like the violent criminal who repeats the well-known cliché, 'my fist hit him on its own', as if that fist was not controlled by his own psyche. Most of these child soldiers did not experience themselves as being the subjects of their violence: 'I feel compelled to go fight'; 'I feel the spirit coming and forcing me to get my knife.' Where we would say he felt anger or any other emotion welling up within him, he says 'I felt the spirit coming ... and compelling me'. But can we blame them for having 'succeeded' in this way in avoiding murderers they were carrying inside themselves? Do we not find here a kind of temporal inversion of Winnicott's famous description in his text 'Fear of Breakdown':

> The patient needs to 'remember' this, but it is not possible to remember something that has not yet happened, and this thing of the past has not happened yet because the patient was not there for it to happen to.
>
> (Winnicott, 1974, p. 105)

Here the child soldiers have taken the regressive path. Winnicott's words imply that the child must be able to represent, symbolise and self-appropriate his experience. This implies that some people cannot self-appropriate experiences because the 'subject', the 'I', is not constituted in such a way as to be able to symbolise it. It is a work of the psychic apparatus to create the 'I'. Here the child soldiers seem to have found the regressive solution of 'disappropriating' what they were experiencing. Their violence was not of the 'I', they were the spectators of it and could avoid seeing themselves as the violent, dangerous beings they had become.

According to our interviews with these children, this regressive movement, both of subjective disappropriation and of desymbolisation, not only allowed them to avoid seeing themselves as killers but spared them from experiencing too much anxiety. Before one of my doctoral students went to live with these child soldiers for a few months and interviewed them, we thought that they would tell us about the fear of death, the emotions experienced when they saw companions or even enemies being killed; the emotions around rapes and killings. The young people we interviewed had all experienced these moments that one might think were traumatic, but only a few spoke of them as memorable and even traumatic experiences. Did they succeed in 'being absent to themselves', to use Winnicott's idea? Whatever concept we use to account for it, the massive defensive process put in place by these children seems to have allowed them not to feel or symbolise anxieties that we imagined to be overwhelming. The effectiveness of this regressive process affecting symbolisation is such that, even once demobilised, these children were not 'aware' of having faced such anxieties. Often they were unable to put into words what they had experienced, and they seemed to be aware of this inability: one of them says, 'I lack the words to express the feelings we had.' Many of them say they were unable to feel emotions in the face of death or battle. One child says, 'Because my heart was no longer beating under the emotion, it is as if I was stabilised and that my emotion no longer existed.' Another child soldier talks about his condition since his demobilisation, saying, 'I stayed like the one who is no longer there', and another says, 'It was like a movie that was playing.'

My proposal is to the effect that subjective disappropriation and desymbolisation are two aspects of a regressive process of protection in these former child soldiers. Desymbolisation and subjective disappropriation make it possible to kill and not be terrified.

Like several Huttus who seemed to be observers of their own acts, and like the criminal who says 'It was stronger than me, my act was too fast for me to do anything about it,' the child soldiers have found the solution of desubjectivation, which is a form of desymbolisation.

Let us now examine the example of a murderer with whom we did about 20 interviews. André is a man who one day decided to commit a perfect crime. He decides to kill someone in such a way that no one could ever discover that he is the perpetrator of the murder. He plans this murder for several months, chooses his victim, the way to kill him, how to dispose of the body. One day he is ready and he sets his project in motion. He invites this man to his home; they drink alcohol, and during the evening André kills him. Then he cuts his body into pieces that he hides in different places in the city. During the following months, André will diligently read the newspapers specialising in criminal news. He is rather triumphant, not only satisfied to find that the investigation is going nowhere but he feels a sense of triumph that he has committed a perfect murder since it is obvious that he will not be traced. But in the months that follow changes occur in his life, and in him, which will completely modify the future. On the one hand, the feeling of triumph fades little by little since the specialist newspapers stop writing about this murder to fill their pages with other sordid stories. André reunites with friends, develops a new important friendship and at the same time begins to feel remorse. So André decides to denounce himself by telephone and he waits at his house for the police to come and make the arrest.

What happened to André for him to commit this murder, to be able to implement such a scenario and even to denounce himself? I cannot present here an exhaustive description of the dynamics that underpinned his gestures, but I will present a few points in relation to the themes of desymbolisation and disidentification.

About 20 hours of interviews make it possible to note some characteristics of André.

When we discuss with him the period preceding the murder, André recounts his life, his work and quite spontaneously he discusses the fact that his love partner had left him several months earlier. But André tells us this fact simply to situate this period of his life chronologically. He will never mention that he committed the murder at a time when he would have been affected by the separation, had been depressed or destabilised by it. The interviewer has these thoughts, not him. But André describes a period when he became unstable; he began to take hard drugs, he spent long periods of time alone taking drugs and listening to loud music. It was around this time that he set about concocting his perfect crime scenario. André had the cognitive abilities to do so; he is intelligent, so he invented several scenarios. But the fact that he has the capacity to imagine and elaborate a crime does not mean that he does not present a difficulty of symbolisation. What develops in his scenario is that the person he is going to kill is not really a person, not really a human being. Yes, André knows cognitively that he is a human being, but this person has lost the meaning of being an 'other like myself' who would have a life, affects, an intrinsic value.

His daily interest, his imagination, are completely at the service of the perfect crime. The choice of the victim, even if it turns out to be a colleague whom he meets on occasion, must not arouse either empathy, pity or identification. For the crime to be perfect, he chose someone who meant nothing to him. His objective motivation was that if he chose a stranger there would be no clue that can connect them in the eyes of the investigators, the police would not be able to trace him. But the interviews also show that the absence of an emotional bond between him and his victim will also ensure that when he kills him, he will not be inhibited, he therefore looked at his victim as an instrument that would allow him to realise his grandiose fantasy and not a human being towards whom he would feel compassion.

André therefore describes a very cold planning. Before that period of his life, André had seemed like a 'normal' man who had the most normal friendship and love relationships. But clearly when his life companion left him there was an upheaval with consequences of desymbolisation and disidentification. In the year that followed this separation, he was visibly deeply shaken even if he did not recognise it. André tells us that during this year, he began to take drugs more and more frequently and that it was the drug that made him suicidal; again without linking his suicidal thoughts to the separation. For him, committing the perfect murder was a way of not committing suicide. Planning this murder seemed to bring him out of his depression. He says, 'The more drugs I took, the more suicidal I became, so I decided to do it.'

We can make the hypothesis that the loss of his life partner left him desperate, and that to overcome the suicidal risk he unconsciously felt (but not mentalised), he resorted to a grandiose fantasy, to completely reverse his helplessness. From our external position, it is possible to think that the person he killed could represent his ex-spouse. But the unconscious process is rather that the objects, the people he met every day and the person he is going to kill, do not represent someone, do not represent his ex-spouse and no longer even represent human beings. There is a regressive process supported by the grandiosity of the ideal ego in which the object is no longer an object in the psychoanalytic sense, the other is no longer a 'similar other' an 'other like me'. The other is only a way in which he would achieve a kind of grandiosity that would magically remove the despair resulting from the abandonment by his spouse.

André says: 'It's still a huge taboo in human beings to kill someone... and to have crossed that taboo ... pride ... that wouldn't be the right term but it's the feeling to have achieved something that very few people have done.' He also says: 'I had gone further than the ordinary mortals.'

At the time of the murder, André says he knew what he was doing, that he knew it was monstrous but that he had managed to put himself in a state where he felt no pity, no hatred, he felt nothing. He saw the face of his victim and yet it was like a stranger, 'As if I had never seen him before, I no longer recognised him.' In front of his victim, he felt nothing. But during this same period, no one mattered to him anymore; his partner had left him, and he lived without any friend, alone, without any significant relationship. A world without an object, or a world in which people had no meaning, were barely human beings. He describes that he was detached and calm at the time of the murder, 'I was there but it's as if I was an observer,' he says.

This state of disidentification and disppropriation persists for a few months during which he thinks of committing a second murder. But according to what he says, he is no longer depressed and has reduced his drug use. Then gradually a series of transformations take place: he finds old friends again, he reconnects with his family, he develops a rather significant friendship with a man, and as people become significant in his life, remorse sets in. People become human again, a progressive process takes place, a resymbolisation process, a re-identification to other human beings, a re-humanisation of the people who are part of his existence, until André denounces himself to the police about a year after the murder. It is impossible from the interviews to truly understand the turning point of resymbolisation, but it seems to be concomitant to a new significant relationship.

In summary then: the interviews show first, a regressive stage during which the ideal ego supports disidentification, the desymbolisation of objects, the overcathexis of the ideal ego reversing the traumatic effect of abandonment and creating a world where objects are dehumanised. Then after the murder, as meaningful relationships are put back in place, a progressive process of resymbolisation and of identification that lead André to see the other as 'another like myself', as a human being, will bring the guilt that was absent during the previous year.

Conclusion

In this chapter, I have tried to highlight some common elements that allow some people to commit acts of incredible violence, in a psychological state that does not reveal significant anxiety or guilt, in a state of remarkable disidentification. What I wanted to highlight is the presence of a process of desymbolisation, which manifests itself in a disidentification and a desubjectivation, supported in certain cases by the ideal ego.

By this regredient process, the identification link is broken between the subject and the object, there is a disidentification, which makes it possible to no longer see the other as a 'similar other' or another subject.

References

Balier, C. (1988). *Psychanalyse des comportements violents* [Psychoanalysis of violent behavior]. Paris: Presses universitaires de France, Fil rouge.

Bion, W. R. ([1958]1967). Attacks on linking, in *Second Thoughts*. London: W. Heinemann.

Bouchard, M.-A., & Lecours, S. (2004). Analyzing forms of superego functioning as mentalizations. *The International Journal of Psychoanalysis*, 85(4): 879–896.

Brunet, L. (2019). They think they find themselves: radical violence and narcissistic-identity suffering. *The International Journal of Forensic Psychotherapy*, 1(1): 21–31.

Casoni, D. & Brunet, L. (2007a). The psychodynamics that lead to violence. Part 1. The case of the chronically violent delinquent. *Canadian Journal of Psychoanalysis*, 15(1): 41–55.

Casoni, D. & Brunet, L. (2007b). The psychodynamics that lead to violence. Part 2. The case of 'ordinary' people involved in mass violence. *Canadian Journal of Psychoanalysis*, 15(2): 261–280.

Daxhelet, M-L. & Brunet, L. (2013). Le vécu des enfants soldats [The experience of child soldiers]. *Cheminement psychique et transformations identitaires, La psychiatrie de l'enfant*, 56(1): 219–243.

Daxhelet, M-L. & Brunet, L. (2014). La pensée magique chez les enfants soldats congolais [Magical thinking among Congolese child soldiers]. *Un processus défensif anti-traumatique, Criminologie*, 47(1): 247–266.

Delisle, G. & Brunet, L. (2011). De l'utilité clinique de la symbolisation [On the clinical utility of symbolisation]. *La Revue canadienne de psychanalyse*, 19: 32–51.

Eissler, K. R. (1950). Ego-psychological implications of the psychoanalytic treatment of delinquency. *The Psychoanalytic Study of the Child*, 5: 97–121.

Freud, S. ([1923]1961). The ego and the id. In J. Strachey (Ed. and Trans.), *The Standard Edition of the Complete Psychological Works of Sigmund Freud* (vol. 19, pp. 3–66). London: Hogarth Press.

Gabrion, F. & Brunet, L. (2014). Une étude des relations significatives d'un ex-détenu: aux sources identificatoires de la conflictualité [A study of the significant relationships of an ex-convict: The identifying sources of conflict]. *Filigrane*, 23(1): 115–135.

Hatzfeld, J. (2003). *Une saison de machettes* [A season of machetes]. Paris: Seuil.

Kaës, R. (1976). *L'appareil psychique groupal* [The group psychic apparatus]. Paris: Dunod.

Luquet, P. (2002). *Les niveaux de pensée* [Levels of thinking]. France: Presses Universitaires de France.

Mailloux, N. (1971). *Jeunes sans dialogue* [Young people without dialogue]. Paris: Fleurus.

Redl, F. & Wineman, D. (1951). *Children who Hate: The Disorganization and Breakdown of Behavior Controls*. Glence: Free Press.

Roussillon, R. (1999). *Agonie, clivage et symbolisation* [Agony, cleavage and symbolisation]. Paris: Presses Universitaires de France.

Roussillon, R. (2001). *Le plaisir et la répétition. Théorie du processus psychique* [Pleasure and repetition. Theory of the psychic process]. Paris: Dunod.

Winnicott, D. W. (1974). Fear of breakdown. *The International Review of Psychoanalysis*, 1: 103–107.

5 Mind, psychoanalysis and law in the line of fire

Plinio Montagna

I

'Mind in the line of fire' can be seen as a state of heightened mental alertness or vulnerability, possibly due to the exposure to some kind of stressful or dangerous agent, which can impact its functions and, consequently, mental state. Military situations with soldiers' lives threatened by enemies that can attack at any moment represent a prototypic model for this metaphor.

Ego integrity is in danger due to external conditions, as it faces challenging circumstances. Its strength is tested, eventually to the brink of actual rupture.

In the line of fire, the first task is to survive. This may involve reducing some tools inherent to the organism. For example, plants subject to high ambient temperatures and dry weather shed their leaves to protect themselves until the next rainy season.

By the same token, the human psyche corollary to this may include the mobilisation of the fight or flight mechanism. The ego can stand and confront the stimulus or it can't bear it and go into a breakdown – focusing on the present moment and skipping long-term planning; focusing on attention and immediate solutions rather than on detailed and deep contemplation, as energy has to be spent to face the present stressful situation.

Thus, the effectiveness of the defences and some aspects of the weakening of the mind may sprout as human resilience is at stake.

As for the former, the vectors of fragilisation can be threatening the mind to its rupture. What remains is its ability to resist this inflection, or to return, after stretching, to the starting point – this is what is usually described as resilience.

The resulting vectors from destructive sets can occur internally in each individual, as the outcome of organisation and arrangements of configurations of internal objects, or by mimicking, mirroring and then introjecting objects from the outside world.

Let's remember Freud:

DOI: 10.4324/9781003646266-8

> Suffering threatens us from three sides: from our own body, doomed
> to decline and dissolution ...; from the external world, which can
> befall us with very powerful, inexorable, destructive forces; and
> finally, from our relationships with other human beings. The suffer-
> ing that originates from this last source is perhaps more painful than
> any other.
>
> (Freud, 1930)

Gampel (2022) uses the term 'radiative' as a 'metaphor of social and
political violence in the external world that enters our psychic apparatus
and our social equipment, without our being able to have any control
over its entry, implantation and effects'; it appears, she says, as 'physical
illness, emotional turbulence, uncontrolled drive, deviation from the
political to the use and abuse of the social context, demanding the
awareness that no individual is safe from the effects of the destructive
events that human beings inflict on other human beings'.

The term radiative is related to the fact that the impact, much like
radiation itself, penetrates our psychic apparatus without us having any
control over its entry, implantation and effects (Gampel, 2022, p. 169). It
reaffirms the concrete experience of possibly destructive effects that
human beings can inflict on others. We are, after all, immersed in the
social culture broth – all in the same boat, even if in different locations in
that vessel.

Harris (2017) stresses the impact of political regimes, particularly the
authoritarian ones, in our personal lives. Faced with a potential or actual
traumatic situation, we can focus on the ego and its disarticulation, as
well as understand the elements that enable resilient responses by the
individual.

Sometimes the collective mind itself can be in the line of fire, such as
when – besides real war – there is a public tragedy, a continuous pressure
perpetrated by some disruptive leader, elected or not. In this case, the main
threat may be that of the complete destruction of the group, or part of it.
Many times, the destruction threat comes from the very persons, institutions
or powers that should protect the individual, in a perversion of their aims.
Omnipotence, stupidity and arrogance are sometimes also thrown into the
mix, causing disasters of great magnitude to follow. Every so often, as Bion
puts it, by certain uses of projective identification, one can put bad parts of
the self into the objects so that these parts may be rendered more tolerable
(Bion, 1967).

In *Cogitations* (1992, p. 143), Bion writes:

> The excess of the death instinct, whatever its reason or duration – in
> addition to contributing to the excess of dead objects – painful and
> proto-non-real – means that animism (an animistic vision) does not
> manage to develop. The need for appeasement contributes to a

complex state, in which objects have to be reanimated and venerated. These objects are not exactly gods or idols, believed to be alive and endowed with human attributes, but objects that are chosen specifically and precisely because they are dead. The essential characteristic of the adored object is that of being dead .... This enables the patient to expiate his crime and obediently devote himself to animating what he knows to be inanimate and impossible to animate.

The arrangements and rearrangements of connections between different elements of the world, and between people, are being configured and reconfigured at every moment in the personal, relational, social, political or any sphere of life. They are in constant motion. At a given moment and under certain circumstances, this movement can exceed the ego's limit of tolerability and characterise the presence of trauma. This, on one hand, refers to a disruption and, on the other, denotes a defensive operation of the ego, with the function of preserving its own existence.

Some of the issues on the agenda will depend on the type of power in question, the person who is in power, his/her goals, and whatever means he/she has managed to use to reach that position.

In 'The Unique and the Singular', Ricoeur (2004, p. 72) points out: 'Where there is power, there is fragility; and where there is fragility, there is responsibility.' This can relate to the legal system itself being confronted with significant challenges, controversies or threats. It may involve situations where the judiciary, legal practitioners or legal processes are under intense scrutiny, pressure or criticism. For example, a high-profile case that attracts public attention and debate, or when the legal system is handling complex and contentious issues, can all be considered 'in the line of fire'. Beyond these lines, various threats to democratic law can be at stake.

In any of these cases, 'law in the line of fire' implies that the individuals or institutions involved are operating in circumstances that expose them to potential harm, harsh criticism or intense scrutiny. Therefore, one must also take into account who makes the law and what sort of law is valid at the moment. If, in addition, we bring psychoanalysis into the picture and connect mind in the line of fire with law in the line of fire, we consequently throw psychoanalysis into the line of fire.

'Psychoanalysis in the line of fire' can refer to the practice of psychoanalysis in situations of intense risk, danger, crisis or high stress. Delving into the unconscious, or sometimes helping to shape the not yet formed unconscious, can help individuals facing highly stressful or traumatic experiences. It might also refer to the application of psychoanalytic principles to understand the psychological impact of being in high-stress or dangerous situations. To practise psychoanalysis in high-stress environments implies using psychoanalytic tools in various scenarios, such as studying the mental health of individuals who work in high-pressure professions like emergency services and law enforcement, or of critical incident response teams.

In either case, 'psychoanalysis in the line of fire' highlights the importance of understanding and addressing the psychological well-being of individuals who regularly face significant stress, danger or trauma. Psychoanalytic approaches can provide insights into the unconscious processes and coping mechanisms that shape human behaviour, helping individuals navigate the psychological challenges they encounter in high-stress environments.

The analyst can also be seen as a kind of resilience tutor for the patient, somebody who brings the possibility of personal development, helping to enhance the likelihood of dealing with matters of life.

II

We are going through a period of considerable global turmoil, as witnessed by urban violence, religious fundamentalisms, migratory tensions and – in several countries – violence arising from the rise to power of totalitarian and anti-democratic groups.

Currently, in some countries, democratic law is or has been threatened by disruptive actions intended to limit people's freedom to choose their leaders. Law has either been in the line of fire or has actually been perversely used by rulers during the last few years, including during the COVID-19 pandemic, either by threat or by denial actions.

This has been the case in Brazil, my country, which had a four-year cycle of a disruptive government that frequently advanced conspiracy theories, instigating institutional rupture and coups, which culminated in the invasion of the palaces of the three powers of the republic – Executive, Legislative and Judiciary – shortly after the inauguration of the new government elected by the people. The action was a local version of the assault on the Capitol in the United States, on 6 January 2021.

Zienert-Eilts (2022) characterises as 'destructive populism' a movement that brutally feeds negative emotions such as deep fears, feelings of disadvantage, persecution, envy and primitive aggression. Its discourse is one of division and polarisation between individuals and society in general, of cultivating disagreement, discussion and disruption. Negative effects are encouraged as brutality and omnipotence are idealised.

Splits and separations occur in groups that previously lived peacefully: families split; some parents and children stop talking to each other; previously peaceful groups break apart with increased intolerance and aggression. This is exactly what happened in my country. As violence was stimulated, some people were even murdered simply because they had different political convictions from those in power. In such an atmosphere, the space for alterity is erased, there is little room for coexistence with the different, who are attacked and ridiculed by those in power.

We cannot forget that the unifying power that hatred of the same object promotes is impressive. This was already understood by fascism and other forms of totalitarianism (Montagna, 2021).

Conversely, the democratic civilising process involves cultivating the primacy of the thinking process, of the egoic sphere, in dealing with the other. 'Everything that is loved in the bosom of the soul and human relationships, the rule of force, but is painfully loved, because of the ever-looming danger of destruction,' writes Simone Weil (1949), addressing human nature, referring to how love and the fragility of human connections are always threatened by destructive forces.

Under the aegis of the death impulse, neo-Pentecostal religious funda-mentalism was stimulated. We witnessed the rise of severe attacks on education and health, which culminated in the denial of science during the COVID-19 pandemic. There was astonishing ridicule of the most elementary protective measures by the population, including the recommendation of drugs for this infection that had been proven useless.

Thus, it is not surprising that Brazil had the third highest number of deaths in the world from COVID during the pandemic, according to the World Health Organization (Wikipedia, 2025). Health and intelligence agents were just ignored by a government that disregarded the severity of the situation and, even more incredibly, mocked the suffering of the people, criticising vaccines and promoting medications against the virus that had been shown to be ineffective.

We can say that, for a time, models close to destructive narcissism – char-acterised by aggression, lack of empathy, some antisocial behaviours, grandi-osity, stimulation to aggression to achieve goals, as well as violence or cruelty towards non-members of that group – came to the fore. And, non-surpris-ingly, the stimulation was directed to a group functioning according to Bion's basic assumptions mode, rather than functioning in an operative way.

An important part of the media systematically adopted an attitude of denying evidence, both in relation to vaccination, as well as in relation to other protective behavioural measures against contact with the virus. Furthermore, recommendations of medications that had been proven ineffective against the virus were being promoted, adding to the creation of a denialist mindset that resulted in catastrophic consequences for the population that relied on the power of these federal authorities.

Denialism has many roots, but in this case ideological motivations played a crucial part, especially the demarcation of opposing groups – us versus them. From the political point of view, denialism is an instrument that seeks to select certain facts while ignoring other relevant ones with the purpose of legitimising an ideological position through the use of half-truths, thus denying elements that threaten this ideology.

Another way to define denialism is the refusal to believe in theories or well-founded scientific demonstrations even when the evidence is irrefutable.

One feature of a broad denialism is the possibility to deny evidence regarding other prejudices, an idea which group members blindly embrace. One of their main motivations is, in fact, to follow a leader so as to feel part of a larger sect. Difficulties with dealing with uncertainties is another element of denialism, much like distrust, misinformation and lack of scientific preparation.

In moments or situations like these, an important challenge to our analytical practice is how to deal with rigidity or fundamentalisms, whatever they may be. It touches us in our rigid and omnipotent areas, making it necessary to get rid of temptations to impose any of our convictions on the patient. In addition, we respect their points of view and seek to understand what may be moving them, from their inner world, to that component.

The fundamentalist patient, rigid, fixed (whatever his/her ideology may be), challenges our foundations because, even if we are not fundamentalists, we nevertheless have our boundaries beyond which we do not allow discussions. Everybody has foundations beyond which there is no arguing about. Not everything, of course, can be negotiated.

Denialists do not consider themselves denialists; they call themselves sceptical, and the definition of scepticism is also distorted since, strictly speaking, they refute any type of evidence that opposes the beliefs adopted (Fancelli, 2021).

We obviously know that denial can be an important defence mechanism of the ego, as suggested by Anna Freud; Kubler-Ross showed its protective role in grief and grieving conditions (Kubler-Ross & Kessler, 2007). But far beyond denial as a softener or avoidant of an emotional impact, denialism is proposed as a pathology of denial. In addition to the emotional escape from the denied fact itself, it has implications for the whole personality, with different consequences. When denialism transcends the individual level, it has political and eventually economic relevant consequences.

Many times, the feeling of belonging to a certain group favours or even sustains the maintenance of denials and denialism, even if this may often occur at the expense of marked cognitive dissonances for the individual. The identification with a group – sometimes to be kept under an umbrella of 'protection' of that group or its leader – is what counts, is what moves the individual, who must hold on to his/her beliefs and positions without any question or doubts. This is the area of the patient where his/her fundamentalism is inscribed.

The Freudian model of the mind has been described as a war of embattled fundamentalisms – the biologically based, unscriptural impulses of the id versus the scriptural and at least partially assimilated moral dictates of the superego. As a result, the ego tries to establish the most harmonious possible relations within the mind (Philips, 2008).

III

Although the term resilience has not been part of Freud's universe, the description of mental plasticity and other ones related to physics has been used by him. In 'Terminable and Interminable Analysis', for example, he refers to cases in which we are faced with 'a certain psychic inertia, a depletion of plasticity, of the capacity for modification and further development', including the very elderly (Freud, 1937, p. 258).

The study of individual or psychosocial factors that favour resilience shows it as a process, a permanent dynamic construction. The analyst can become, by providing and sustaining the patient's development, a resilience tutor par excellence. When the procedural nature of resilience and psychoanalysis intertwine, the maturation of the individual's potentials in a psychoanalytic process is always on the horizon.

Resilience must be distinguished from what is known as pseudo-resilience; the psychic counterparts are different from each other, although in the face of traumatic situations the responses may be competent in both cases.

Unlike the resilient response, the pseudo-resilient one is particularly dissociative, in which the body is used as a substitute for psychic processes, thus causing somatic symptoms and physical complaints. The resilient person, in turn, shows a high capacity to tolerate and integrate a range of affections, frustrations and conflict management at a symbolic level.

Other characteristics of resilience itself include the non-passivity in accepting reality, the belief in the value of life and the ability to improvise. Inventiveness and creativity are processes that accompany the adaptive process, with the reconfiguration of oneself in the face of adversity. Creativity introduces a playful element that allows a distancing from reality. In addition, it shows an active self that supersedes any possible passivity during the trauma period. Freud's insight into the spool game, the fort-da, is exemplary (Freud, 1937).

Resilience requires the existence of an internalised good object, based on the prior existence of a real good object; it also depends not only on the fact itself that occurred, but also on the interpretation given to it. That is to say that the meaning given to the fact matters as much as, if not more than, the fact itself.

In the resilient response, the individual is affected and modified by trauma, adversity or a stressful condition. Such a response allows the individual to bend but not break. In fact, not only is a breakdown avoided, but the reversal takes place with *restitutio ad integrum* and the experience results in learning and emotional growth. In this sense, the question of how to turn a bad deal into a profitable one is key.

The existence of some kind of attributed meaning, of a coherent version of the facts, is significant. It is interesting to remember that it is often as or more important for the patient to feel understood by the analyst as the content of the understanding itself.

Resilience must be seen as occurring and developing in a process, within an affective, social and cultural context. It concerns the capacity to metabolise the psychic trauma.

IV

If we ask what kind of questioning would make it possible for psycho-analysts to be useful for the practice of law, we must consider, as Legendre (2001) does, that 'the idea of law depends on the idea societies themselves make out of their notion of life'.

Concerning group processes, Freud (1912–13), in *Totem and Taboo*, points out that 'for the first time I based my position on the existence of a collective mind, in which mental processes occur in the same way as in the individual mind'.

Collective processes create social norms and laws, which represent the individual on the social plain: the individual is at the same time assimilated into the group while maintaining his/her autonomy. The law carries with it aspirations, desires, ideals and values. It also defines and circumscribes the limits of what is and what is not acceptable to everyone. They protect personal safety and safeguard social institutions. Relations are mediated by ideologies.

When the institutions themselves are threatened by destructive populist ideological movements that propagate, for example, denialism (as mentioned above), a concrete threat of social disruption, pain and intense suffering is on the agenda. If disruptive movements start from the 'status quo' itself, we are facing what Zienert-Eilts (2022) understands as a perverted continent, with the idealisation of aggressively destructive and omnipotent affections, and the deformation of democratic societies. Beta elements, she says, are fed, limiting their metabolation to alpha elements.

The need to put in motion all the resources of social resilience is on the agenda.

References

Bion, W. (1967). *Second Thoughts*. London: William Heinemann.

Bion, W. R. ([1967]1992). *Cogitações* [Cogitations]. Rio de Janeiro: Imago.

Fancelli, U. B. (2021). *Populismo e Negacionismo* [Populism and denialism]. Curitiba: Ed. Juruá.

Freud, S. (1912–13). Totem and taboo. Some points of agreement between mental lives of savages and neurotics. In J. Strachey (Ed. and Trans.), *The Standard Edition of the Complete Works of Sigmund Freud*, vol. 13, London: Hogarth Press, pp. 1–162.

Freud, S. (1930). Civilization and its discontents. In J. Strachey (Ed. and Trans.), *The Standard Edition of the Complete Works of Sigmund Freud*, vol. 21. London: Hogarth Press. pp. 1–53.

Freud, S. ([1937]1975). Analysis terminable and interminable. In J. Strachey (Ed. and Trans.), *The Standard Edition of the Complete Works of Sigmund Freud*, vol. 12. London: Hogarth Press, pp. 213–226.

Gampel, Y. (2022). A Dor do Social [The pain of the social]. *Livro Anual de Psicanálise*, 36: 163–182.

Harris, A. (2017). O tanque no quarto [The tank in the room]. *Revista Brasileira de Psicanálise*, 21(3): 151–166.

Kubler Ross, E. & Kessler, D. (2007). *On Grief and Grieving*. New York: Scribner.

Legendre, P. (2001). The other dimension of law. In Goodrich, P. & Gray, D. C. (Eds), *Law and the Post Modern Mind*. Ann Arbour: The University of Michigan Press, pp. 175–192.

Montagna, P. (2021). A Lei, ora a Lei? [The law, now the law?]. In Vianello , *Vozes do Dante*. São Paulo: Ed. Colégio Dante Alighieri, pp. 50–53.

Philips, A. (2008). Sobre o fundamental. *Ide*, 31(47): 16–23.

Ricoeur, P. (2004). *Ethical and Theological Writings: The Unique and the Singular*. London: Continuum.

Weil, S. (1949). *L'Enracinement: Prélude à une déclaration des devoirs envers l'être humain* [The need for roots: Prelude to a declaration of duties towards human beings]. Paris: Gallimard.

Wikipedia (2025). COVID-19 pandemic in Brazil. *Wikipedia*. https://en.wikipedia.org/wiki/COVID-19_pandemic_in_Brazil#cite_note-Template:COVID-19_data-1

Zienert-Eilts, K. J. (2022). Populismo Detrutivo como 'Continente Pervertido: Olhar Psicanalítico sobre a Atração por Donald Trump'. *Livro Anual de Psicanálise*, 36: 139–161.

6   Radicalisation and delusions of sanity?

Carine Minne

Given the current sorry state of our world, the extreme eruptions of violence in so many parts and the atrocities being carried out, those of us interested in human beings must find ways of contributing to understanding how all this happens – often repeatedly. Hence, I suggest we take a glimpse into the radicalised and/or psychotic mind. I come from a clinical background, not as a researcher but as a forensic psychiatrist and psychoanalyst, who has assessed and treated hundreds of young people, mainly men, who have carried out atrocities. Most of them have been diagnosed with psychotic illnesses, many with personality disorders and a few labelled as radicalised terrorists.

My hope is to illustrate the similarity in their background histories, the blurred boundary between what is considered psychiatrically psychotic and psychoanalytically psychotic and how the general public tends to hate 'mad' in cases of terrorist atrocities and prefer 'bad'; and consider what, if anything, we can do about this to contribute to understanding, and especially to prevention. I will also refer to psychoanalytic researchers' views of the narcissistic identity suffered by 'lone wolf' terrorists.

In order to protect the confidentiality of patients and prisoners, I will use the case of Anders Breivik, based on information that was available in public and publications by the Norwegian psychologist and psychoanalyst, Siri Gullestad (2017), who was involved in the ferocious public debate over this case at the time of the trial.

On 22 July 2011, Anders Breivik massacred 77 people in Norway, stating that his motivation for this was ideological, driven by anti-multiculturalism and anti-feminism, with the aim of reasserting a patriarchal and white Europe. Just before carrying out the killings, he sent out a manifesto of 1,500 pages to over 1,000 recipients, in which the main message was that a revolution was required in order to save Norway from 'Eurasia'. He then travelled to central Oslo where he set off a bomb in government headquarters, killing eight people and maiming many more. He went on, travelling to the island of Utoya, 40 km away, where the former female Prime Minister of Norway was giving a speech to 600 young members of the Social Democratic Party attending a summer camp

DOI: 10.4324/9781003646266-9

there. His intention had been to decapitate her on video but a delay in his journey meant she was gone before he arrived. He proceeded to kill 69 children and young people over a period of one hour, shooting them in the head or chest, reportedly smiling as he did so, before finally being arrested.

Soon after these atrocities, several media reports echoed the general public's main response, which was to label him 'bad' and not 'mad'. A psychiatric report presented at his trial referred to a diagnosis of psychosis; hence, there was a recommendation for sentencing to a high security hospital. This apparently led to a public outcry and, unusually, a second psychiatric report was commissioned stating that he had a narcissistic personality disorder and no psychosis. The degree of shock and rage induced by such horrendous acts may have contributed to the polarising of views thereby preventing a more dialectical approach. Interestingly, and also unusually, it was the prosecution service that focused on his psychopathology and need for hospitalisation, whilst he and his defence team insisted on his sanity, with him apparently stressing his moral justification, possibly wanting to be a heroic political prisoner.

Much information regarding his early years became available due to the leakage of childhood clinical records to the press. This included references to the loss of his father in toddlerhood, a mother with whom the relationship was both suffocatingly close and aggressively distant as well as sexualised, an inability to make friends, his failure to manage adolescent developments leading to independence, failed attempts at joining masculine groups such as gangs including Asian gangs, confused sexuality and an eventual immersion into a life online including playing violent games and joining extreme right-wing ideologists' groups. His own rationalised explanation and professed ideologies for carrying out these horrific acts cannot simply be accepted as he stated. It is crucial to dig deeper in order to understand the multi-factorial ingredients that could lead a man to behave in this obscene way as this is one way towards prevention. One could hypothesise that the early loss of his father, the complex and sexualised relationship with his mother, his difficulties developing a self-identity, trouble establishing a career for himself, combined with a confused sexuality, occurred at a time when the Internet enabled him to 'find' an ideology supporting his unconscious conflicts arising from the personal history described above (anti-women, anti-non-whites). Finding a secure, ideological anchor could have enabled him to experience a sense of belonging to a group as well as apparent confirmatory clarity of thought of being right. In reality, both of these functioned merely as sedatives to personal psychical turmoil – identity confusion, the threat of mother/women and the more general threat of 'others'. Yet, providing psychoanalytic understanding as one part in the dialectic can be misconstrued as excusing or, worse, condoning his dreadful actions.

The manifest politicisation of his likely psychopathology seemed to be connected to a generalised collusion with his 'delusion of sanity', a term coined by the late Dr Leslie Sohn (personal communication, 1998). This type of collusion is promoted by the longing in many people for a rational explanation for such terrible violence and can serve as a way to gratify the need for retaliatory punishment whilst avoiding thinking of how someone could do such a heinous thing, or to avoid imagining the state of mind of a person like Mr Breivik, who reportedly laughed while shooting his victims. Rationalisations and denials are the most common symptoms of psychoses as opposed to delusions and auditory hallucinations (Lucas, 2008). These can come across as plausible even if obscene. When the public and criminal justice system both collude with such rationalisations and denials, the disturbed psychotic mind of the perpetrator is overlooked and the person dealt with as if of sane mind – bad, not mad.

What is also overlooked is the troubled personal history in individuals who end up perpetrating severe violence, often starting with unnoticed depressions in babies and toddlers. Every patient I have assessed and treated over three decades in secure psychiatric settings and prisons suffered from often extreme babyhood and childhood traumas. These are then referred to as the 'ghosts from the nurseries' when their impact appears later on in those highly disturbed babies and toddlers now manifesting in big adult hairy bodies. This is one reason why it is so easy to forget the 'roots of evil'. Disturbed babies and toddlers evoke tremendous compassion but their adult equivalents don't.

Despite the vast amount of knowledge regarding the development of the human brain and mind from *in utero* onwards, and how vital the first 1,000 days are in any person's life (Gerhardt, 2003), a recent survey carried out by The Royal Foundation in the UK found that only 25 per cent of the general population considered the first two years of a child's life as important for future development (Royal Foundation Centre for Early Childhood, 2023). The myth continues to be held that if they can't remember, it won't affect them. The reality is that most of the seeds for one's future personality-functioning are laid down by the environment and the nurturing one receives on the background of one's genetic predisposition. I have never yet met an offender patient whose dream as a 10-year-old was to become a serial killer, a paedophile or a terrorist. I realise that to rehumanise the dehumanised can be considered abhorrent by many. It is convenient for us to separate 'them' from 'us'. But which one of us has never had a murderous thought? The difference is that most of us only think it, whereas a few others actually go out and do it. This difference stems from a consequence of the early traumas combined with epigenetics; hence the reason why many people traumatised in early childhood do not become violent later on.

What is of importance therefore is prevention. Psychosocial knowledge is available to allow massive impacts in prevention if the focus of public, physical and mental health services is on the first three years of life. This should begin with school education, at antenatal clinics and with an expansion of highly psychotherapeutically trained health visitors and family therapists. In Germany, a nationwide universal psychosocial health system approach, named 'Nobody Slips through the Net', involves the publically funded training of midwives in further parent–infant training, who remain with the expectant families identified as in need of help, from the antenatal period until the child is at least one year old (Sidor et al., 2015). Funding such very early interventions has also been calculated by Nobel Prize-winning economist James Heckman as cost effective (Heckman et al., 2010), and referred to as the Heckman effect, which illustrated graphically is described as 'The Heckman Curve'. It shows that the highest rate of economic returns comes from the earliest investments in children, providing an eye-opening understanding that society invests too much money in later development when it is often too late to provide great value. It also shows the economic benefits of investing early and building skill upon skill to provide greater success to more children, as well as greater productivity, and to reduce social spending for society.

Early interventions antenatally, at baby and toddler clinics, could make all the difference in preventing such cases and other types of violence, be they 'lone wolves', certain terrorists, gang members, stranger killings or domestic violence abusers.

It is dreadful that confidential clinical information was leaked to the press about Mr Breivik's childhood psychiatric input, and while I would never condone such breaches, the information confirms that he too was another man whose childhood traumas activated such violence in his adult life under a cloud of serious mental disorder; just like so many patients and prisoners who have been violent. Without having assessed this man, I am still of the mind that someone with this history did likely develop a psychotic illness on the background of a highly disturbed personality, that enabled him to present himself as if he were sane. His own wish to be considered sane was colluded with, and I suspect that the trial, media representation and sentencing to prison will all have contributed to gratifying the likely grandiose part of Mr Breivik's disordered personality (Minne & von der Tann, 2011). It is likely still of little comfort to surviving victims, or family and friends, of those youngsters who died so barbarically. This man will have sought out an ideology that fitted with his unconscious criteria; hence the importance of a multi-faceted approach in such cases, including the unconscious motives, but more importantly prevention by improved psychosocial services for babies, toddlers and their families.

In the words of Louis Brunet, Canadian professor of psychology and psychoanalyst who has researched terrorists (2019, p. 26):

> There exists beforehand among the violent fanatics and especially the terrorist radicals, even before their radicalisation, an identity

wandering and a narcissistic suffering that must be denied, compensated and reversed by specific processes, including self-idealising processes. And processes of de-identification and de-objectivation (dehumanisation) of the 'other-not-me' which are the two visible parts of the process. Often processes of reversal succeed in hiding the narcissistic wandering even to the radicalised person himself. And the ultimate reversal of this underlying narcissistic suffering will manifest itself through the use of the destructiveness of the other at first, but in some cases going as far as self-destruction.

We have thus seen in many violent radical young persons and especially those who are called lone wolves, previous signs of identity disorganisation, the presence of a feeling of insignificance, the search for a borrowed identity to put on as a piece of clothing, long before their destructive gesture and even well before what is known as their 'radicalisation'. Because their radicalisation is their illusory solution, it is the process in which they adopt an identity, a mission that will make them heroes. This terrifying lack of meaning and significance often goes unnoticed by most clinicians who are looking for clinical entities with definite and obvious symptoms such as a DSM diagnosis.

Despite the focus in this chapter on an individual's likely psychopathology, it is essential, in the search for understanding individual, group and mass atrocities, to examine the role of group dynamics as well as state terrorism. Bandy Lee (2022) has coined the term 'social disorder' to refer to ill societies that produce atrocious, polarising, dangerous leaders, rather than the other way round. I would stress the importance of inequality and poverty as known drivers for this too.

However, I must refer to Freud and Einstein's correspondence regarding 'Why War?' (Freud, 1933). In a request by the League of Nations to communicate with a chosen professional, Einstein asked Freud for his thoughts on whether there is any way of delivering mankind from the menace of war and achieving world peace. The response remains so painfully relevant today, even when we readers have the benefit of subsequent writings on this subject, such as those of Bion, Klein, Segal, Volkan and others. Einstein's own suggestion to Freud was, acknowledged as unrealistic, of an international administrative legal body to settle conflicts as and when they would arise between nations, although he rightly suspected certain psychological obstacles to this, including the major problem of such a body being run by humans. Most of those in leadership positions would be reluctant to give up their autonomy, or their nation's sovereignty, for peace and security provided in this way. Furthermore, due to the inevitable inequalities between the minority leaders and the majority led, the minority leaders would retain a paranoid stance in fear of being ousted by several of the led coming together and over-powering them. This led Einstein to a further question to Freud of whether it was possible to proof man against his innate hatred and destructiveness.

Freud rephrases the first question to become how war can be avoided rather than extinguished and this, in my view, is important to stress and hints at prevention being the best approach. He summarises the evolution of winning wars, starting with muscular superiority, to tools and weapon superiority, meaning that intellectual superiority overtook muscular superiority. However, he reminds us that any victor needs to obliterate or subjugate the opponent and how any victory provides deterrence alongside a satisfying of the destructive impulses, but the loser becomes filled with revenge, waiting for the opportunity for this to be unleashed. Herein lies a description of the endless cycle and hence, the contagiousness of violence.

It is interesting to note that Freud references a colleague of Einstein's, a physicist, Lichtenberg, and the Compass of Motives, as an analogy when he describes the essential working together of the Life and Death instincts, Eros/Thanatos, Love/Hate and the importance of not conflating judgementally these polarities with Good/Evil. No action is the work of a single instinctual impulse but rather a compound of motives. His description of peaceful times is of communities being held together by emotional ties between their members – identifications – alongside the threat of violence via the law or the 'Right'. The problems inevitably arise with the 'Right' (Mighty, Rulers) becoming violent within the context of the community's group dynamics, where inevitably, self-centredness, narcissism and paranoia are present – the psychotic basic assumptions of groups waiting to surface and dominate. There is a further compound here, of individual dynamics of leaders with group dynamics of the communities led.

Freud therefore stresses that the aim towards peace ought to be via diverting humans' destructive inclinations that are present in all individuals and groups, rather than trying to rid humans of these. Anything that encourages emotional ties between people is a step away from violent conflict. Leaders of groups, communities and nations will always be needed but he recommends better 'training' of our leaders before they become leaders. Here, I was reminded of an exchange with Lord Alderdice, a politician and psychoanalyst known to many readers, and my question to him of whether all politicians ought to have a personal psychoanalysis before their bid for leadership positions.

Such an idea could inadvertently seem to idealise psychoanalysis, but it could actually be a tool for moderating the destructive impulses, and the impact of negative group dynamics, in those individuals that communities and nations choose to be their leaders.

I would also like to quote Segal (2002, p. 35), who said the following:

We are again at a crossroads. Panic has subsided. Apparently, we are 'winning' the war against the Taliban – another pyrrhic victory. At this moment, we still have the choice of remembering the lessons of the Gulf War or blindly repeating our disastrous mistakes. We cannot annihilate all evil and terror without destroying ourselves, because it's a part of us. Even a 'crusade against terrorism' to obtain freedom and democracy is as dangerous and illusory as other fundamentalist beliefs that we will attain paradise if we destroy the evil that we attribute to others.

The real battle is between insanity based on mutual projections and sanity based on truth. How is it that terrorism can get such massive support? I think part of the problem is that we submit to the tyranny of our groups. If we project too much into our group, we surrender our own experiences and the group tyrannises us; we follow like blind sheep led to the slaughter. This does not mean that we should insulate ourselves and enjoy some superior ivory tower of our insights; we are all members of some group or other and share responsibility for what 'our group' does. Even when we are passive and feel detached, our apathy abandons the group to its fate. But speaking our minds takes courage, because groups do not like outspoken dissenters. We are told, 'Ours not to reason why, ours but to do [to kill] and die' (Tennyson, 1854). But we have minds of our own. We could say, 'Ours is to reason why, ours is to live and strive.'

So, returning to radicalisation and delusions of sanity, I hope to have shown a high degree of overlap also with psychosis. Freud's reference to 'divert instead of get rid of' destructive impulses, implies that there is no cure for violence or war but there are many treatments that can really help prevent symptoms arising or, if that fails, after they erupt. Violence is a bit like a societal 'diabetes' – insulin-dependent diabetes can be a devastating illness but it can be well treated and managed (contained) with insulin, because at present, pancreatic transplants remain mainly in the realm of research. Destructive impulses, as a societal illness, can be treated with the 'insulin' equivalent, which is talking-, listening-, identifying with- and other de-othering, dependent. As psychoanalytically oriented people, we really ought to make ourselves much more available as one important facet in striving for and/or reclaiming peace by facilitating communications at those deeper wavelengths between people and peoples, the leaders and the led. If prevention is the best form of treatment/management/containment of violence, then this ought to start right from the beginning, *in utero*, with the parents, family, baby and child services, local communities, schools, places of work, health systems as well as political systems.

References

Brunet, L. (2019). They think they find themselves: Radical violence and narcissistic identity suffering. *International Journal of Forensic Psychotherapy*, 1(1): 21–31.

Freud, S. (1933). Why war? Correspondence between Freud and Einstein. In Strachey, J. (Ed.), *The Standard Edition of the Complete Psychological Works of Sigmund Freud*, Vol. 22 (1932–1936), London: Hogarth Press, pp. 197–215.

Gerhardt, S. (2003). *Why Love Matters*. London and New York: Routledge.

Gullestad, S. (2017). Andres Breivik, master of life and death: Psychodynamics and political ideology in an act of terrorism. *International Forum of Psychoanalysis*, 26(24): 207–216.

Heckman, J. J., Moon, S. H., Pinto, R., Savelyev, P. A., & Yavitz, A. (2010). The rate of return to the High/Scope Perry Pre-school Program. *Journal of Public Economics*, 94(1–2): 114–128.

Lee, B. X. (2022). Societal disorder as a precursor to dangerous minds in politics. *International Journal of Forensic Psychotherapy*, 4(2): 184–191.

Lucas, R. (2008). *The Psychotic Wavelength. A Psychoanalytic Perspective for Psychiatry*. London and New York: Routledge.

Minne, C. & von der Tann, M. (2011). We must focus on Anders Behring Breivik's personality as well as his politics. Opinion. *The Guardian*, 22 August.

Royal Foundation Centre for Early Childhood (2023). *Public Perceptions Survey 2022. Understanding Public Perceptions of Early Years Development*. Ipsos. https://shapingus.centreforearlychildhood.org/wp-content/uploads/2023/01/Royal-Foundation_EYD-Qualitative_Final-Report_220123.pdf

Segal, H. (2002). The mind of the fundamentalist/terrorist. Not learning from experience: Hiroshima, the Gulf War and 11 September. *IPA Newsletter*, 11(1): 33–35.

Sidor, A., Fischer, C., & Cierpka, M. (2015). The effects of the early prevention programme 'Nobody slips through the net': A longitudinal study in an at-risk sample. *Mental Health and Prevention*, 3(3): 103–116.

Tennyson, A. L. ([1854]2007). The charge of the light brigade. In *Selected Poems*. London: Penguin Classics.

7 Oedipal complex

Collective conspiracy theories and individual delusional beliefs

Ronald Doctor

In this chapter on collective conspiracy theory and individual delusional beliefs, I will try to show how the urgency of a need for relief from apparently intolerable mental states involving intense but diffuse anxiety seems to be critical in the development of both psychotic states and conspiracy theories, as a defence against primitive anxiety. Bearing the anxiety and confusion seems to be impossible and leads to either a psychotic organisation with individual delusional beliefs, or collective conspiracy theories, coupled with omnipotent certainty. Both delusional beliefs and conspiracy theories may lead to violent murderous forms of action, which seem to be the only means available to the individual, or group, that can bring an immediate relief to what is otherwise an unbearable form of anxiety.

Individual delusional beliefs and collective conspiracy theory have been described as a template imposed upon oneself or the world to give the appearance of order to events. They appear to make sense out of a world that is otherwise confusing and perplexing and do so in an appealingly simple way by dividing the world sharply between the forces of light and darkness.

It is remarkable how often patients in vague and ill-defined persecutory moods with terrible levels of anxiety and depersonalisation may become calm when these anxieties become organised in a delusional system or conspiratorial theory. Both Freud and Bion saw psychosis as a two-stage process: a dynamic coexistence, in which there is an initial psychic catastrophe, a terrifying anxiety, manifested as a fear of death or annihilation, or to quote Bion, 'a nameless dread' ([1961]1988, p. 183). Similarly, this can also be seen in psychiatric nomenclature, 'a *delusional mood*', 'wahnstimmung', or a feeling of something strange in the atmosphere, with feelings of intense anxiety, depersonalisation and derealisation, which precedes the actual delusional belief. These processes are characterised by a denial of an unacceptable reality, followed by the creation of a substitute reality with delusions and hallucinations that 'make good the damage done' (Freud, 1924). The delusional beliefs that we take to be the pathological product are an attempt at recovery, a process of reconstruction (Freud, 1911).

DOI: 10.4324/9781003646266-10

Like the individual delusion belief, the collective conspiracy theory can be seen as a two-stage process, in that, according to authors Douglas, Sutton, and Cichocka (2017), people appear to be drawn to conspiracy theories when they promise to satisfy important social-psychological motives that can be characterised as *epistemic*, i.e. the desire for *understanding, subjective certainty* and appear to provide broad, internally *consistent explanations* that allow people to preserve beliefs in the face of uncertainty and contradiction. There may be *existential motives* where people may also turn to conspiracy theories when their existential needs are threatened, associated with feelings of powerlessness, to compensate for those threatened needs.

Clinical material

The material I am going to present follows my attendance at an 'Expert Witness Masterclass' in a court case that involved the killing of a father by his son. The class started with a slight commotion in that the eminent psychiatrists acting as expert witnesses in a court case they were about to discuss had just received the news that the verdict had been given against their expert advice. This is very unusual, and their confusion as to why the verdict had been given against their expert advice became my puzzlement; and on the way home from this bewildering masterclass, I bought four newspapers to read to try to understand my confusion. The newspapers were filled with the script from the court trial of this young man, and detailed information about the case, and I have used this script today to try to understand my and the expert witnesses' non-comprehension.

Mr A was a successful captain of a local rugby team; he was bright, handsome, disciplined, mature and highly regarded among his peers and teammates. The 19-year-old, the youngest of three children, was at the centre of a loving family, and proudly involved in the rugby club in a rural village in the UK. To everyone, his life seemed happy and trouble free, but late in 2012 something in Mr A changed that led him to kill his father in early 2013. Father and son had a mutual love for rugby and their shared passion meant they were continually together.

In the summer of 2012, Mr A began to experience a buildup of stress that damaged his outlook and led to devastating consequences. Mr A was deeply affected after breaking up with his girlfriend, his first serious relationship, when she suspected that he had been unfaithful. This relationship started soon after Mr A's grandfather had passed away – the first time he had experienced the loss of a close relative. He became unsure about whether he should drop out of a technology course he had started in September 2012. He also began to feel quite pressured competing in high-level rugby. He resorted to excessive drinking on nights out with friends, and online gambling, and later admitted to having suicidal thoughts. He then lost interest in rugby; he faked injuries and was pleased when he received text messages saying that training had been called off. Something had changed for Mr A over a couple of months.

His family noticed that he had become quiet and withdrawn, often opting to sit alone in his bedroom, and he appeared as if he were 'in another world'. But the devastating extent of his so-called depressed mood only became clear during an incident at the family home in October 2012 shortly after the Sunday dinner. Mr A coaxed his mother into the garage and attempted to strangle her with a TV cable. 'It was in my head to do it – I was going to kill my mum,' he told a psychologist. 'I had the cable in my hand, I raised the cable and put it around her neck.' His mother told the court: 'He said he wanted me to go to heaven. He said I could look after him better there.'

His mother said that she was in total shock and arranged for him to see the GP the next day. The GP referred him to a counsellor at an addiction awareness charity. He was diagnosed with depressive disorder that impaired his mental functioning. The GP said that Mr A came to believe that killing one of his parents would resolve his unhappiness by making them his 'guardian in heaven'. Mr A, himself, would later say that he felt that: 'Killing someone would settle me down a lot more. I was going to kill someone. I knew it was going to be one of my parents. When I had these thoughts, it seemed as if all my problems would go away, that I would be happy, that I could carry on with my life a bit longer.' However, his health was not assessed by a psychiatrist before tragedy struck. Mr A felt the counselling session did not help, he only had one session, and thoughts of killing one of his parents soon began to resurface again.

He managed to get hold of a gun, and three months after the attempted strangulation of his mother, Mr A again harboured thoughts of killing his mother as he worked alongside her at a shop. He appeared his usual self, chatting with customers and later playing pool with friends. However, he felt unable to go through with his plan and instead he decided to kill his father on his return home. He lay outside with his gun, 'My heart went fast; I felt powerful,' he said, and as his father came home and got out of his car, Mr A shot him. He knelt beside his father, said sorry and considered taking his own life but decided against it. He drove to the neighbour and said, 'Daddy is dead.'

He initially told the police there had been a burglary at the home, but later the same night, sitting on the edge of his bed, Mr A confessed to the killing. Before being taken away by the police, Mr A was allowed to speak to his mother. 'We just lay on the bed, we hugged and cuddled each other, we were both crying,' she later told the court.

The trial

I am going to present some of the aspects of the trial in which conflicting details of Mr A's mental state and events in the weeks prior to killing his father were given.

. Asked by *Prosecuting Counsel* whether the accused could form rational judgements, *the consultant forensic psychiatrist*, Dr B replied, 'Yes, he is able to.' Mr A had told him he never thought about the consequences of killing his father. Then counsel asked Dr B if Mr A's behaviour around the time of the shooting was irrational. He replied: 'It's certainly not normal thinking; it's abnormal ... but certainly not indicative of mental illness.' The psychiatrist was also asked if it was possible Mr A was developing schizophrenia, to which he replied that he was satisfied that at present there were not sufficient features to make a diagnosis of schizophrenia.

Prosecuting Counsel referred to Mr A's behaviour around the time of his father's death, including a loss of interest in rugby, heavy drinking and suicidal thoughts. *The psychiatrist Dr B* responded by saying that the 'overall picture' of depressive symptoms was not strong enough to make a depressive episode diagnosis. *Defence Counsel* put it to Dr B that he was 'going to the book and seeing what boxes could be ticked.' Dr B added, 'My view is that he does not meet the criteria for a major depressive episode, even a mild depressive episode, but I accept he does have depressive symptoms.' Questioned on Mr A's suicidal thoughts, Dr B added that one would not diagnose depressive illness based on suicidal thoughts alone.

Mr A's mother said in the trial that he 'never gave us any bother' until she noticed he had become withdrawn. His mother said she was in the garage with her son examining a 'leaking tumble dryer' when he began sobbing and told her he had split up with his girlfriend. She said she told her son not to worry as he was still a young man and would find someone else. She said he replied, 'I don't want anybody else.' She added: 'I was turning to go out of the garage when I felt a cord being thrown over my head. I ran out of the garage door and Mr A was saying, "I didn't mean it, I didn't mean it." I said to him: "You did mean to do it. What's going on?" He said that he wanted me to go to heaven to look after him and granddad.' The sobbing mother said that her son's grandfather had died some time before and Mr A was very close to him. I told him: 'I don't want to go to heaven. I want to stay here with you. He said, "I hope you will always be very proud of me." I said that I would always be proud of him.'

When Mr A's mother was asked if she could explain what had happened, she said: 'There is no reason at all as to why he would want to kill me. I thought there was something seriously wrong with him. We were very concerned. We didn't know what we were dealing with. We were the perfect family. He loved his dad and his dad loved him.'

She said she and her son drove separately to the appointment with the counsellor, where he spent around an hour and a half; he only saw the counsellor once. She said that following the incident in the garage, she had found her son had changed and would increasingly spend more time out of the house. 'He would keep himself to himself. He would be very snappy at times and very vague in his answers,' she added.

She said that after her son was remanded in custody, he was granted compassionate High Court bail to attend his father's funeral while accompanied by his solicitor. The court heard the family had been told that Mr A had written a letter while on remand and wanted it read at the funeral. She then read the letter to the jury. It said: 'To my special dad. This is just a few words I want to say to you as we send you to rest in heaven. Throughout my life you have been a gentleman, a role model, manager and an inspirational figure to me. All that I have done and achieved in my life I offer up to you. It is you I must thank. This is just a short note. You have been a great dad, I love you and I will miss you in my life.'

The court had also heard from a rugby colleague, who described the teenager as 'a quiet, unassuming, lovely young gentleman … very warm and very caring, and anything but "cold and uncaring" – totally opposite to that description'.

In his summing up, *the prosecution barrister* described Mr A as 'brutally selfish' in killing his father in order to get over whatever upset he had in his life. He said it gave the accused feelings of control and excitement and he had shown little empathy for his victim. The prosecution barrister told the jury that although the teenager was a gifted rugby player and a good sportsman with a good life given to him by a good family, Mr A was a treacherous man. Beneath his smiling face was a 'wicked, planning, manipulative killer', the lawyer said. He added that the one voice they had not heard in the courtroom to tell them his thoughts and feelings was Mr A, himself. In a case that 'cries out for him to get into the witness box and explain to you what he did, silence is what he has given you', the barrister told the jury. The teenager had described the killing to police as an 'incident', but the prosecution barrister said, 'It was not an incident, it was the slaughter of his father, planned and executed meticulously by him.' The prosecution barrister said there was no evidence that the accused was suffering from mild depression, nor that his alleged mental condition had an impact on his understanding, rational judgement or ability to demonstrate self-control, which would provide a defence to the murder charge. He said, Mr A, feeling a bit down, following the breakup with his girlfriend, was not an excuse for murdering someone.

Mr A admitted killing his father, but his *defence team* said it was 'a very clear case of diminished responsibility.' *Mr A's barrister* said a *manslaughter verdict*, as opposed to *murder*, would be the 'right, just and proper thing to do'. He said the central question was how a teenager of impeccable character, with everything in the world to live for, came to develop bizarre notions that killing one of his parents would help him to cope with his problems in life. The teenager shot his father shortly after breaking up with his girlfriend and throughout the trial the jury heard expert testimony about the state of Mr A's mental health.

But Mr A's *defence barrister* said that not once during the trial had the prosecution suggested any motive for murder. He told the jury not to be blinded by expert evidence and asked them: 'Do you really need to be a psychiatrist to know that something in this young man's head was badly wrong?' Mr A's attempt to strangle his mother ten weeks before the shooting was a 'dreadful spine-chilling incident' that was 'every mother's worst possible nightmare'. This incident was 'the window that sheds light on this whole case; it shows beyond all doubt that he was suffering from deluded thinking and abnormality of mental functioning', he said. Manslaughter was not a soft option, but his responsibility for his father's death was diminished by his mental state at the time of the killing.

In the end *the jury* accepted the findings of the *defence team's* forensic clinical psychologist who said he was suffering from a recognised mental condition; while Mr A knew his plans to kill either of his parents were both highly illegal and morally wrong, he was nevertheless driven to commit the slaughter to put his parents in heaven as a solution to his unhappiness and teenage problems. The jury found him not guilty of murder but guilty of manslaughter and he was given a life sentence with a minimum of ten years. This was later reduced by three years after he appealed on the grounds of diminished responsibility.

Discussion

It seems that Mr A feels people are concerned and caring about him, but they also abandon him; his grandfather died, and his girlfriend rejected him. At the same time, he feels intensely dependent on his family, but they will also abandon him. He initially has to run away or isolate himself; and though the family feel very supportive, he seems to feel that they will abandon him and thus he will be annihilated. This is the beginning of a vicious circle in that the more he depends on his family the more he will become weakened, and thus to overcome his feelings of weakness, smallness and dread, he must take control and develop an idea (delusional) and he resorts to an idealised and omnipotent solution:

> To place his parents in heaven where they will always look after him and in that way 'he can live happily ever after' with no anxiety and convinced that he will be looked after forever.

Thus, psychosis can be considered a two-stage process: initially there is a 'psychic catastrophe', characterised by a 'denial or disavowal' of unacceptable reality with a resulting feeling that there is something in the air, an oppressive tension, a strange feeling; this is followed by the creation of a substitute reality in the form of delusions and hallucinations to 'make good the damage done', and with a feeling of relief from the unbearable tension (Freud, 1924).

Thus, his family noticed that he had become quiet and withdrawn, often opting to sit alone in his bedroom and he appeared as if he were 'in another world'.

Freud (1911) emphasised that many of the symptoms of psychosis arose from attempts on the part of the patient to restore his damaged ego and to reconstitute a world, which had been destroyed. 'The delusional formation which we take to be the pathological product, is, an attempt at recovery, a process of reconstruction' (Freud 1911).

Mr A's mother said: 'He said he wanted me to go to heaven. I could look after him better there.' The GP said that Mr A came to believe that killing one of his parents would resolve his unhappiness by making them his 'guardian in heaven'. Mr A said that he felt that: 'Killing someone would settle me down a lot more. I was going to kill someone. I knew it was going to be one of my parents. When I had these thoughts, it seemed as if all my problems would go away, that I would be happy, that I could carry on with my life a bit longer.'

Later, Freud (1924) noted that the anxiety that accompanied the symptoms of psychosis suggested that this was due to the hated and denied reality continuing to force itself upon the mind.

The idea that his parents had to go to heaven to look after him seemed to resurface after his attempt at strangling his mother, but with much more force. He seemed more determined to move into the realm of concrete action and obtained a gun to evacuate the tension of his overwhelming anxieties that he would remain alone and completely vulnerable forever.

Steiner (1993) argues that in such circumstances of overwhelming confusion, uncontrolled panic and intense anxiety, the only solution is to turn towards a *psychotic organisation*, which even if recognised as mad, offers relief from the catastrophic anxiety experienced outside. The psychotic part of the personality relieves the patient's anxieties by providing an omnipotent retreat where these anxieties can be organised into a delusional system where the source of persecution becomes clear. This provides relief from anxiety but at the disabling expense of having to live in a psychotic world.

Lucas (2009) drew attention to how clinicians had to be alert to how the psychotic part of the personality could cover up its murderous activity by appearing calm and reasonable, and how this had major implications for the ongoing management of these types of cases. In particular, each time we make an assessment of a patient with a suggested history of psychosis, he asked us to consider whether we are hearing a straightforward communication from the non-psychotic part or being invited to accept a rationalisation from the psychotic part. Psychosis can be conceptualised as a lifelong battle between the psychotic and non-psychotic parts of the personality. Lucas' (2009) important contribution to this was to coin the phrase 'tuning into the psychotic wavelength', which succinctly encapsulated the task of trying to differentiate which part of the personality one was dealing with. Furthermore, he highlighted how difficult this task could be and how it was quite possible for the psychotic part of the personality to try to impersonate the non–psychotic part so that one could be duped into feeling that one was dealing with a rational and sane part of the personality instead (Lucas, 2009).

'He was referred for counselling at an addiction awareness charity,' thus minimising the seriousness of the initial event with his mother.

Duncan Cartwright (2002), in talking about rage murder, also describes how people keep their murderousness concealed and out of sight by a particular use of projective identification. The self identifies with idealised people who are psychically held 'outside', so as to keep them away from the buried and unseen badness or murderousness inside; he called this a 'narcissistic exoskeleton'. Thus, it is the projection of idealised goodness outside, with badness internalised and hidden, commonly inducing in the treatment team the belief that the person is not a killer and that he is, in fact, nice and reasonable.

'The 19-year-old, the youngest of three children, was at the centre of a loving family, proudly involved in the rugby club in a rural village in the UK. To everyone his life seemed happy and trouble free. He was described as a quiet, unassuming, a lovely young gentleman … very warm and very caring.'

Psychotic states arise when ordinary defensive measures fail either under pressure or as a result of anxieties from internal or external factors such as severe loss, which trigger an imminent threat of annihilation.

Mr A was deeply affected after breaking up with his girlfriend, his first serious relationship, when she suspected that he had been unfaithful. This relationship started soon after Mr A's grandfather had passed away – the first time he had experienced the loss of a close relative. He was unsure whether to drop out of a technology course. He also began to feel quite pressured competing in high-level rugby.

In these concepts of *buried badness or murderousness* there is always a psychically traumatic and indigestible experience to do with loss and death and a failure of symbolisation (Sohn, 1995). Thus, a patient provoked by some particular trigger, usually to do with loss and the fear of death, and the consequent weakening and complete collapse of his defensive structure or 'narcissistic exoskeleton', shifts from identification with a previously idealised version of the self to identification with a previously buried bad version of the self. The latter is experienced as an unbearable and intolerable intrusion of the self, which threatens survival. Either it can lead to suicide or it is evacuated and projected into a victim who is then experienced as life threatening. The murderous attack is represented as an attempt to destroy the threat of the bad object, which at that point is experienced concretely as the fear of death or annihilation or possibly the preservation of the good object. Paradoxically, the act of murder is to preserve the good object. To quote Leslie Sohn (1995, p. 574), 'It seems to me that concretisation is specifically to keep the good object in concretely and by the act of murder it is to preserve the good object.'

Perelberg (1999) put forward her hypothesis that violence, and thus murder, relates to a *core phantasy* that involves both the primary relationship with the mother and phantasies about the primal scene, i.e. the original act that created the individual. She states that violence has the function of allowing the perpetrator to believe that he can create a space in which he can survive in the face of an object that is experienced as terrifying. Violence or murder is the acting out of a narrative; it is thus a communication about these patients' belief systems about themselves, about their relationships with others and about their origins. The patient may be communicating a belief that the truth is unbearable, and that distortion of the truth is the sole means of surviving and preventing a catastrophe. The violent act or phantasy tells a tale that represents their personal or collective myth of creation and contains both pre-Oedipal and distorted Oedipal theories.

Mr A, after killing his father, lay in bed with his mother, hugged and cuddled and they just cried together.

James Gilligan (2011) makes the point that classical myths and tragedies may have originated not so much as products of fantasy or as the symbolic, conscious representation of fantasies that are unconscious in the minds of healthy people, but rather as attempts to describe and represent, to cope with and make sense of, to reconstruct their genesis. Indeed, to survive emotionally and mentally, the actual crimes and atrocities that people have inflicted on one another reach as far back into history as our collective memories extend.

Perhaps what is lacking in this narrative is his developmental history. According to Walter Benjamin, in 'Theses on the Philosophy of History' (1940, p. 249): 'Personal narratives can become fragmented, psychotic and appear like a pile of debris.' In fact, this chaotic fragmentation can become organised through the dominance of an omnipotent narcissistic organisation. The psychotic experience can become reified and occupy a disproportionately pre-eminent and significant position in a person's autobiography and its translation by acute psychiatry. The patient's *personal history* can become devalued and the meaning of the story, in their own words rather than in psychiatric translation, is too often disregarded (Doctor, 2008). For them, the relative vividness of the psychotic experience, in this case the Oedipal complex with the killing of his father and joining with his mother, can stand out against a background of impoverishment; it can form a powerful, collective historical continuum that subsumes the individual personal history. At this point, the ability of the individual to maintain a view of himself that is distinct from the image offered to him by the psychotic spectacle begins to fade. Perhaps the act of murder is such an image, the 'sudden flash of recognition' (Benjamin, 1940), which passes from the patient to us in a moment of extreme conflict. However, this is also the moment of its passing, unsustainable in the aggression that has produced it.

History is not revealed by the momentous events but by the ones that lie hidden in their shadows. This is what brings alive the past in the present, shifting the lens from the subject of history to the history of the subject. Telling stories can be an important source of meaning for patients. Their exploration offers opportunities for individuals with experiences of psychosis to reclaim a sense of their own identity and biography and to escape, at least to some extent, the one-dimensional narratives of pathology. Murderers become barely recognisable as human; in other words, the crime keeps getting in the way, concealing them, so to speak.

Conclusion

It is a sign of the deepening irrationality of the times that we are beset by conspiracy theories. In periods of great cultural stress, like now, some people try to explain the terrifyingly inexplicable by creating a neat story to tell themselves, that seems to make sense of it all. I think that my curiosity in this endeavour in finding the truth at all costs was helped by a paper by Civitarese (2021), which *helped me to see how* I may barricade myself behind causal theories of what happens in analysis, *and how one* thinks that one possesses the truth and insists on explaining verbally the nature of *the patient's* problems. I think it is not only Oedipus who has to find the truth by enacting his mad phantasies, so I as the analyst, like Oedipus, may *also* put my psychosis into wanting to tell the patient what he believes is the truth. *In other words, there is* too much emphasis on the epistemic side of representation, i.e. the desire for *understanding, subjective certainty* that appear to provide broad, internally *consistent explanations* that allow people to preserve beliefs in the face of uncertainty and contradiction. As Bion (1958, p. 144) says, 'The discovery of "cause" relates more to the peace of mind of the discoverer than to the object of his research.'

References

Benjamin, W. (1940). Theses on the philosophy of history. In *Illuminations*. London: Pimlico.
Bion, W. R. (1958). On arrogance. *International Journal of Psychoanalysis*, 39: 144–146.
Bion, W. R. ([1961]1988). A theory of thinking. In Bott Spillius, E. (Ed.), *Melanie Klein Today. Volume 1*. London: Heinemann, pp. 178–186.
Cartwright, D. (2002). *Psychoanalysis, Violence and Rage-Type Murder: Murdering Minds*. London: Brunner-Routledge.

Civitarese, G. (2021). On the limits of interpretation; a reading of Bion's 'On Arrogance'. *International Journal of Psychoanalysis*, 102: 236–257.

Doctor, R. (2008). The history of murder. In Doctor, R. (Ed.), *Murder: A Psychotherapeutic Investigation*. London: Karnac.

Douglas, K. M., Sutton, R. M., & Cichocka, A. (2017). The psychology of conspiracy theories. *Current Directions in Psychological Science*, 26(6), 538–542.

Freud, S. (1911). Psychoanalytic notes on an autobiographic account of a case of paranoia (dementia paranoides). In Strachey, J. (Ed.), *The Standard Edition of the Complete Psychological Works of Sigmund Freud*, Vol. 12. London: Hogarth Press, pp. 3–82.

Freud, S. (1924). Neurosis & psychosis. In Strachey, J. (Ed.), *The Standard Edition of the Complete Psychological Works of Sigmund Freud*, Vol. 19. London: Hogarth Press, pp. 149–153.

Gilligan, J. (2011). *Violence: Our Deadly Epidemic and Its Causes*. New York: Grosset/Putman.

Lucas, R. (2009). *The Psychotic Wavelength: A Psychoanalytic Perspective for Psychiatry*. London: Routledge.

Perelberg, R. J. (Ed.) (1999). *Psychoanalytic Understanding of Violence and Suicide*. London: Routledge.

Sohn, L. (1995). Unprovoked assaults – making sense of apparently random violence. *International Journal of Psychoanalysis*, 76: 565–575.

Steiner, J. (1993). *Psychic Retreats: Pathological Organisations in Psychotic, Neurotic and Borderline Patients*. London: Routledge.

Part 3

Society and the law

Introduction

Massimo De Mari, in 'The Crime of Being a Stranger' (Chapter 8), explains the difficulties of working with refugees who have committed crimes and are not identifiable with documents of any kind. In this case, Italian law used to consider their mere presence in the territory a crime. So, once they were free from prison, there was no way that any other institution could take care of them. This contradiction led to a lack of identity which could be another burden on the shoulders of people who are often escaping from war zones and have risked their lives to reach Italy.

In Chapter 9, 'Rules, Poetry and Truth-telling in Psychoanalysis', Alex Winter states that the aim of his chapter is to delineate the different kinds of rules that apply to analytic work and to form a view about the ways in which these may be either a help or a hindrance to the analytic practitioner. Attempts at truth-telling are identified as a central tenet of psychoanalysis. Poetic thinking will be drawn on to illustrate, by analogy, an approach to truth-telling, in which ambiguity is valued and taken account of within the clinical encounter. This will be contrasted with the kind of legal thinking that underpins the formal regulatory environment in which psychoanalysts do their work.

Shimpei Kudo's chapter, 'Voyeuristic Photography (*tosatsu*): Liberation in the Claustrum' (Chapter 10), describes how the law imposes prohibitions on individual behaviour, but where there is a prohibition, there exists a wish. Contemporary forensic psychotherapy, however, has argued that this desire rises out of anxiety and fear. Furthermore, given that crime is a social affair, social and cultural influences on the development of individual psychodynamics cannot be ignored. The chapter discusses these issues through the problem of 'to(u)satsu', voyeuristic photography, as seen in Korea and Japan, where the shutter sound of smartphone cameras cannot be turned off.

Adrienne Harris, in Chapter 11, 'My "Back-alley" Abortion', writes that the term 'back alley' is surely native to her generation; 'it provoked in me a set of memories of my own abortion at the age of 19 in Canada, where, as in the United States, abortion was illegal. Technically undertaken in what was presented as a legitimate medical office in urban Toronto, it was in all other respects, including its unconscious meaning to me, an event in a "back alley"'.

DOI: 10.4324/9781003646266-11

8　The crime of being a stranger

Massimo De Mari

In this chapter, I explain the difficulties of working with refugees who have committed crimes and are not identifiable with documents of any kind. In this case, Italian law used to consider their mere presence in the territory a crime. So, once they were free from prison, there was no way that any other institution could take care of them. This contradiction led to a lack of identity, which could be another burden on the shoulders of people who are often escaping from war zones and have risked their lives to reach Italy. Only recently has this serious contradiction been removed from the criminal code, but the bureaucratic difficulties associated with the problem of residence in the territory remain.

Introduction

Working as a psychiatrist and psychoanalyst in prison is a difficult task because of the struggle to find a mental space within often dilapidated and unliveable facilities and to devise a reintegration project that has any chance of success. In recent years, the impact of the sharp increase of refugees in Italy has led to a percentage of non-EU inmates inside prisons of about 75 per cent. Prison work thus constitutes in some ways a 'line of fire' comparable to that of a border between two warring countries. This is because within the prison situation refugees bring their stories and experiences that inevitably clash with the often-contradictory reality of their host country.

The migratory phenomenon in Italy

In the last 20 years, we have witnessed a dramatic social imbalance following the wave of migration from neighbouring countries that have brought large numbers of immigrants, mostly undocumented, to Italy. This imbalance starts from a necessary sociological premise concerning the general population; that is, the gradual abandonment of certain work activities, which are considered too tiring and unrewarding by the job-seeking population, mostly of a young age. Thus, the demand for unskilled labour has increased, which has led to Italy being considered a

DOI: 10.4324/9781003646266-12

country where it is easier to find unskilled work. This migratory flow, which we might call 'physiological' from poorer countries (in particular, initially, Albania, Poland and Morocco), grew exponentially as a result of the well-known international political and economic turmoil, justified no longer only by economic reasons but by those fleeing countries at war or with dictatorial regimes.

> Anger may become, in some cases, a desperate striving to feel alive and escape innermost death. The refugee may thus end up feeling remote and isolated, while in fear of the company of otherness. Feeling different, refugees become isolated or relate only to those who share a similar trauma. This is the reason why the earliest sign of recovery is to be found in a renewed search for others who differ from the self.
>
> (Castriota, 2022, p. 113)

The first generation of immigrants also brought with them a significant criminal drift, for crimes involving drug dealing and the management of prostitution. The criminal phenomenon resulting from the numerically less and less sustainable entry of immigrants came largely from the countries of origin; at that time Italy constituted a mirage of freedom and job opportunities for many but also of easy gains on a criminal basis for others. All this aroused no small amount of social alarm, prompting successive governments over the years to draft a series of laws to calm the population and contain the phenomenon.

The legislative issue

Law no. 189 (30 July 2002), called 'Bossi-Fini', replaced law no. 39 (28 February 1990, called 'Martelli') and law no. 40 of 6 March 1998 (called 'Turco-Napolitano'), which set out the general outlines of public policies on immigration in Italy by establishing the crime of clandestinity. The mere fact of being present in the country without documents, including arriving as an illegal immigrant, was considered a crime. This then led to the real possibility of these people being arrested and finding themselves in jail for this reason. This meant that a considerable number of immigrants from the countries mentioned above were sent to prison, and were also convicted for other petty crimes (especially drug dealing) in addition to the crime of illegality. What happened was that these people had just arrived in a country where they had no recognised rights and where they lived in poor conditions. Consequently, they were forced to ask for help from their compatriots who were already living in Italy, most of whom were involved in illegal activities.

After the first few days of their stay without being able to be a legal resident in Italy and thus have a job (because in order to have a job it is necessary to possess documents and have a written proposal from an employer), these people were then forced to commit crimes. One of the easiest opportunities was drug dealing, a crime for which the Bossi-Fini law had established very high penalties. For a first episode of petty dealing it was possible to be sentenced to as little as two years in prison, while recidivism for the same crime carried a four-year sentence.

Recently, under a government formed by centre and right wing parties (2018–20), a 'security decree' tightened immigration regulations and limited the right to asylum, making the expulsion of migrants and revocation of citizenship easier. The decree was ultimately overturned in 2020, but by that time it had already served as a symbolic victory for the right wing parties, which won the last general election.

These laws stem from a grassroots movement that sees illegal immigration as the main cause of instability and the rise of micro-crime in the country.

In the last few years, there has been a shift from the primacy of sociology towards a primacy of criminology. This is due to an increase of social insecurity, especially economic. This means that people began to consider a whole range of sociological issues related to marginalisation as pertaining to criminology, not only in the noblest meaning of the term, i.e. related to crime prevention, but in a punitive sense towards behaviours considered on the margins if not against the law.

Statistics have since shown that the number of crimes has not particularly increased as a result of the increase in the number of immigrants. There has even been a general reduction in the crime index; for example, since 1990 there has been a 50 per cent reduction in homicides. What has happened, however, is that public opinion considered the presence of immigrants a danger regardless of why they were in Italian territory, and this was naturally amplified by the mass media.

Criminology has become very popular in the media, and this has led to criminal policy and legislation with the following changes: 1) Raising penalties as a priority; 2) Increasing the space given to 'victimless' crimes. These are crimes where the danger comes from the stranger just by the fact that they are one, even without them having committed any crime – the willingness to penalise non-harmful behaviour against another just by existence itself.

An illustrative example of this policy is the so-called 'Urban DASPO', an administrative and criminal penalty for loitering.[1] It is also not surprising that in a state such as Italy, which is strongly conditioned by the presence of the Catholic Church, there is the crime of blasphemy for which a fine of up to 4,000 euros was recently established.

How the prison population has changed

When I started working in prison as a psychiatrist, the population con-
sisted almost entirely of Italian citizens, with a few rare exceptions. The
spread of drugs was not yet a social problem as they were not easy to
obtain and were quite expensive on the market. The most widespread
and cheap psychoactive substance was alcohol, but not to the point of
significantly characterising criminal behaviour. At that time, each inmate
was allowed to have a quarter of a litre (about 10 oz) of wine available
every day, while now alcohol is strictly forbidden.

According to Erving Goffman's definition, prison is a 'total' institution,
because of its 'encompassing' characteristic. The individual in it has all
his vital needs cared for but finds an 'impediment to social exchange and
exit to the outside world' (Goffman, 2003). Unlike other total institutions,
such as the convent, the barracks, the boarding school, people do not go
to prison because of a vocation, a professional choice or to recover from
some disease but are locked up there forcibly, to serve the sentence prescribed for a crime they have committed.

In the 1800s, prison provided corporal punishment up to and including
the death penalty. Suffering was inflicted on the offender's body as
expiation for the crime he had committed, a solely afflictive punishment
that had no re-educative or re-integration prerogative for offenders. With
the Enlightenment, prison began a progressive transformation from a
place of expiation and punishment (the old diction of the penitentiary
was 'House of Punishment') to a place where a mental suffering (caused
by the loss of freedom) is inflicted (Foucault, 1975). Beside the suffering,
however, the offender has a chance to rehabilitate along a path of
gradual awareness, leading to the so-called 'critical review' of the crime
committed, a term that could be translated, in psychological language, as
'insight'. The first prison regulation is contained in law no. 354 (26 July
1975). This is still the law that regulates the penitentiary institutions to
which, in accordance with the times, updates are made, such as during
the COVID-19 pandemic, for example, when many inmates were given
the opportunity to access home detention. Another important law is law
no. 663 (Gozzini, 10 October 1986), which introduced premium permits
and other forms of rewards, effectively giving the prison a concrete
rehabilitative function. There are two types of prisons in Italy: the first is
called Casa Circondariale, where people accused of a crime are remanded
in custody, waiting for the charge to be formalised. When the three levels
of trial have been carried out, reaching the final judgement, the prisoner
may remain in the prison to serve the sentence if this is not longer than
five years. For sentences exceeding five years, the designated facility is
the second type of prison, which is called Casa di Reclusione (De Mari,
2018).

Prison as a possible moment of growth

From a psychoanalytic point of view, some characteristics of prison could be seen as symbolic aspects, some more evident, others less so. The first possible association is with a paternal, judgemental and competitive masculine self to which one has transgressed and towards which one can channel the aggressiveness of the power struggle. It is well known how, in the prison subculture, those who have committed the most serious crimes are the ones who gain the highest place in an unwritten hierarchy. The competition is therefore manifested both vertically (I-father-god) and horizontally (I-brothers-society) and is fostered by the structural organisation within the prison. The organisation of each prison has a pyramidal structure with the warden on top. Under his command there is a predominantly male staff, which only in the last 20 years has seen, with much resistance, the entry of female workers. The prison is a house that could be perceived as a home, with a containing 'protective' side, both with respect to the society that rejects the offender and towards the possibility of relapse. We might consider it a kind of maternal 'holding', lately improved, as I mentioned earlier, by the increasingly numerous presence of female workers such as psychologists, school teachers, social workers, volunteers and also police women.

The potential educational function of the prison implies some unwritten duties that have the function of fostering coexistence, to find a good relational balance with peers. It is important to establish a constructive relationship with educational figures, which include in-house educators and teachers of various degrees, and maintain relationships with outsiders, particularly family members. Inmates are allowed to have access to personal or online meetings, epistolary or telephone contacts, and this is facilitated by the collaboration of educators and cultural mediators. The inmate population in the prison where I work is largely made up of young adult males (statistically a higher percentage among offenders), a population that in the last 20 years has taken on a very different connotation if compared with the decades of the 1980s and the 1990s. Back then, the inmates were all Italians, with a few rare exceptions, and the toxic and drug addiction was restricted to alcohol abuse; today, 70 per cent of the inmate population is composed of non-EU nationals and 30 per cent are drug addicts. There used to be a prevalence of so-called 'common' crimes (theft, robbery, extortion); today, crimes against the person, violent and often heinous, prevail.

The crime as a symbolic equivalent

Psychoanalysis speaks of transgression of the rules imposed by the superego, thus taking us back to a pre-Oedipal stage of psychosexual development; the anal phase, in particular, when the concept of the superego begins to take shape. According to Freud, the anal phase follows the oral phase and precedes the phallic/genital phase. Sometimes, as we know, the obstacles that get in the way of these phases do not allow for a linear overcoming, so that some open questions remain in the ego unprocessed (Freud, 1905).

The personality structure that is being formed may be deficient of some fundamental components that provide stability and balance, and enable the individual to make choices, facing a realistic perspective. The lack of security, often of affection, in the early stages of life, produces an attachment deficit that then carries over into difficulty in handling life's frustrations, and the resulting aggression is not tolerated and turns into distress. Insecure attachment, added to genetic personality traits, data biological constituents and environmental influence, can lead to pathological forms of dependency. When distress prevails, aggression is no longer contained within the mind and is acted out in the external reality. This leads to behaviours that tend to bend reality to one's own needs, necessarily, therefore, limiting others' need for freedom. Crimes are themselves transgressions of social rules that are precisely meant to preserve the individual freedom. We have seen a recent example of this kind of transgression in the denial of the risks connected to the COVID-19 pandemic. To wear or not to wear a mask, to follow or transgress the rules imposed by scientific committees; these decisions have become social and even political topics, clearly indicating that the line between expressing one's own freedom and respect for the freedom of others is very thin and precarious.

'When people who have committed a crime are arrested' – as the late Italian psychoanalyst Gino Zucchini used to say during his seminars – 'they are put in handcuffs, which serve concretely to block their ability to convey anguish in a violent act. From a symbolic point of view, the handcuffs allow them to contain the anguish and bring it back to the mind, where it can be contained, in order to be able to process it into "healthy" pain' (personal communication, Zucchini, 1995–99). Psychoanalysis has for many years now been paying increasing attention to the so-called 'serious pathologies', those that were once considered completely insensitive to the psychoanalytic approach. It has always been held, in the wake of what Freud himself argued, that patients with severe mental disorders such as autism, schizophrenia or other forms of psychosis did not have the proper prerogatives to use the psychoanalytic tool. These prerogatives, as it is well known, include: 1) A certain cultural and intellectual level that allows the expression of, through language, one's own deep suffering and to grasp the metaphorical and symbolic meaning of words. According to Franco De Masi:

> In severe pathologies we find an inhibition of language and ideation coartate, that is, limited, conditioned by deep psychic suffering, an

anguish that becomes tolerable only through the use of equally strong defence mechanisms ranging from removal, splitting, denial, projective identification … from which then result symptoms such as obsessive ideation and, to follow, hallucination or delirium. These patients have, therefore, an altered view of reality.

(De Masi, 2012, p. 2)

A capacity for empathy such that they can enter into a relationship with the therapist and thus allow the establishment of the transference and countertransference necessary for the interpretation of what happens in the 'hic et nunc' situation of the session. 'Patients with severe pathologies,' says De Masi,

suffer serious deficiencies at the affective level, from the earliest stages of attachment. Such primary deficiencies lead to the structuring of a fragile, introverted personality, locked in an autistic affective and relational, often characterised by a latent depressive background in which anger and aggression find a fertile breeding ground.

(De Masi, 2012, p. 3)

The ability to tolerate the frustration of analytic work that tends to drop psychic defences and bring out from the unconscious latent conflicts. 'The internal arrangement in severe pathologies,' points out De Masi,

can be located at a primary level of functioning, where needs and desires rule, the heritage of a higher developmental set-up, are too distant and frustrating a goal (let's think of the great problem of drug addiction). The process of subjectification, the dynamics of separation-individuation and finally the capacities of autonomy and relationship. The experience toward the other is thus characterised by feelings of envy, the result of a narcissistic pathological, which is known to have destructive characteristics.

(De Masi, 2012, p. 3)

From these brief hints, we therefore easily understand how patients with serious illnesses are, by definition, the least likely candidates for psychoanalytic treatment understood in the classical sense of the term.

It is therefore fair to ask whether it is possible to use, with this type of patient, the tools and method that classical psychoanalysis provides us with and, if the answer is positive, whether it is still psychoanalysis that we are using or is it not something else that has nothing to do with classical psychoanalysis anymore?

The work of a psychoanalyst in prison and the patient–therapist–society triad

1) Personality characteristics and defences: the personality of the individual who commits crimes presents aspects of particular complexity and is difficult to frame from a diagnostic point of view. The most used unconscious psychic defences are the more archaic ones, splitting and denial, but also the rational and conscious ones such as lying and not remembering play, especially in the early stages after the arrest. They have an important role because they respond to a need for self-defence and are used as levees to save oneself from too severe a punishment and try to get out of the crisis situation in the best possible way.

2) The therapeutic relationship: for the therapist, it is never easy to accept the idea of entering into a relationship, sharing one's feelings and thoughts with someone who has been responsible for morally reprehensible and sometimes destructive behaviour towards others. These acts are, in some cases, directed against unknown people, encountered by chance so their victims may be people well known by the therapist or even friends or relatives, or even people who may recall their loved ones.[2] Since the first moment I started working in the forensic field, I have been asking myself whether some criminal behaviours might be foreseeable, and whether psychoanalysis would be a possible treatment. Of course, the answer is not easy, just as it is not easy to answer the question of the judge who needs to determine whether the individual who committed a violent crime, like a murder, was 'at that time' (weeks, months, sometimes years before) capable of understanding.

One of the crucial questions about violent crimes like murder is if they always have a connection with hate.[3] As Patrizio Campanile says:

> Ruthlessness, ferocity, and brutality are combined, in the case of cruelty, with indifference and insensitivity to the victim's physical or moral pain. There's a link that acting with cruelty may have to the sublimation process and therefore to forms that the system of ideals can take in the individual. The possibility of sublimating is certainly a great opportunity for the individual and for humanity, but it can also pave the way toward the destructiveness in individuals, groups, and society gaining the upper hand. The individual and the masses can resort to extreme cruelty as a possible way to avoid the anxiety of helplessness (Hilflosigkeit) that in the life of each individual and in groups can have many faces.
>
> (Campanile, 2017, p. 38)

I believe it is essential that the therapist is able to recognise and find within themselves a similar complexity and verify the presence of their own balance that would make it possible for the patient to feel recognised and find a foothold for their own dissociated aspects. I am convinced that, long before any social rehabilitation and re-educational project, the goal is to help the patient who acts out violently to be aware of their dissociated parts in order to be able to follow a difficult path that tends to establish a new balance, and is able to recognise, manage and process aggression.

Working on the patient's history from a reintegrative perspective

Dealing with mental pathologies could be, in some ways, easier when working as a psychiatrist: it is just a matter of making a diagnosis and then you can count on a wide range of medicines that help the patients to improve their symptoms and to regain contact with reality. It is quite different when you have to deal with personality disorders, which keep the patient on a border between the possibility of keeping life's frustrations in mind rather than acting them out, often violently, and committing crimes. In many cases these personality disorders are not present with only one characteristic (i.e. narcissistic, borderline, dependent) as we might find traits of different kinds together in the same person, which makes the description of that personality more complicated. Moreover, working psychoanalytically with these complex personalities is a particular challenge as transference and countertransference are deeply involved and sometimes hard to recognise.

Refugee, foreigner, stranger: living without an identity

THERAPIST (T): Is it the first time you have been in prison?
PATIENT (P): Yes.
T: How long have you been in Italy?
P: About ten years now.
T: Are you here on a regular basis? I mean, have you any documents or a temporary work permit?
P: Nothing.
T: You mean you have never been legal in this country?
P: No.
T: Is there anyone from your family here?
P: No, they are in my country.
T: Are you married?
P: Yes.
T: Have you got children?
P: Yes, I have two little children. They are six and four years old.
T: What do you and your wife do for a living?
P: My wife is a housekeeper, and she's paid under the table and I ... have no regular job ... so ...

T: So you have been doing something wrong ... that's why you are here?

P: Yes.

T: Have you attended school in your country or here?

P: Primary and secondary ...

T: Do you use drugs?

P: Yes, mostly cannabis and sometimes cocaine ...

T: Alcohol?

P: Of course, a lot ... mostly beer ...

T: How did you manage to live here for so many years without documents, that means living without medical assistance ... nothing?

P: Fortunately we are all in good health, doctor; when we need medical help we ask some friends from our country or we can go to the emergency room.

This is a typical first session with a patient, during his first experience in prison, which is the male prison where I work in Italy. This patient might come from Maghreb regions (Tunisia, Morocco, Algeria) or from east European countries (Romania, Albania, Serbia, Croatia), and sometimes from far east countries (India, Pakistan, Afghanistan) or central (Senegal) and South Africa.

'From a psychological point of view,' quoting De Zelueta,

> racism implies that the 'black' is legitimately dehumanised and can therefore be physically and psychologically exploited. Racism therefore begins, as in all other acts of dehumanisation, with a distortion of perception: the 'other' is really perceived as different, filthy, stupid, bad, childish. Scapegoats then become as essential to the maintenance of law and order as armies and police forces.
>
> (De Zelueta, 2009, p. 275)

A patient from Tunisia, married with three children and working regularly in Italy, as a result of some economic problems, found himself involved in drug dealing and was therefore confronted with the experience of prison. This event was particularly catastrophic for the patient since it led to, as a consequence of separation from his wife, the loss of parental authority and of his residence permit, which was also a consequence of the loss of validity of his identity documents, which had expired. When he was only a few months away from being returned to freedom, this patient developed an acute psychotic decompensation for which urgent hospitalisation to a psychiatric service was necessary, where a diagnosis of acute psychotic breakdown was made. In the weeks prior to his being released, the treatment team tried hard to safeguard this patient's mental health by trying to find him a possible residence, where he could live, at least temporarily, until he could regularise his documents and a local mental health team could take over. But in the absence of valid identity documents and a regular residence, according to current laws in Italy, this was not possible.

All the heads of territorial institutions (social services, psychiatric services, police headquarters) looked for a solution during interdisciplinary meetings, albeit a temporary one, that would allow them to solve this patient's problem regardless of the law. In the end, when a viable solution was somehow found, the police headquarters took the decision to send this patient back to his homeland, after which nothing more was heard of him.

This seems to me a typical example of the situation in which the marginalised foreigner, from whatever social and political situation he comes from, is in Italy at this very difficult social political moment. I believe that beyond all political and social issues, we, as psychoanalysts, must necessarily confront the issue of the 'other' as the stranger; what Freud calls 'the uncanny' (Freud, 1919). Stranger means 'someone not known or not familiar'. If the unambiguously familiar is heimlich (homelike), then its antonym, the uncanny, is unheimlich (unhomelike).

In the prison population, particularly among immigrants, it is common to observe certain pathologies related more to altered personality. The most common personality disorder is the antisocial, which can evolve into full-blown psychopathy. Other forms of psychiatric pathologies are comparable to those also common in other segments of the population, but what may strike the psychoanalyst most is to see how, behind the histories of these personality disorders, there is a series of traumatic episodes.

The first moment of trauma is often related to early developmental issues in troubled and dysfunctional families, to which all those events related to social and political turmoils become the second and even the third moment of trauma. Thus, several traumas join together and lead to the formation of unbalanced, if not disturbed or pathological, personalities.

It is commonly believed that when we talk about psychopathy and deviance, we refer to mental pathologies; while, instead, it is important to emphasise that these aspects of personality, which we can find in various psychopathological syndromic pictures, are also present in 'healthy' people. The diagnosis of these disorders is complicated by an apparent normality of behaviour and a high cognitive and intellectual level, often above the average, in the face of a distorted view of the relationship from a moral and especially affective point of view.

Therapy can therefore rely little on the contribution of psychopharmacology, as very often we find no symptoms; these are people who report well-being and avoid confrontation with 'psy' professionals as much as possible. We observe, then, conscious defensive attitudes (pathological lying, adapting to prison subculture patterns, a tendency to give a positive self-image) related to the logistical situation in which we find ourselves establishing relationships with these patients, i.e. prison or psychiatric-judicial facilities. Such attitudes aim to downplay one's responsibility as much as possible and opportunistically obtain as many secondary benefits as possible; first and foremost, a reduction in sentence. As a result, the therapeutic relationship, rather than being sought in order to clarify one's reasons for committing a crime and deepen one's psychic issues, may be commodified, become the object of manipulation or be experienced in a judgemental and persecutory manner. Here, then, the first therapeutic approach with these patients must be one of acceptance. It is, especially, necessary to address the experience of feeling 'foreign' therefore 'different'; an experience that as we have seen has to do with different psychic and intra-psychic levels.

It is very common to see initially defensive or aggressive behaviours from people who feel judged by prejudices. Quite often the therapist, as a representative of the institution, may initially be considered by the immigrant inmates as a racist, precisely because laws and public opinion express fear of being subjected to an invasion. The presence of the 'strangers' in the Italian territory is perceived as an intrusion by outsiders (unheimlich) who have nothing to do with the Italian culture. Moreover, if they decide to remain in Italy, the most common concern is that they would probably steal jobs from Italians (which is one of the most common slogans of the right wing political parties), or to commit crimes.

Conclusion

We live in a time when each individual's life is affected by social, health and international political issues that have had, and still have, profound effects on everyday life. The prison perhaps represents a model in which several 'lines of fire' are intertwined, a prototype that can be taken as a model of all the possible dynamics that the psychoanalyst is confronted with. The challenge then will be to continue to work psychoanalytically, seeking, beyond the obstacles and difficulties that these situations entail, an openness of thought that will then allow the psychoanalyst to work on the relationship and thus to bring to these patients that specific help that the psychoanalytic method has as its main characteristic.

So, the questions I ask myself every day are as follows:

1   How can psychoanalytic theory, with the necessary adaptations of method, be used with this kind of patient and what kind of help might it offer in prison or in other settings in the line of fire?
2   Can we still call psychoanalysis this adapted method we are using, or is it something else that has nothing to do with classical psychoanalysis anymore?

I am convinced that every psychoanalyst must build his or her own mental setting that will enable him or her to work analytically in all conditions, even extreme ones in which he or she may find him- or herself. Just like many colleagues who serve on International Psychoanalytic Association committees working with refugees or in other extreme situations have shown, if the psychoanalyst has a sufficiently stable mental setting, he or she will be able to continue to work analytically in all those off-the-couch activities that everyday reality offers us today.

Notes

1 Anyone who does certain actions in the territory can receive a de facto DASPO: whoever engages in conduct that restricts free accessibility and enjoyment in specific areas of urban space in violation of specific prohibitions on parking or occupation of designated spaces.
2 'Neurotics,' says Arthur Williams, 'generally suffer and fail to carry out most of their projects due primarily to the anxiety and inhibitions that plague them. Criminals, on the other hand, take action and often commit crimes. Examining the stages of "emotional development through which all human beings pass" allows us to identify the moments when the person who will become criminal and the person who will become neurotic deviate from normal psychic maturation' (Williams, 1983, p. 191).
3 In a 1971 article, Kurt Eissler relates the death drive to ambivalence and narcissism, and says: 'The death drive, within the organism, by means of the life process, reinforces differentiation, that is, structural growth. When this structuralization has reached its maximum, psychobiological unity decays. Part of this death drive is diverted and, in the form of aggression, placed in the service of man's survival and his protection against danger. Ambivalence stands in the way of object fixation. Narcissism, through the reinforcement of self-esteem, is the first requirement for survival. Aggression, when it is necessary and useful in itself, also becomes the primary means by which to gain narcissistic gratification. Ambivalence becomes a guide for the discharge of aggression against beloved objects, and man becomes destructive precisely where he loves. Man's problem is not his aggressive drive but rather the fact that his aggression is driven not by self-preservation but by narcissism and ambivalence and therefore, unlike the animal, poses a supreme danger to his own species and culture. Man does not use his aggression primarily against the enemy or probable enemy; instead, ambivalence compels him, as mentioned earlier, to use it precisely against his own love objects. The one area where, in most cases, the clinician has an opportunity to observe something to do with the cultural effect of ambivalence is in the parent-child relationship. It is no exaggeration to say that very frequently parents are the bane of their children even though they are what is closest to their hearts. There seems almost to be a secret tendency in man to destroy what he loves most' (Eissler, 1971, p. 27).

References

Campanile, P. (2017). *La crudeltà, il paradosso della sublimazione e la paura* [The rawness, the paradox of the sublimation and the fear]. Raffaello Cortina.
Castriota, F. (2022). Psychoanalysis and the drama of refugees in Italy. In Elton V., Leuzinger-Bohleber, M., Schlesinger-Kipp, G., & Pender, V. (Eds), *Trauma, Flight and Migration: Psychoanalytic Perspectives*. Routledge.
De Mari, M. (2018). *L'Io criminale* [The criminal ego]. Alpes.

De Masi, F. (2012). *Lavorare con i pazienti difficili* [Working with difficult patients]. Bollati Boringhieri.

De Zelueta, F. (2009). *Dal dolore alla violenza. Le origini traumatiche dell'aggressività* [From pain to violence]. Raffaello Cortina.

Eissler, K. (1971). Death drive, ambivalence and narcissism. *Psychoanalytic Study of the Child*, 26: 25–78.

Foucault, M. (1975). *Sorvegliare e punire. Nascita della prigione* [Discipline and punish: the birth of the prison]. ET Saggi.

Freud, S. (1905). *Tre saggi sulla teoria sessuale* [Three essays on the theory of sexuality]. OSF4. Boringhieri.

Freud, S. (1919). *Il perturbante* [The uncanny]. OSF9. Boringhieri.

Goffman, E. (2003). *Asylums. Le istituzioni totali: i meccanismi di esclusione e della violenza* [Asylums. Total institutions: mechanisms of exclusion and violence]. Einaudi.

Williams, A. (1983). *Nevrosi e delinquenza* [Neurosis and delinquency]. Borla.

Zucchini, G. (1995–99). Lectures during the psychoanalytical training seminars. INT – Istituto Nazionale del Training della Società Psicoanalitica Italiana, Sezione Veneto-Emiliana.

9 Rules, poetry and truth-telling in psychoanalysis

Alex Winter

There appear to be things called 'rules' in psychoanalysis. These represent the law. The law in turn stands for something parental, which is never fully intact inside the patient. Freud gave it various names: a censor, a critical agency, the ego ideal and, eventually, the superego. The ego is subject to pressure from this agency. On a societal level, realities of rule-following or rule-breaking, dealt with through the legal system, provide a collective externalisation of psychic processes which exist within us all. It will be my argument that when these external structures re-establish contact with the place from which they came, our inner worlds, the consequences can be jarring and even brutal. I believe this has important implications for the regulation of psychoanalysis.

The significance of rules within psychoanalytic theory

Questions about rules are fundamental to psychoanalytic theory and psychopathology, because they are inherent to the Oedipal situation.[1] The paternal function, which devises and imposes rules, allows the mother–infant dyad to progress towards a three-person relationship and the broader social world. In the classical Freudian view, castration anxieties underpin every child's position within the family and constitute the source of all law-making. Incest is the original crime and castration is the sanction threatened by the authorities. It is also the keystone to what will become a mature personality, in that it is fear of punishment that leads to the development of the superego. Subsequent developments in psychoanalytic thinking might characterise these matters somewhat differently, questioning the phallocentric genesis of law-making[2] and deepening the concept of castration into a range of feared outcomes, including shame, disintegration, loss of the object or loss of its love;[3] but the essential point remains the same – in the neurotic realm, crime and punishment are close to the heart of the internal drama being played out.

Psychosis, by contrast, exposes a chaotic world, characterised by denial of reality. Laws and their enforcers may exist, but in extravagant and persecutory form. The anxiety which is at work centres less on punishment and more on a complete collapse of the self. Psychotic functioning is, however,

DOI: 10.4324/9781003646266-13

connected to the concept of rules insofar as these relate to boundaries and the organising nature of the ego. Psychotic and borderline patients are often preoccupied with basic questions of reality-testing, self-other differentiation or distinguishing between what is internal and what is outside. These fundamental laws of reality are precursors to laws in the ethical sense. They may appear in the clinical situation by reference to features of the frame or setting, which themselves stand for time and space.

In a related way, rules can be thought about in the context of early developmental situations, where aspects of reality are being encountered by the growing child. A primitive form of rule-making is introduced by Freud in *Negation* (1925). The infant engages with reality through its mouth, ingesting and spitting out, dictating in relation to good things, 'It shall be inside me', and in relation to bad things, 'It shall be outside me'. These processes form the basis of what will develop into more complex forms of thought, building from the basic binary of the yes/no judgement, which equates in the mind of the infant to in/out.[4] Klein developed ideas about splitting, projection and introjection forming the early foundation for normal mental functioning, as long as these processes are not too pronounced and give way to more integrative ones in the depressive position (Klein, 1975). In 'The Psycho-Analytic Study of Thinking' (1962a), Bion posited the creation, through projective and introjective communications within the mother–infant dyad, of a thinking apparatus to cope with the problem of thoughts, an aspect of the container–contained model (Bion, 1962b, ch. 27). Whether such a process proves successful depends on if the infant comes to feel, with her mother, that modification of frustration, as opposed to mere evasion, is possible. Bion calls this the 'crux' of the matter.

Winnicott's work on play and transitional phenomena is relevant here. If psychoanalysis offers the potential of a transitional space, in which play *may* become possible, then we ought to attend to Winnicott's frequent warnings about the importance of a child, or patient, being protected from encountering too much external reality. Fragments of external phenomena are brought into the play space and invested with dream-thoughts, but the quantity and nature of such phenomena have to be chosen spontaneously by the child or patient, not (super)imposed; otherwise, external reality will interfere with, and potentially arrest, the process of play. Rules have a delicate status in this area. On the one hand, they are needed in order to provide a holding environment in which anxieties can be explored without becoming overwhelming; on the other hand, they can themselves become a form of external impingement, if imposed in the wrong way. Here is a passage from Winnicott's 'Playing: A Theoretical Statement' (1971: 50):

> Games and their organization must be looked at as part of an attempt
> to forestall the frightening aspect of playing. Responsible persons

must be available when children play; but this does not mean that the responsible person need enter into the children's playing. When an organizer must be involved in a managerial position then the implication is that the child or the children are unable to play in the creative sense of my meaning in this communication.

Rules of analytic technique compared to legal rules

Rules are odd, in that some of them are silent and others get proclaimed loudly. The common law is like this. Large parts of trust and property law, for instance, are known only to specialist lawyers. The technical rules of psychoanalysis are a little like this too. There is the so-called *fundamental rule*, which may get broadcast at one of the first meetings between analyst and patient: that the patient ought to try to speak their thoughts without holding anything back. This is a rule about truth-telling and one which is quite radical. Is it more fundamental than the several other rules which also exist? In no particular order, here are some other examples of (possibly unspoken) rules which exist in the consulting room, subject to limited exceptions:

(A) A private and reasonably comfortable setting will be provided.
(B) The patient's confidentiality will be maintained.
(C) The analyst will not agree to meet the patient outside a session.
(D) Bills, or other arrangements for payment, will be managed in a timely way.
(E) Although some verbal abuse may be tolerated from the patient, destructive action has to be kept within manageable bounds.

In setting out rules at this behavioural sort of level, however, one risks engaging in a narrow kind of thinking. There are also other rules, or principles, by which the analyst abides, which are just as important as those set out above:

Trying to understand what the patient is communicating.
Identifying where the patient is refusing, or failing, to communicate and wondering why this might be.
Aiming to convey interpretations, whilst recognising that the patient may need time and help in developing a capacity to receive these.
Tuning into our feelings and trying to sort out whether and how these might relate to the patient.
Maintaining our analytic position and noticing with interest when we seem to have been moved away from it.
Favouring thought over action.
Acknowledging that thoughts can be a cloak for emotional states.

At some point, what might have been phrased as rules come out better as musings, or even fragments of poetry. It is possible, come to think of it, that poetry is the more natural expression of these analytic concepts than prose. We may feel drawn back to the idea of *attempts at truth-telling* as indeed being fundamental to psychoanalysis and to the various technical considerations which Freud suggested for the management of sessions (Strachey, 1958). Poetry, unlike prose, is in a sense incapable of lying. It may recite or work over lies, as is the way in many of Shakespeare's sonnets (for example, No. 138, part of which is quoted below); but the poem itself places a frame around its pronouncements which is interested in what is really going on: who is lying, what about and why? That is close to the idea of the analytic frame.

What we have so far been calling 'rules' are perhaps better thought of as incidents of the psychoanalytic situation. From the patient's perspective, rules which the analyst appears to follow can act as vehicles for potentially very primitive, unconscious fantasy. These may in due course become accessible to analysis (Bleger, 2013). From the analyst's point of view, whatever rules of technique she adheres to are an expression of her own ethical attitude. This develops partly out of the culture in which she trains and practises, but also out of her own capacity for care and concern. We are not talking here about a kind of rule-following which is imposed from outside, but one which grows from within, albeit based on experience. In each case, this way of looking at analytical rules engages a poetic sensibility, where rules are not of interest primarily for their normative value, but instead for their symbolic importance as this relates to the inner worlds of both patient and analyst.

Legal prose is very far away from poetry.[5] In analytic discourse, ambiguity interests us, potentially revealing unconscious processes with which the analytic couple are seeking to make contact. Verbal formulations within the law are, by contrast, wedded to consciousness and do not value ambiguity, which might be condemned by a judge as either evasiveness or sloppy drafting. The whole purpose of the trial process is to force suspected wrongdoers to state their position clearly, with no hiding place. Those drafting legislation are also astute to avoid double meanings. The underlying premise is the same and is directed at wrongdoers. The draftsman allows as little 'wriggle room' as possible. A sense of tightness and control, along with the prospect of infraction, characterises the whole situation.

This distinction between poetical and legal pronouncements shows up in the consulting room from time to time. Some patients may wish to frame either their own or the analyst's utterances as legal, rather than poetical. In this way, they can resist encountering their own vulnerability and attempt to enact a power struggle, through pedantry and with the hope of 'catching the analyst out'. An example of this is given in Edna O'Shaughnessy's paper, 'Relating to the Superego' (1999), where her patient, Mr B, tells her two dreams which he had, unusually, taken the trouble to write down. He then takes pleasure in telling O'Shaughnessy she has got various details of these dreams wrong in her interpretations, as if she had not been listening properly. She writes:

> At one point, I referred to the uphill (his second dream had begun: 'It was uphill'). Very superior, he said: 'No. You are wrong. In the dream I began uphill, but then I turned left, and it was downhill when I was sweeping the leaves.' I felt nastily reproved and tricked.
> (O'Shaughnessy, 1999, p. 867)

It is striking that Mr B had written his dreams down. Perhaps this was the first stage of his transforming what had been a poetical representation (his dream) into a word-bound, secondary process one. In the session he went further, insisting that the analysis ought to proceed in a pseudo-legal manner; things were to be split into either 'right' or 'wrong'. Beneath a purported concern with accuracy or justice, such patients frequently twist language, using a sphincter-like mentality to cut off words from the truth which they are supposed to communicate. Words then become things-in-themselves rather than bearers of meaning and, as such, are weaponised in the service of a sado-masochistic struggle. When this occurs in the consulting room, it has the intended consequence of patient and analyst becoming adversaries instead of collaborators. The analysis becomes a trial, inquisition or, eventually, torture chamber. As well as creating resistance to genuine analytic enquiry, this constitutes an enactment of persecutory anxieties, with the roles of victim and aggressor often becoming reversed.

Professional regulations

Having gone this far in a critique of the pseudo-legal mind as it manifests within the consulting room, we now meet with an unsettling fact. In addition to clinical thinking about frame, setting and technique, there exists another kind of psychoanalytic rulebook: that of the analyst's professional duties. These are created by the analyst's regulator and written down. Unlike the analytical rules mentioned above, with which they blur and overlap, these professional regulations are *defined* by their documentary form and are drafted in legal prose. They are entirely bound by what Freud called secondary process thinking (which is always and only linked to word-presentations) and in that way are alienated from the unconscious. Unlike the rules of technique, which can be described in all sorts of different ways, professional regulations take on a particular form which, once written down, cannot be changed without an authorised process of revision. They become reified as rules which exist in a binary state, to be obeyed or disobeyed. This causes a difficulty for analysts, who want to try to maintain contact with clinical reality, which as I have suggested is to be found more in the poetical than the legal realm.

These professional regulations have, at a few degrees of separation from the statute book, the force of law. This is important. It is, in the end, why such formal duties exist. These are rules which need to be interpretable in accordance with legal, rather than psychoanalytic, method. Moreover, such rules may be enforced by punishments, the potential end point of which is actual violence (the strong arm of the law). Given that actual, as opposed to symbolic, violence is a threat to the analytic relationship, this presents a problem for psychoanalysis.

Received wisdom would seem to suggest that rules of technique are about clinical skill, as opposed to ethics, which are the preserve of professional regulations. Freud and the first few generations of analysts, who were not subject to any psychoanalytic regulatory regime, might have been surprised to hear this, albeit Freud favoured considerations of practical efficacy over moralising (Freud, 1915b). It can be said that those early practitioners' ethical attitude was largely imported from the medical field. Yet this overlooks the unique stance of psychoanalysts towards their patients, which Freud understood was different from that of the medical doctor (Freud, 1917, 1926b). That analytic stance, in its willingness to observe phenomena without judgement and its commitment to truth-telling, is a profoundly ethical one (Levin & Amzallag, 2010). Professional regulations are, by comparison, more like a set of minimum requirements, which the analyst must take care not to infringe. Their concern is rooted in society's views about how all professional people should conduct themselves, rather than anything distinctly analytic coming from within the discipline itself.

This external aspect of the regulatory framework within which we all practise is one which is worth emphasising. Is there a place *within* the analytic situation itself for such a superstructure of written rules? Or, if they come into contact with the analytic couple, are regulations of this kind liable to be experienced as an environmental impingement, with potentially traumatic consequences?

Testing a regulation which governs psychoanalysis

To explore the implications of this, I refer to a professional regulation: paragraph 1(e) of the Ethical Guidelines of the British Psychoanalytic Council (BPC, 2011). This rule states:

> There must be no financial dealings with a patient except with regard to agreed fees.

A lawyer can immediately start imagining a variety of factual scenarios in which questions might arise about this prohibition. But what can a psychoanalyst imagine about such a rule? This is a very different question. Psychoanalytic practitioners could easily lose their analytic capacity if they were suddenly asked to consider the meaning of this rule, especially in circumstances where the outcome might make the difference between them facing disciplinary action, or not (see Stokoe, 2015, p. 199).

I will now describe a clinical scenario, which is fictional, through which this rule can be tested.

A man who was unhappy in his marriage came for five times a week analysis with a female analyst. He was a creative person, who was an artist in his spare time. He had various anxiety-related symptoms and the beginnings of a drink problem, which he told the analyst about and hoped might be alleviated. He came to see the analyst for several years. During that time, he made contact with fantasies and feelings which he had been troubled by, but not very in touch with, before the analysis. He felt helped by the analyst and managed to get his drinking under control. Towards the end of the first year, he was surprised and worried to feel at some point that he was falling in love. And it was not just love, but lust too. He fantasised about sexual encounters with his analyst. Eventually, he was brave enough to tell the truth about some of this in his sessions.

The analyst was brave too. These confessions made her feel anxious and stirred up in ways that were hard to admit. She found herself making mistakes in sessions, referring to the 'importance of boundaries' in a rather sententious way and pretending to herself that she was making interpretations about her patient's unconscious when she was really saying something like, 'Stay away from me!'

After a few sessions, this analyst was able to accept her own feelings of panic and triumph, with the help of her supervisor and some self-analysis. She created a space in which to think about what was going on, rather than merely reacting. In the sessions which followed, she succeeded in conveying to the patient that she was interested in what he was saying. Symbolically, she was telling him that she was open to libidinal contact with him. As long as this communication could be mutually understood as symbolic, that was alright and it could be worked with in the analysis.

The opening lines of Shakespeare's Sonnet 138 operate in a very similar way to what was going on:

> When my love swears that she is made of truth,
> I do believe her, though I know she lies …

The analyst had to be the 'maid of truth', the chaste virgin, who is conjured up by the pun in the first line, in that she was someone who was truthful and obeyed an analytic rule about not touching her patients in a sexual way. On the other hand, in order to help her patient, she also had to be able to 'lie', or sleep with him, in the transference. She then had to do her best to open up this area for discussion between them. This is how we might read Shakespeare's second line, as applied to the analysis, 'I do believe her, though I know she lies.' The patient had to feel that his analyst was straightforward and reliable, but also that she had the capacity to take in and make contact with his fantasies in a way that was not overly defended in regard to her own position as an object of desire.

This episode had significant consequences. In due course, the patient stopped feeling sexually excited by his analyst and became very tearful, as he found that, somehow, what had taken place between them had opened up feelings of grief about his older sister, who had died in an accident when he was 11 years old.

Gradually, as the analysis went on, the man found himself making more art than had previously been the case. Many of the pieces he developed reflected his thoughts and feelings about his past, but also about his analyst and about the space they had created together. He even began being represented by an online gallery, finding that his pieces attracted some interest, and he was able to sell them for modest amounts.

At the end of the analysis, the man presented his analyst with a parting gift – a small line and wash sketch, which was abstract, but carried echoes of both the patient's childhood home and the analyst's consulting room. He did this with apparent sensitivity, mentioning several months before the agreed end date that he had created this artwork and would like to give it to her, but he was not sure if that was alright and he did not want to do anything that would be inappropriate. He hoped it was something they might be able to think about together.

For the analyst, this moment brought back some of the turmoil of the original sexual revelations. She wondered about the ways in which this patient seemed to want to intrude, and not to intrude, into her private life. Would she like the sketch? Or dislike it, but feel obliged to take it? What would it mean to accept, or not accept, this offering? Was this a situation, created by the patient, in which inaction would amount to rejection? They talked together in the sessions about some of these questions, while she continued to take the patient to her supervisor.

In the end, the analyst accepted the gift.

The potential breach of the regulation and its consequences

Given how well everything seems to have worked out in the analysis up to this point, it may seem churlish to start talking about infractions of the rules. However, the analyst's acceptance of this small sketch from her patient was a potential breach of rule 1(e).

Imagine now that for some reason the situation turned sour. It transpired that the analysis had not worked out as well as first appeared. A few years later, the patient's marital troubles resurfaced and led to him and his wife getting a divorce. He could not cope with the situation and felt unable to ask for help. He was so invested in the idea of a happy ending to his analysis, that he could not bear to admit that it had not been so. His drinking got bad again and he now became fully alcoholic. Because of this he lost his job and got into financial trouble. He no longer made art, but his remaining pieces still sometimes sold online for a little money.

He now re-contacted his former analyst. He explained his situation and said that he would like to see her again and try to come to terms with what had happened to him, although he might struggle to afford a full fee. The analyst responded that she was very sorry to hear of his troubles but, unfortunately, she had no vacancies at the present time. She offered to see him for a consultation and to try to find someone else he might be referred to on a reduced fee. He was upset and did not take her up on the offer. Instead, he asked her to return his sketch, claiming that he now needed the money that it might be sold for.

The analyst was troubled by this request and took it to supervision. She decided that she was not inclined to return the sketch, at least not without considerable further thought, as doing so seemed like a collusion with something vengeful and destructive which had taken hold of the patient. The making of this gift had carried important meanings for him and returning it would involve a symbolic rejection of him and a denigration of the analysis. She wrote to him, now offering a series of consultations at a low fee, as a chance to try to think about what was happening, and hopefully with a view to the patient restarting analysis with her once a vacancy opened up. She received no response.

A few months later, the analyst learnt that a complaint had been made to her regulatory body about the sketch which she had accepted from her former patient. This culminated in a hearing by a disciplinary tribunal to which both she and the patient gave written evidence. The collaborative analysis which had taken place was broken apart by this adversarial process. After some legal arguments about the definition of the term 'financial dealings', the analyst was found to have committed a material breach of rule 1(e) of her professional code. She was formally reprimanded, required to undertake a course of ethics training and ordered to return the sketch. This outcome was published on the regulator's website for all to see.

Reflections on the analyst's conduct

However much we might sympathise with this analyst, perhaps we cannot help feeling that she and her supervisor overlooked some important matters. The little sketch seems to have been a kind of Trojan horse in this case. Was there any way to apprehend that possibility before things went wrong?

It is notable that the sketch was something which carried potentially manipulative qualities from the beginning. The patient told the analyst that he had created this artwork for her, with the intention of its being a gift. The patient's creative renaissance was a sign of his supposed therapeutic progress. So, the pressure to accept this physical embodiment of such progress was quite powerful. Rejection would be a terrible narcissistic wound! However, if analyst and supervisor had looked carefully enough, they might have been able to see that there was an element of misdirection at work here. The patient linked the gift to the termination of the analysis and raised it for consideration several months before the agreed end date. This looked like thoughtfulness, as if the patient was open to any outcome and did not bring an agenda. However, that impression was misleading. The patient did not mention the sketch before or during the process of its creation. From the first moment the analyst knew about the sketch, she was also told that her patient had made it for her. All of this was communicated under the fig leaf of a purported interest in consideration of whether the gift should be given at all. However, the truth was that the patient was subtly pressuring his analyst to take the gift without thinking, or whilst only pretending to think.

With the benefit of hindsight, we can see that the patient was not ready for an ending. His desire to make this gift might have been interpreted as an unconscious communication, along the following lines: 'Despite what has been achieved in the analysis, there is something disturbing about my feelings for you that has not yet been understood. You should not accept my wish to terminate the analysis, any more than you should accept this gift.' The analyst failed to consider the possibility that, by accepting the gift, she was in fact rejecting a disturbed part of her patient.

There is also the artwork's monetary value to consider. Although certainly not worth a great deal, this gift could not be said to be something of nominal value, like a box of chocolates, or a bunch of flowers (which, by the way, might well not engage rule 1(e)). Instead, it was a work of art, which might at least potentially be sold. The analyst may have been blinded to the reality of this, because the fact that this patient's artistic work held some monetary value had implicitly been used to measure his therapeutic progress. That state of affairs in turn touched on the analyst's own narcissistic needs. However, in a situation of this kind, monetary value is an aspect of external reality which should be considered alongside, not overlooked in favour of, its symbolic meaning. In light of the events which happened, we can be certain that the patient did not overlook it.

The question of whether it may be appropriate to accept a gift from a patient is a controversial one in the analytic literature (see Talan, 1989; Smolar, 2002; Akhtar, 2003; Evans, 2005; Schaverien, 2011). Some analysts have argued – and I agree – that, in appropriate cases, gifts, including artistic ones, may need to be accepted. This is dependent on whether the acts of giving and receipt, as the patient unconsciously experiences them, have been thoroughly analysed. Certainly, monetary value makes that more complicated – but, although it is significant, surely this cannot be the yardstick of whether or not an analyst accepts a gift. The main question is whether or not, taking unconscious factors into account, acceptance would be beneficial to the patient. Such views might be at odds with rule 1(e). They are more directly in conflict with a new rule on this subject upon which the BPC (2023) is currently consulting (draft Standard 1.4), which expressly outlaws gifts 'except token gifts of nominal value'. Whatever view one takes, could this be an example of a regulator encroaching on questions which ought to be a matter for clinical judgement in individual cases?

In any event, it can be seen that in this case treatment seems to have been ended prematurely, with what may have been a perverse aspect of the patient's character remaining unanalysed. We cannot be sure what the patient's subversive attempt to force a 'gift' on his analyst meant to him, but it seems from the events which transpired that it might have involved an exciting fantasy of violation. If so, then this was successfully enacted in the disciplinary proceedings and the forceful contact to which they gave rise between patient and analyst, now re-named 'complainant' and 'registrant'.

Returning to the argument

I began by identifying the importance of rules, and particularly truth-telling, to psychoanalysis, in both theory and clinical practice. I went on to suggest that there are two different sorts of rules within psycho-analysis: technical ones deriving mainly from Freud ('rules of technique') and disciplinary ones imposed on each practitioner by their regulatory body ('professional regulations'). These rules overlap and often reiterate one another, creating a sort of palimpsest. Despite their apparent similarities, however, the two sets of rules are profoundly different.

Rules of technique are embedded in clinical practice and oriented towards unconscious processes. A breach of these rules can have manifold consequences, including but not limited to: a temporary loss of analytic stance (which can hopefully be recovered), a serious therapeutic rupture, a boundary crossing or – most likely – a merely unproductive session. Any of these outcomes might, upon subsequent reflection, lead to new insights in a given analytic case. Professional regulations, by contrast, are oriented towards external reality, consciousness and secondary process thinking. They are binary in nature and do not value ambiguity. A breach of professional regulations leads to only two possible outcomes: punishment or non-punishment.

I have made the claim that rules of technique are in touch with something like a poetic sensibility, whereas professional regulations belong in the legal realm. Another way of describing the distinction might be to view it through the lens of Winnicott's ideas about playing. Rules of technique are comparable to the rules of whatever game a child might be playing: they arise from within the game itself and form an inherent part of the process of play. Professional regulations are more like the person in a managerial position whom Winnicott described as having to intervene when playing has got out of hand – with the fact of such intervention unfortunately meaning that the children are no longer able to play creatively. These aspects of the difference between the two kinds of rules have significant and unsettling implications for their relationship with clinical work. This is particularly the case bearing in mind that certain patients may adopt a pseudo-legal mode of thinking in the service of resistance and sado-masochistic enactment. If it is true that, within the consulting room, 'legal' states of mind often work to undermine analytic insight, then what are we clinicians exposing ourselves to, when we allow our behaviour to be governed by them, under pain of punishment?[6]

In the clinical scenario that is set out above, there may have been a breach of a rule of technique, in that the analyst accepted a gift from her patient in circumstances where this constituted an enactment of a perverse fantasy. The acceptance of the gift also turned out to constitute a breach of a professional regulation to do with financial dealings. At first blush, it may seem reassuring that, in this case, the professional regulations appeared to be in harmony with the rules of technique. On further reflection, it ought to be clear that the harmony was merely superficial. From an analytic perspective, it is not satisfactory to think that this analyst was punished for an infraction in relation to financial dealings. The heart of the complaint against the analyst was not that she accepted something that was of monetary value, it was that she failed to *think* in an effective way. It was this which her supervisor ought to have identified and helped with, particularly in relation to drawing a distinction between the communication which the patient was attempting to make and the physical object which he was pressuring her to accept. If any consequence was going to be visited on the analyst, it ought to have been self-reflection, with the hope that this might reveal what blind spots had caused her to overlook the perverse nature of her patient's conduct and to collude in the premature termination of his treatment. This might have been an opportunity for development, which could have worked for the benefit of both analyst and patient, if the treatment could somehow have been sustained, or recommenced. Even if that was not possible, at least the analyst would have learnt something and perhaps become a more effective clinician for future patients. A professional sanction for accepting financial benefits was not a helpful or appropriate outcome. On the contrary, it was unhelpful. This was not a corrupt or venal analyst, who needed to be brought to heel. It was an analyst who had made mistakes and become confused about a patient, but had done so in good faith. The tribunal which dealt with the patient's complaint seems to have become the unwitting tool of a disturbed analytic patient, allowing him to realise a fantasy of violating contact with his analyst, under the auspices of a legal dispute.

Concluding thoughts

The use of complaints as sado-masochistic transference enactments is something which comes up fairly frequently in practice. Regulation of psychoanalytic treatment has, over the past quarter of a century, increasingly become the subject of comment and sometimes concern (Figlio, 2000; Ikkos & Barbenel, 2000; Merlino, 2006; Levin & Amzallag, 2010; Stokoe, 2015; Parker & Revelli, 2018; Sachs & Sinason, 2023). The problem may be that the legal quality of analytic professional regulations – their binary, adversarial nature, their focus on conscious thinking, their orientation towards punishment and their conversion of thought into action – lends them to potentially damaging enactments, unless the relevant tribunals are unstintingly analytic in their approach. Those who bear the task of adjudicating on the conduct of analytic professionals will already be alive to the dangers of a legalistic approach to clinical questions. However, the distinction to which I have drawn attention, between rules of technique and professional regulations, may not have previously been articulated in quite this way.

Professional regulations (and, indeed, the strong arm of the law) are essential in dealing with analysts who are suffering from perverse or narcissistic disturbances which make them a danger to patients.[7] In cases of that sort, the clinical frame has irretrievably broken down and external intervention becomes necessary, because clinicians cannot be trusted to police themselves or keep their patients safe. In most other situations, however, I would suggest that the appropriate response to an error is not a publicly humiliating sanction, but further analysis and better supervision. It is essential that the tribunals that adjudicate on these issues are astute not to allow professional regulations to be used as a vehicle for enactments. Therefore, to the extent that a registrant needs help, whether with improving their analytic capacity, or indeed reflecting on whether an analytic career is in fact the right one for them,[8] it is better, if at all possible, for this to be offered as pastoral support from colleagues, rather than as a kind of judicial verdict.[9]

All of us make mistakes, or take missteps, in our psychoanalytic practices from time to time. This is part of the nature of analytic work and, although we do our best to avoid it, sometimes it can be helpful in identifying the unconscious issues with which a patient might be struggling. The key aim of psychoanalysis, which is to foster an environment conducive to truth-telling, is not assisted if either patient or analyst has to work in a climate of fear. Given the unhappy history of psychoanalysis as regards self-regulation (Sandler, 2004), this may appear an unattractive argument. It is, however, in the interests of both analysts and patients that, wherever possible, the analyst's own superego should be the primary guardian of the analytic frame, rather than this being effectively outsourced to a legal system to which the dynamic unconscious is an alien concept.

Appendix

Four areas of disturbance and some thoughts about their relationship to rules

Narcissism. Perhaps the only general principle which the narcissist recognises is that rules created by other people are not acceptable. A narcissist wants to be sole legislator, advocate and judge. Therefore, if he does follow a rule, that is likely to be because he is able to experience it as his own creation. More often than not, he will feel that the usual rules do not apply to him.

Obsessionality. For obsessional patients, rules can be regressively invested with anal-sadistic libido. The conscious experience is that, by rule-following, anxiety is managed and feelings of apparently inexplicable guilt are fended off. Unconsciously, however, an obsessional person may find rule-following an exciting vehicle for letting out aggression. All of this is well concealed. The idea of being well behaved or law abiding shuts off awareness of sadistic motives.

Perversion. This is directly related to the subject of rule-twisting and, in particular, to deceit and breaches of trust. Concealing and revealing the shocking truth are, for the pervert, sources of special sado-masochistic pleasure. We can think of this in connection to all sorts of perverse activity – 'heavy breathers' on the telephone, 'flashers' who expose themselves in wooded areas and paedophiles who groom children and their families by pretending to be helpful, friendly and above all law-abiding adults.

Delinquency. The need to break rules emerges in very direct form in the context of anti-social behaviour, where authority figures and their laws come under attack from a child or adolescent who may be expressing feelings of severe deprivation and the hope of getting hold of the love or attention to which they know they have a right.

Notes

1 See the Appendix for some examples of areas of disturbance which can be seen as rule-related.
2 See, also, Juliet Mitchell's invocation of the 'law of the mother' operating between siblings (2022).
3 Not least to deal with the fact that the castration-as-punishment paradigm does not work in the same way in relation to little girls. Freud himself was aware of many of these aspects: see for example, *Inhibitions, Symptoms and Anxiety* (Freud, 1926a) at p. 82.

4   See also *Instincts and Their Vicissitudes* (Freud, 1915a) pp. 119 and 134 ff and chapter I of *Civilisation and Its Discontents* (Freud, 1930).

5   Judges have often given in to a temptation to quote verse (particularly Shakespeare), as if out of a longing for a sensibility they feel is absent from their work. To take just one Shakespeare play, *King Lear*, as an example, see: *Gabb v Farrokhzad* (2022); *R. (Miller) v The College of Policing* (2020); *Chambers v DPP* (2013); *Brewer v Mann* (2010); *Sharp v Adam* (2006); *Yorkshire Bank plc v Tinsley* (2004); *Gaspari v Iarnrod Eireann* (1996).

6   I would like, in this context, to note an important paper by the Jungian analyst John Miller (2018), for a radical case against regulation which includes some thinking along similar lines to mine. I do not, however, agree with his conclusions, which, as I understand them, entail an outright opposition to regulation or institutionalism of any kind.

7   See, for example, the discussion of the notorious Masud Khan case in Godley (2001), Sandler (2004) and Joyce et al. (2019) (where, as it happens, gift-giving by the analyst was an early boundary breach), and see generally Gabbard and Lester (1995).

8   According to Paula Heimann (1978), 'whoever has mistakenly entered the profession should get out again as quickly as possible, in his own interest and in that of his patients'.

9   Philip Stokoe (2015, 2023), drawing on Bion, has argued that professional regulation can be understood as a kind of secondary container, acting as a further area of psychic support which can be turned to by both patient and analyst in cases where the primary container, the clinical situation, has cracked. I think this is an appealing idea. It will, however, be apparent that I have doubts about how effectively such a concept can be realised in practice. This is due to the profound differences between these two forms of container, as well as the tendency of the regulatory regime to become alienated from clinical practice and to be experienced by both patient and analyst as an impingement, rather than a support.

References

Akhtar, S. (2003). Things: Developmental, psychopathological, and technical aspects of inanimate objects. *Canadian Journal of Psychoanalysis*, 11: 1–44.

Bion, W. R. (1962a). The psycho-analytic study of thinking. *International Journal of Psychoanalysis*, 43: 306–310.

Bion, W. R. (1962b). *Learning from Experience*. London: Heinemann.

Bleger, J. (2013). Psychoanalysis of the psychoanalytic setting. In Churcher, J. & Bleger, L. (Eds), *Symbiosis and Ambiguity: A Psychoanalytic Study*, The New Library of Psychoanalysis,79, pp. 228–241.

Brewer v Mann. [2010] EWHC 2444.

Chambers v DPP. [2013] 1 WLR 1833.

British Psychoanalytic Council (BPC). (2011, February). Ethical guidelines. https://www.bpc.org.uk/download/747/4.2-Ethical-Guidelines-Feb-2011-no-numbers.pdf

British Psychoanalytic Council (BPC). (2023). Draft updated Standards of conduct, performance and ethics of the BPC (consultation period: 28 April 2023 to 9 September 2023). https://www.bpc.org.uk/consultation-on-standards-of-conduct-performance-and-ethics/

Evans, M. O. (2005). Gift-giving in psychotherapy: Layers of meaning and developmental process. *British Journal of Psychotherapy*, 21(3): 401–415.

Figlio, K. (2000). Registration and ethics in psychotherapy. *British Journal of Psychotherapy*, 16(3): 327–334.

Freud, S (1915a). Instincts and their vicissitudes. In Strachey, J. (Ed.), *The Standard Edition of the Complete Psychological Works of Sigmund Freud*, Vol. 14. London: Hogarth Press, pp. 109–140.

Freud, S (1915b). Observations on transference-love (further recommendations on the technique of psycho-analysis III). In Strachey, J. (Ed.), *The Standard Edition of the Complete Psychological Works of Sigmund Freud*, Vol. 12. London: Hogarth Press, pp. 157–171.

Freud, S (1917). Introductory lectures on psycho-analysis (part III). In Strachey, J. (Ed.), *The Standard Edition of the Complete Psychological Works of Sigmund Freud*, Vol. 16. London: Hogarth Press, pp. 243–256. Lecture XVI, 'Psycho-analysis and Psychiatry'.

Freud, S. (1925). Negation. In Strachey, J. (Ed.), *The Standard Edition of the Complete Psychological Works of Sigmund Freud*, Vol. 19. London: Hogarth Press, pp. 233–240.

Freud, S. (1926a). Inhibitions, symptoms and anxiety. In Strachey, J. (Ed.), *The Standard Edition of the Complete Psychological Works of Sigmund Freud*, Vol. 20. London: Hogarth Press, pp. 75–176.

Freud, S. (1926b). The question of lay analysis. In Strachey, J. (Ed.), *The Standard Edition of the Complete Psychological Works of Sigmund Freud*, Vol. 20. London: Hogarth Press, pp. 177–258.

Freud, S. (1930). Civilization and its discontents. In Strachey, J. (Ed.), *The Standard Edition of the Complete Psychological Works of Sigmund Freud*, Vol. 21. London: Hogarth Press, pp. 57–146.

Gabbard, G. O. & Lester, E. P. (1995). *Boundaries and Boundary Violations in Psychoanalysis*. New York: Basic Books.

Gabb v Farrokhzad. [2022] 1 WLR 2842.

Gaspari v Iarnrod Eireann. [1996] IEHC 8.

Godley, W. (2001). Saving Masud Khan, *London Review of Books*, 23(4), 22 February.

Heimann, P. ([1978]1989). On the necessity of the analyst to be natural with his patient. In *About Children and Children-No-Longer*. Abingdon: Routledge, pp. 239–249.

Ikkos, G. & Barbenel, D. (2000). Complaints against psychiatrists: Potential abuses. *Psychoanalytic Psychotherapy*, 14: 49–62.

Joyce, A., Thomson, N. & Abram, J. (2019). The Winnicott Archives: A consideration of some preliminary findings. *Bulletin of the British Psychoanalytical Society*, 55(1).

Klein, M. ([1958]1975). On the development of mental functioning. In *Envy and Gratitude and Other Works 1946–1963*. The International Psycho-Analytical Library, 104, pp. 236–246.

Levin, C. & Amzallag, Y. (2010). The liminal smile: Ethics in psychoanalysis and the problem of regulation. *Canadian Journal of Psychoanalysis*, 18: 60–85.

Merlino, J. P. (2006). Psychoanalysis and ethics – relevant then, essential now. *Journal of the American Academy of Psychoanalysis*, 34: 231–247.

Miller, J. (2018). Why is psychoanalysis not in trouble? In Parker, I. & Revelli, S. (Eds), *Psychoanalytic Practice and State Regulation*, ch. 4, London and New York: Routledge.

Mitchell, J. (2022). Why siblings? Introducing the 'sibling trauma' and the 'law of the mother' on the 'horizontal' axis. *Psychoanalytic Study of the Child*, 75: 121–139.

O'Shaughnessy, E. (1999). Relating to the superego. *International Journal of Psychoanalysis*, 80: 861–870.

Parker, I. & Revelli, S. (Eds) (2018). *Psychoanalytic Practice and State Regulation*. London and New York: Routledge.

R. (Miller) v The College of Policing. [2020] 4 All ER 31.

Sachs, A. & Sinason, V. (Eds) (2023). *The Psychotherapist and the Professional Complaint*. London: Karnac.

Sandler, A. M. (2004). Institutional responses to boundary violations: The case of Masud Khan, with a commentary by Wynne Godley. *International Journal of Psychoanalysis*, 85: 27–44.

Schaverien, J. (2011). Gifts, talismans and tokens in analysis: Symbolic enactments or sinister acts? *Journal of Analytical Psychology*, 56: 160–183.

Sharp v Adam. [2006] WTLR 1059.

Smolar, A. (2002). Reflections on gifts in the therapeutic setting: The gift from patient to therapist. *American Journal of Psychotherapy*, 56: 27–45.

Stokoe, P. (2015). Ethics and complaints procedures for psychoanalytic organisations: Some thoughts about principles. *Couple and Family Psychoanalysis*, 5: 188–204.

Stokoe, P. (2023). The unique nature of boundaries in psychoanalytic therapy and the implication for ethics and complaints procedures. In Sachs, A. & Sinason, V. (Eds), *The Psychotherapist and the Professional Complaint*. London: Karnac.

Strachey, J. (1958). Appendix: List of writings by Freud dealing mainly with psycho-analytic technique and the theory of psychotherapy. *SE* 12: 172–174.

Talan, K. H. (1989). Gifts in psychoanalysis – theoretical and technical issues. *Psychoanalytic Study of the Child*, 44: 149–163.

Winnicott, D. W. ([1971]1991). Playing: A theoretical statement, in *Playing and Reality*. London and New York: Routledge.

Yorkshire Bank plc v Tinsley. [2004] 3 All ER 463.

10 Voyeuristic photography (*tosatsu*)

Liberation in the claustrum

Shimpei Kudo

Law, crime and psychoanalysis

In the face of a criminal offence, one is forced to ask, 'Why?' Why could such an outrageous act be committed, and why did they do it? The question of 'Why?' is sometimes unanswerable, yet asking it is a manifestation of the mind's creativity to face difficulties without losing one's sanity when encountering things that are incomprehensible and beyond the imagination. Why do people break the law? Psychoanalytic understanding contributes to such enquiry.

The word 'crime' has two meanings: 'an illegal activity or an illegal act' or 'an unacceptable or very unreasonable act or situation' (Cambridge Dictionary, n.d.). If we ask 'Why?' in the former sense, then we must consider the following: Without desire, there is no prohibition. In *Totem and Taboo*, Freud (1912–13) discerned that a prohibition is what conceals a desire, just as there is no law against putting one's hand in the fire. Laws are destined to be broken.

Thus, the more essential question concerns the latter: 'Why does one conduct an unacceptable or very unreasonable act?' Above all, by asking 'Why this person?' we are beginning to psychoanalyse the motives of the offender.

To this, Freud gave a somewhat perplexing and paradoxical answer. He asserted that people commit crimes out of a sense of guilt (Freud, 1916). Punishment does not only come after the crime, but because they want to be punished, they do evil. They do not feel guilty because of their evil deeds, but they conduct wrongdoings because they have a guilty feeling. To escape internal persecution, one exposes oneself to external persecution. It must be significant.

Therefore, the analysis of the psyche should be directed to this original guilt or persecution. What was 'it' for which the evil was done? Freud here rediscovered the primitive patricide identified in *Totem and Taboo*; the fear of retaliation for marrying one's mother and murdering one's father for it. He illuminated the trajectory that the child's desire created anxiety, and the anxiety created a desire for punishment, which, in turn, led them to commit a crime.

DOI: 10.4324/9781003646266-14

Forensic psychotherapy

Here are multiple elements that lead to later forensic psychotherapy. First, the understanding that crime is a result of anxiety and psychic pain. It is a phenomenon that can be described as immorality, lack of norms, lack of empathy, etc. The offender may appear selfish, self-centred and narcissistic. However, at unconscious motives, one is trying to protect oneself from internal anxiety and psychic pain. In society, crime is a 'problem', but in the individual, it is a 'solution'.

Second, the finding that a moral operation exists here. The agency that brings about this function is called the 'superego', and it is often assumed that the criminal does 'not' have this superego. However, if, in fact, the retaliation is more than one can bear, then it is 'excessive'. Crime creates a crisis in society, and criminals are seen as dangerous. Yet the crisis or danger is already present in the person as the harsh superego.

Third, the common perspective in all psychoanalytic understandings is that the origin is in childhood. One does not suddenly become a criminal at some point in one's life. And there is no break in human nature between those who commit crimes and those who do not. In the process of development, people are driven by the need to protect themselves from crisis and danger, and in some sense, probabilistically, they become pathological and criminal. Without that internal and/or external developmental history, motives cannot be comprehensible.

Fourth, relationship to society. The wish to marry one's mother and murder one's father may seem extremely immoral. However, if a young child loves his mother and thinks, 'I want to be with my mom, go away daddy,' it may be cruel and ruthless, but at the same time, it is innocent. If this innocent love and hate is responded to by the outside world as a target of punishment, or if it actually ends up affecting the outside world, it will cause a strong fear. Thus, crisis and danger arise at the point the child's inner world meets the outer world. Crime is a pathology in which personal problems are acted out at the point of contact with society, but it can be said to be one of the repetitions.

On the other hand, forensic psychotherapy, as a psychoanalytic approach to the problem of delinquency and crime, has added new perspectives in parallel with the development of psychoanalysis after Freud. One is that its scope extends to the inner world of infancy as early childhood; the nature of the father–mother–child triad (Oedipus complex), which Freud identified as the source of guilt, came to be considered as a consequence of the preceding period, and the nature of the mother–child dyad is under question (a discussion may occur as to whether the 'mother' here should be a mother). Another is the shift in emphasis from wish to anxiety and fear. Freud argued that the primary process of the mind functions according to the principle of discharging unpleasure and seeking pleasure, which is controlled by a secondary process that takes reality into account. Thus, it was 'desire' that was found in the oldest layer of the mind, beyond the anxiety and sense of guilt behind external problems. Nevertheless, important concepts in forensic psychotherapy, such as the core complex (Glasser, 1979) and the death constellation (Hyatt-Williams, 1998), indicate that it is anxiety and fear (especially of death) that organise and drive one's mind and behaviour.

Furthermore, another perspective can be added. If the source of the motivation for crime lies in the encounter with the external world, there may be social and cultural factors at play. How is the love and hate of an innocent child reacted to, and how is this anxiety and psychic pain resolved? One cannot become a criminal independent of the outside world. I shall discuss here its influence on the formation of the motivation for crime.

Voyeuristic photography

'Japan and South Korea are among the only countries in the world to regulate camera shutter noises on mobile phones' (Growcoot, 2023). In both countries, camera shutter sounds cannot be turned off. As Freud says, where there is a prohibition, a desire is hidden, and this prohibition is based on the wish for sneaky photography. A kind of voyeurism called '*to(u)satsu*' ('*tou*' means steal and '*satsu*' means taking photographs or recording) in Japan or '*molka*' (a coined word from '*mollae-kamera*' which means hidden camera) in Korea refers to photographing under skirts of (mostly) women on public transportation, at commercial facilities, on stairways, etc. or capturing them undressing or using the toilet by hiding cameras in toilets, bathrooms, locker rooms, etc. In 2022, the number of arrests in Japan was nearly 4,000 (National Police Agency, 2023), which is comparable to the number of arrests for crimes of obscenity (4,890).

Although not an uncommon crime, voyeuristic photography was treated as an incident under the nuisance prevention ordinance rather than as a crime under the laws and regulations until July 2023 in Japan. There were few studies, a limited number of hits in publicly available literature databases, and only one useful article was found: a paper by a group of family court investigating officers in Tokyo (Sugiyama et al., 2009). This was a study of juvenile delinquents, but it did not examine the psychological aspects; only demographic characteristics were found: parents present, no family problems, no problems with the juvenile's academic record and low likelihood of re-delinquency. At first glance, it is noteworthy that it gives the impression of a child from an intact family, but it can be assumed that some problems exist as long as there is illegal behaviour. This apparent 'no problem' characteristic seems to me to contribute to the formation of cultural anxiety and psychodynamics.

Case A

Mr A, a male in his twenties, was referred to my office by a counsellor at his organisation after he was arrested for *tosatsu*. Mr A had a girlfriend, but she had spoken openly to him about having sexual relations with an unspecified man, and he was distressed by this. Although he sometimes accused her in strong tones, she was in distress at such times remembering her dominant father, and Mr A could not stay angry. When he was away from her, he worried about where she was and with whom, but when he was with her, he could not say what he wanted to say. I felt that he was in a suffocating and constricting world.

Mr A became addicted to *tosatsu* to escape from painful experiences with his girlfriend. He took pictures of underwear from under skirts at shopping centres, public facilities and other places, and masturbated with them. There was no consistent portrait of the victims, and their ages ranged from the twenties to the fifties. Mr A could not answer why he did *tosatsu*. He later stated that seeing what was hidden was an accomplishment, but he had no idea of the emotional or symbolic meaning of seeing and photographing concealed things.

This was the second time that Mr A had been caught for *tosatsu*. The first happened, two years after he had failed his college entrance exam, while he was attending cram school to prepare for the following year's exam. His parents wanted him to study hard for the exam when he was home, so he continued to study in his room. However, he was quite poor at remembering letters and may have had a disability in this respect. As a result, his performance did not improve as he expected, but he still felt that he was not allowed to stop studying. This had been the case since he was in middle childhood. At this time, the only thing he could do was to stay in his room and indulge in masturbation. He repeated *tosatsu* and was eventually caught by the police. He was not charged and, for the next several years, he did not engage in *tosatsu* again.

When asked when his *tosatsu* began, Mr A said that he had learned it from older boys at high school, that they and their friends were taking voyeuristic pictures for fun, and that he thought to himself, 'This is how boys play'. It sounded like a liberating narrative that he had discovered a new fact of life, strangely accompanied by an impression of liveliness. Mr A then became addicted to taking voyeuristic photos on buses and trains for a while, even when he was by himself.

Mr A's parents were conservative and inflexible. His father worked for a company, and his mother was a housewife. Mr A had siblings, and they all lived together, which is not unusual in Japan. There were rules in his house: everyone had to eat dinner together, and they had to be home by dinner time, even on the weekends. The family were required to stay together as much as possible, and for this reason there was no air conditioning installed in the children's bedrooms. This was to prevent them from staying in their rooms for too long. The mother did not appreciate Mr A having a girlfriend and told him, 'don't get busy' when he was in high school. His mother had a similar attitude towards his father and seemed to think that 'don't get busy' was the way to respect someone, Mr A said.

At the first session, Mr A showed up with his mother. He talked about the crime in front of her and said he thought perhaps a sexual desire was the reason he couldn't leave his girlfriend. 'The counsellor said so,' Mr A said. He told me that he read books on sexual crimes and how to live every day and wrote reflection papers. He said that he wanted to quit *tosatsu*, but his words were strained, as if he were trying to take someone else's words and force himself to fit into them. I asked him if he had any difficulty talking about these issues in front of his mother, to which he replied that he had already told her everything and that he would be fine. I wondered if that was really true. It seemed odd.

Once a week, face-to-face psychoanalytic psychotherapy started. His mother gave him a ride to and from the office to prevent him from recidivism on the way. Since she tried to ask about the sessions during the ride, and because Mr A was becoming more and more constricted in the sessions, I arranged a meeting with his mother about a month later. His mother apparently thought Mr A was adorable as a young child. She had noticed that he was not good at learning, but when I told her about the possibility of a specific learning disability, she did not seem to understand the suffering that Mr A must have gone through. She also told how Mr A admired his father's work. However, the father did not want Mr A to follow in his footsteps, as he was having a hard time as a manager after receiving a promotion at work. The mother seemed satisfied with the recognition her husband had gained, but when I pointed out his struggle and suffering, she changed the subject, saying, 'Well, I guess that's his business.'

Although these were casual responses, they seemed cruel, and an understanding began to arise in my mind that Mr A was trapped inside his mother, who had no heart. Mr A also talked about how his mother had prayed for an hour every day since his arrest, which made him feel guilty. He also reported that he felt he could not argue with his mother because she borrowed people's words to say what she wanted to say. There was only indirect communication. It seemed to imply that he was enclosed within his mother's world. However, Mr A himself did not think this was a problem; rather, he was trying to adapt to it. Mr A was trying to be a 'good boy'.

Mr A was stuck in an unanswerable impasse in therapy, trying to figure out what he had to do to be the right person. His topics were limited, and he tended to be speechless. I asked Mr A to live an ordinary life so that his mind could work; and after three months, I introduced the couch to let him be free in the session, even though it was only once a week. Mr A responded immediately, and treatment progressed through his realisation that he was trapped in the world of his parents, especially his mother, and his gradual breaking of family rules.

Mr A began to sort out what were actually his own thoughts and feelings among those that felt like they were not his, regaining his own wishes and boundaries. There was one time when the pathology for *tosatsu* and masturbation returned, and the risk of reoffending increased, but that was when he was in a training programme requiring an overnight stay for a week and could not go out during his free time and had nothing to do. Mr A understood that this was a risk, and since then, at least three years have passed without reoffending.

Discussion

Psychodynamic interpretation of voyeuristic photography

Tosatsu is a crime that is not common outside of Korea and Japan, but voyeurism might be. It is a kind of perversion. Perversion is considered to be the sexualisation of aggression (Stoller, 1975), where the hatred is so intense that a defence is made by sexualising it to avoid the killing occurring. Mr A could have had some kind of resentment towards women, but this did not manifest itself clearly. Rather, the absence of anger characterises him, and one can detect a sign of strong castration there (remember that Mr A talked about his own relationship with his girlfriend and his crimes in front of his mother, that he was unable to direct his anger towards his girlfriend, and that his home life and age-appropriate sexual interests were restricted in terms of freedom and independence).

Mr A's desire for voyeuristic photography was heightened when he was enclosed by others and thereby made impotent. It goes beyond the partial experience of genital castration, in which the whole being is placed in a suffocating and cramped state. The suffocating impression at the beginning of treatment probably derived from this. Such an understanding was confirmed in a situation of heightened risk during treatment. I would say that Mr A was in the claustrum (Meltzer, 1992).

His communication of emotions, such as anger, sadness and anguish, was rejected by the recipient. The mother's indifference to her husband's sufferings at work, contrasting with her admiration of him, is an illustration of how Mr A's pain is not metabolised by the object. If we take the perspective that communication is a sort of projective identification, it was as if the lid was closed on the container into which he had attempted to throw himself. Or, attempting to get inside the container, he could not proceed and was trapped. Given the nature of the object, Mr A was engulfed by the object, yet the communication was non-responsive.

According to Meltzer, Mr A was struggling in the rectum, and masturbation was a release there. This could be described as a sexualisation of security, following the term sexualisation of aggression. Stuck in the rectum and unable to reach the breasts (relief), sexual pleasure brought him consolation (in Japanese, masturbation is called *jii*, where *ji* means self and *i* means comfort). One might also say that there was a geographical confusion between the rectum, the breast and the genitals, but either way, the problem was that he could not reach the breast.

In this light, voyeuristic photography may be an act of self-comfort to alleviate the agony of the claustrum and, at the same time, that of pleasure that brings the satisfaction of having successfully intruded into a place where no further entry was permitted. It might be suggestive that in Japan, the arrest of a 'gutter man' was reported, who repeatedly lay in the gutter, sometimes peeping, and did *tosatsu* for more than four hours.

It must also be pointed out that the engagement with the object (underwear) here is non-contact and at a distance, as with other forms of voyeurism, in particular through the camera in voyeuristic photography. It was not real. Often, *tosatsu* offenders say, 'It wouldn't be a crime if the victim didn't know they were being photographed.' Despite his regret for the incident and his efforts to prevent recidivism, Mr A said the very same thing. This denial is, on the one hand, a self-centred defensive justification, but the relationship whereby seeing does not mean seeing, and photographing does not mean photographing is also a repetition of the incommunicable relationship with the object, which we can again interpret as a sign of castration.

Socio-cultural effect on psychodynamics regarding anxiety

So, why does this act occur in certain cultures? Several factors could be considered. One, for example, is the restraint of children, known as educational maltreatment. In both Japan and South Korea, family pressure for achievement in education is high, and children are prepared for university entrance examinations from an early age for a long period of time. 'Good' children are mass-produced, and some children cannot bear the burden. It may be said that Mr A was a victim of such burdens. If we take Welldon's (1988) argument that female masochism narcissistically turns into sadism towards children who are an extension of the self, we can assume that sadism manifests itself in the form of such maltreatment in Korea and Japan. Education is often something women are deprived of. Providing it to the child as an extension of the self would be a recovery from castration through the child. On the other hand, the pressure for achievement, the expectation of high standards of academic performance and study effort, is for children not as aggressive as harsh discipline but rather tormenting by slow degrees. Children can grow up to be 'good (obedient)' in such cultural sadism that binds them by love.

It may be a cultural feature that this castration is often carried out by the mother. In Japanese mythology (*Kojiki*), there is a story of a goddess sending her son from heaven after the unification of the land by a male deity and making the throne pass from the male deity to her son. The descendant of the son is the Emperor of Japan, according to the myth. But notice that there is no Oedipal struggle here, in which the male god fights and governs (and gets the female). For Japanese boys, it is the mother who carries the castration and the bestowing. If castration by the father is a product of rivalry and conflict, that by the mother is a rejection of desire itself. For the mother, her son's desire is the desire of the male who castrated herself. At the same time, as an extension of herself, she wants her child to succeed. Consequently, an obedient boy who lacks desire as an individual is demanded to fulfil the mother's desires. Being a 'good boy' is a sign of castration but is also underpinned by the 'prohibition of desiring' (Kudo, 2024).

Thus, claustrophobic anxiety arises in the relationship with the primary object, being affected by social and cultural features. Then, why does its resolution (satisfaction of intrusion, i.e. sexualisation of security) have to be voyeuristic photography? Mr A's personal history shows that it was taught by his seniors as a boys' game. This is not an unusual situation, and it would be widely accepted that the direct reason for voyeuristic photography is because it is familiar to boys. The more important question, however, is why it is so prevalent.

First, it is probably due to the fact that seeing is more distant from the object than touching (having sex). The prohibition of desiring prevents an individual from sexually approaching the object. Even if it is possible to have sex with a lover, as Mr A did, the claustrum, the imprisonment, is there. Second, because it is covert. Peeping does not require exposing oneself to others. This implies that one does not need to expose one's desires to others. Achieving one's desires without being castrated is a kind of triumph. Offenders are often addicted to this sense of achievement and triumph. A third reason may be that it is an intrusion. At the same time as being imprisoned in a world with the object, these people are blocked from communication with the object. Approaching with anger and longing would require an intrusion to see what is not supposed to be seen. Fourth, there may be a detachment of desire. In Japan, direct expression of one's own wishes is regarded as shameful. They can only be fulfilled with the consideration of others. Therefore, 'good' children detach themselves from desiring. In voyeuristic photography, the subject is projectively identified with the seeing device, the camera, where the perpetrator can experience his desires. Cameras were used to slip under skirts, were hidden in toilets and bathrooms, or, before the advent of smartphones, placed on the tip of a shoe that was positioned under the skirt. The self is projected onto a small object in a small space, and the offender indulges in the pleasure of intruding into places that should not be entered and seeing things that should not be seen within this small, confined space. Prohibited and hidden desires are perversely liberated in the anxiety of claustrum.

Conclusion

It was in Japan that cameras were installed in mobile phones for the first time in the world. Since that time, they have had a shutter sound. *Tosatsu* has been a familiar problem from the beginning. Children's creativity is castrated, and their mothers' true desires are locked away in a hidden world. The desire to peek into the hidden is also hidden, projectively identified with the camera, and in the claustrum it gains the freedom of masturbation. *Tosatsu* seems to be an act of sexualised security, protecting the offender from the despair and anxiety of the claustrophobic world.

Crime is a pathology, the dynamics of anxiety and agony that arise when the individual's inner world meets the outer world, which unfolds at the point of contact between the individual and society. The influence of culture cannot be ignored here. Laws are prohibitions established on the basis of these factors, but at the same time crackdowns are reenactments of former anxieties and anguish. The psychoanalytic approach opens a new path to get out of this vicious circle, not by aiming for compliance with the law but by breaking into criminality, approaching the source of the anxiety and unfolding the spontaneous creativity that was supposed to be there. Responding to the question of 'Why?', psychoanalysis contributes to this realm.

References

Cambridge Dictionary. (n.d.). Crime. In *Cambridge Dictionary*. Retrieved 8 April 2024, from https://dictionary.cambridge.org/ja/dictionary/english/crime

Freud, S. (1912–1913). Totem and taboo. In Strachey, J. (Ed. and Trans.), *The Standard Edition of the Complete Psychological Works of Sigmund Freud*, 13. London: Hogarth Press, pp. 1–162.

Freud, S. (1916). Some character-types met with in psycho-analytic work. In Strachey, J. (Ed. and Trans.), *The Standard Edition of the Complete Psychological Works of Sigmund Freud*, 14. London: Hogarth Press, pp. 311–333.

Glasser, M. (1979). Some aspects of the role of aggression in the perversions. In Rosen, I. (Ed.), *Sexual Deviation* (2nd ed.). Oxford: Oxford University Press.

Growcoot, M. (2023, 6 November). Korean smartphones have mandatory shutter sounds, 8 in 10 want it muted. *PetaPixel*. Retrieved 8 April 2024, from https://p etapixel.com/2023/11/06/korean-smartphones-have-mandatory-shutter-sound s-8-in-10-want-it-muted/

Hyatt-Williams, A. (1998). *Cruelty, Violence and Murder: Understanding the Criminal Mind*. London and New York: Routledge.

Kudo, S. (2024). Amae and attachment: Their conceptual and cultural organisation and clinical implications. *The Journal of The Japan Psychoanalytic Society*, 6: 71–83.

Meltzer, D. (1992). *The Claustrum: An Investigation of Claustrophobic Phenomena*. Perthshire: Clunie Press.

National Police Agency. (2023). Number of arrests, 2022. *National Police Agency*. https://www.npa.go.jp/bureau/safetylife/bouhan/chikan/chikan.tousatu.pdf

Stoller, R. J. (1975). *Perversion: The Erotic Form of Hatred.* London: Karnac.

Sugiyama (2009). An empirical study of Chikan and Tosatsu by juveniles. *Kachokyo Journal,* 37: 110–125.

Welldon, E. (1988). *Mother, Madonna, Whore, The Idealisation and Denigration of Motherhood.* London: Free Association Books.

11 My 'back-alley' abortion

Adrienne Harris

How has it taken me 60 years to be able to write this story and need to write it? I think the title is a clue. This past spring, I was in an online meeting of a group of women, all of us having written essays in an edited book, *What Do Women Want Now?* At that meeting, during a discussion of the rejection and destruction of legalised abortion through the erasing of *Roe v. Wade* (1973), one woman referred to the returning danger of 'back-alley' abortion. I felt an acute startle. That term 'back alley' is surely native to my generation; it provoked in me a set of memories of my own abortion at the age of 19 in Canada, where, as in the United States, abortion was illegal. Technically undertaken in what was presented as a legitimate medical office in urban Toronto, it was, in all other respects, including its unconscious meaning to me, an event in a 'back alley'.

It is actually, on reflection, not hard to answer why this has taken 60 years to write and publish this story. This speaks I think to the particular potency of the issue of illegality. It created and will create again the fears and shames of criminalised actions in the doctor and the patient. It would be impossible for me – at the time or retrospectively – to parser out my shame and fear from the doctors. Both of us were united in 'criminality', however we parsed it. I know more about the unconscious now than I did at 19, but I feel that the mix, mix up, mélange or shame and fear in both participants is a crucial element in the unpacking of meaning in abortions undertaken outside the law.

I am now finally feeling the need/requirement to write about this event and its meaning to me as we enter a new and terrible era post *Roe v. Wade* (1973). As in the earlier days of illegality, this experience, the presence and condition, and availability of abortions will not feel equal across our North American culture. Race and class will determine the how, the where, the cost and the consequences of 'back-alley'. Because abortion has been legal (even if unequally available and safe) in the United States since 1973, it is falling to women of my generation to write about the history, the ordeal and danger of illegal abortions – 'back-alley' as my colleague rightly noted.

I published an earlier version of this chapter in a journal room. It seemed so fitting. A room can easily be made into a 'back alley' if we

DOI: 10.4324/9781003646266-15

think of 'back alley' as conjuring up: danger, unpredictability, illegality, exclusion from social protection, outlaw, criminal, homeless and helpless and above all the violently destructive effect of shame... Let me bring you into the room that was my (and other women's of the era of the 1960s) back alley... It's a clinical operating room in a private office in midtown Toronto. It has a space to lie down. Other than that, the room is bare. I am tempted to use the word 'barren', which I think captures a fear I could not then and barely now articulate. All I can feel is how afraid I am. What am I wearing – a surgical gown? Perhaps just a slip and underwear. I remember already feeling shame and fear. I don't or can't really take in the specifics of my surroundings. I am terrified, shame-ridden, more singularly alone than ever in my life, though my life is not very long at this moment. I am 19, a sophomore at an Ivy League college, where one should surely be able to manage one's life. But, at that moment, late fall 1960, I have left my quite luxurious and sociable dorm room to come north to the city I grew up in, where an older woman friend – the only person I can speak to in any confidence – has put me in touch with a doctor. I say that so easily. Maybe really a doctor? Many years later I learned that this person did indeed have a medical licence, but during that first encounter, I knew almost nothing.

When I called my friend to say I was pregnant, she was kind and comforting. She clearly knew what that meant or could mean. Been there. Done that. She took a very strictly practical stance, and she helped me find the right person for that moment of legal, moral and psychological uncertainty. Or so I had to believe. So, I sit in the waiting room and then the operating room under the control of a man who is mocking, sneering, subtly but clearly insulting, and shaming. He does his work. No anesthetic, no language, nothing comforting is said or intended. No pain meds. I walk out of the room onto the street not sure I am viable or safe. I feel damaged and bad in mind, spirit and body. The physical pain of the experience must surely be carrying the negative and self-hating emotions I was experiencing. I cannot sort out if I should and will die, or if I have escaped some human female requirement for suffering. Am I bad? Damaged? Lucky? All of the above?

My older friend takes care of me for a week, and I go back to college. I have a different life from the one that would have unfolded had I not had access to abortion, however terrifying. And through some mix of luck and biology, my experience at 19 does not consciously or critically destroy or fatally disrupt a later history of fertility and family. Yet I am aware that the emotional cost has taken a lifetime to process. I don't want to exaggerate but that experience lived a virulent life in my unconscious. I think the criminality of that situation contributed significantly to my feeling criminal. I feel it is important to speak about now, as abortion seems, with sinister determination, to be moving into criminalised spaces (inside one's mind and in the world). In the decades following my illegal abortion, whenever I drove down that street in Toronto, I felt a stab of shame – mild, subtle, but inevitable. Consciously, I practised consistent support for women's freedom. Unconsciously, a slower more insidious process took place, regarding my own characterological 'badness'.

But to go back to that room is something I still do reluctantly. Everything was at stake, and everything altered in that painful, frightening space. One remnant reappeared. Over a decade later, I am in Toronto with my family: my parents and my children. All seems easy. My father, his face oddly strained, asks to speak to me alone. He has had a call from someone in the police department. My name has turned up in the records of a man arrested for illegal abortions. My father looks anguished. I feel the world opening under my feet. I make up some story as to why I would have been in that person's office. My father, I suspect, is relieved not to have to hear or say any more.

What discursive scene has been enacted? I feel the interwoven strands of hatred and fear of women and sexuality, of the haunting that accompanies action. But mostly I feel my intense commitment to erasure and refusal. Nothing happened. I am struck by the intense intrusion of criminality into my unconscious and conscious assessment of this event and my actions. I can insist on my rights and freedoms. The life and practices of my generation were all about rebellion, reclaiming rights for oneself and others. My unconscious tells a different story and I write this today in order to insist that we examine the ways that social control, legality and bodily management haunt women in particularly insidious ways and do so across class and race and many forms of identification and female subjectivity.

And in a sense, that refusal, that denial, holds to this day. Everything worked out. No one was hurt. I stay in control. Refusal, resistance, repression. In one sense, this is a story of the bad old days, when abortion was not a right but a theft, a crime, an erasure.

A number of years later, probably close to 25 – a quarter of a century – I take up reproductive rights activism in a group called CARASA, the Committee for Abortion Rights and Against Sterilization Abuse. We hold demonstrations and sit-ins. The Black women in this battle with us are inevitably more injured and harassed, and whenever we are arrested in the course of demonstrations, they inevitably get longer sentences and larger fines. At the sentencing after one of the arrests, the White women are sent to take care of the Black families whose protesting mothers are serving time in jail. I arrive at the house of one of the jailed women. Her children – four and eight, perhaps – await me. We shop; we go to the park. The older child is so grown-up, so parentified and he helps me care for his little brother.

But this neglect and loss sit in me alongside relief, enigma and mourning. At the time, I was most conscious of shame and terror. Later I thought about the dangers I had not even dared imagine: death, sterility, never having or knowing that child or having the child come to a space of meaning.

I bring myself and my reader back to that room at this moment in a radically and dangerously changed world for women. Now that *Roe v. Wade* is dismantled, what will poor women and young women and women whose class, race and situation limit massively what actions are possible do? The *New York Times* the other day had a picture of a young, white, middle-class woman reflecting on the current (but surely endangered) possibility of taking medication – abortion by pills – to induce miscarriage. We surely know that whatever technology can generate, its availability will still function by class and caste and privilege.

I have relived that experience so many times in my imagination. This is the first time I write it down. Something of the return to the nightmare of illegal abortions requires me as a witness.

Because I could act and make my own determination about the outcome of pregnancy, I continued various forms of privilege: college, graduate education, a new relationship and marriage, a whitewash that at that time had something crucial to say about class and privilege.

I got to choose to keep the pregnancies I wanted to. My shame stayed hidden.

That shame-ridden scene in Toronto, now over 60 years ago, awaits many women in many difficult and dangerous situations. In thinking and talking about the destruction and dismantling of *Roe v. Wade*, the memories of that period of shame and fear came back. At a Zoom conference on abortion, a colleague, a woman of my generation, spoke of the history of reproduction and the times of 'back-alley abortions'. I shuddered. The room I went to in 1960 was in a polished, upstanding, reputable medical building. Who knew the actual practices of the doctor I was visiting? Yet it was 'back-alley', covered up with veneers of legitimacy. But in the consideration of danger, legitimacy and the shame so easily attached to female sexuality and embodiment, it was 'back-alley'. As I reread this account, I have to notice that there is no trace of a partner, shared responsibility or mutual care. I think that was true throughout that experience. My older friend stood by me, helped, contained, and comforted me, and was never judgemental. But it is clearly in retrospect an experience that was mine alone to bear and manage and work through. This must be part of my character, but also, I think, part of the era. How do we go forward maintaining the deep capacity for supporting other women that feminism and the women's movement gave us? How not to live always alone in a frightening and dangerous room?

That is one of my worries for the women, now three generations younger than me, who have an increasingly shaky access to means of being in control of their bodily, sexual and reproductive lives. And as we learn, over and over, that danger falls unequally on women of different classes, races, social groups and castes. We – all women – are again at the mercy of the 'back alley', but we are not equally vulnerable.

I also worry that the focus of this chapter is too exclusively on the situation for middle- and upper-middle-class women and their families in

North America. It is imperative that any work on abortion take in the larger global picture. At a recent online Zoom conference organised by Lynne Zeavin and COWAP, I listened to Dayna Tortorici, who is providing a wide vision of the impact of abortion availability and ideology on women, on children and on families.

Tortorici starts in an intense and determined voice: 'there is no term in American politics that is more mendacious than *"pro-life"'*. She questions whether the antagonism to abortion is about children or about the control of the bodies of all and any persons: cis, trans, child, non-binary, female – in regard to pregnancy. She is adamant that we should appreciate the virulence and control entailed in laws that put human organs 'in service to another human life against their will'. In her view, Alito, who wrote the majority opinion in DOBBS, writes an opinion oblivious of any legal history of equal protection under the law (McGrath, 2024).

The data Tortorici reports for America and beyond is harrowing: 'Pregnancy is 30 times more dangerous than abortion .... A nationwide abortion ban would cause pregnancy-related deaths to increase by 24%.' Material from the Guttmacher Institute tells an even darker story globally. Unintended pregnancy rates are highest in low-income countries yet abortion rates are significantly lower in those regions compared with middle-income and high-income countries. The documentation closes with an appeal indicating a need for greater action to achieve global equity in sexual and reproductive health. For a comprehensive approach, see Guttmacher Institute (2022).

References

Guttmacher Institute. (2022). The disparities in unintended pregnancy and abortion among low-, middle- and high-income countries. Fact sheet. *Guttmacher Institute*. https://www.guttmacher.org/fact-sheet/induced-abortion-worldwide

McGrath, S. (2024). Samuel Alito's Dobbs opinion and the resurrection of second-class citizenship. *Pace Law Review*, 44(2): 331.

Roe v. Wade (1973). 410 US. 113.

Part 4

The pandemic and the law

Introduction

Rakesh Shukla's chapter, 'COVID, Control and Rule of Law: The Unconscious and Irrational at Play' (Chapter 12), describes how the COVID-19 pandemic hugely impacted the rule of law in India. The pandemic and the lockdowns witnessed the passage of new legislations and sweeping amendments in agricultural laws, citizenship laws, industrial laws, federalism, judiciary, jurisprudence and minority rights. This chapter explores the socio-political and psychological factors at play at an individual, societal and institutional level. This psychological state of having no agency and being attacked and vulnerable through the very air we breathe may have played a role in the ease of the abrogation of old and the introduction of new legislations. In the context of the clinic, COVID resulted in a situation where shared realities of the client/patient and therapist could not be denied and compelled therapists to confront and articulate their own anxieties and fears about illness and death. The onset of COVID accentuated intolerance and homogenisation, decreasing the space for rights, dissent, difference and diversity but the fault lines in society and the legal system run deeper and need to be addressed in our quest for a better tomorrow.

Cândida Sé Holovko and Jurenice Picado Alvares's chapter, 'Domestic Violence and Pandemic: Horror and Hope' (Chapter 13), describes a project that was formalised in February 2020 between the Brazilian Society of Psychoanalysis of São Paulo and the Domestic Violence Against Women Court, with the objective of offering a psychoanalytic psychotherapy approach to women in a state of vulnerability. The psychoanalytic approach emphasises the importance of attentive listening to conscious and unconscious traumatic experiences and the psychic elaboration of the consequences on women's bodies and subjectivities. It also highlights the role of power and cultural differences in the universe of gender violence, where patriarchal masculinity prevails, oriented to domination and often violence, as a hegemonic pattern. Two clinical situations are described, emphasising how gender violence embraces imaginaries socially shared

DOI: 10.4324/9781003646266-16

and how pulsion drive dynamics are present in this type of intrapsychic and interpsychic pathological links.

Osamu Kitayama and Kai Ogimoto's chapter, 'COVID-19 and Japanese Tragedies: Looking Forward to Our Happy Endings' (Chapter 14), states that Japan's countermeasures against COVID-19 focused on the government requesting the people to implement self-restraint and self-quarantine, rather than enforcing legal control in the first year of the pandemic. Although the situation was unpredictable and did not allow anyone to relax, these measures seemed to work effectively. They discuss the principle that made this possible and the mythological thought patterns of Japanese people that function on public relationships.

12 COVID, control and rule of law

The unconscious and irrational at play

Rakesh Shukla

The novel coronavirus (SARS-CoV-2) that causes COVID-19 first emerged in the Chinese city of Wuhan in 2019 and was declared a pandemic by the World Health Organization (WHO).[1] The first COVID case in India was reported on 20 January 2020 in Thrissur, Kerala, with symptoms of a dry cough and sore throat.[2] On 24 March 2020, the Indian Prime Minister, Narendra Modi, called for a complete lockdown of the entire nation, closing all industry and suspending train and bus services.[3]

The COVID pandemic has hugely impacted the rule of law in India, leading to unprecedented changes in laws over large swathes of the legal domain. The concept of rule of law derives from the French phrase 'La principe de legalite' or the principle of legality. It refers to governance based on principles of law and not on the arbitrariness of men. Equality, justice, fundamental rights, common good, accountability, independence of judiciary and presumption of innocence are the broad ingredients of the rule of law. The period during the pandemic and subsequent lockdowns witnessed the passage of new legislations and sweeping amendments in agricultural laws, citizenship laws, industrial laws, federalism, judiciary, jurisprudence and minority rights. These far-reaching changes display an instrumentalist use by the ruling Bharatiya Janata Party government of the conditions prevailing during an unprecedented public health crisis. This chapter explores the socio-political and psychological factors at play at an individual, societal and institutional level.

COVID, impact on psyche and role of leader

The COVID pandemic induced a psychological state of being under siege, particularly in the deadly 'second' wave in April 2021. On 26 April 2021, the number of recorded cases, at 360,960 in India, was the highest in the world. Reuters reported that just in the capital city of New Delhi, four people were dying every minute. In the six weeks from 1 April, the official COVID-19 death toll had risen by 2.2 times from the start of the pandemic. On 10 June 2021, India reported 6,148 deaths, the highest death toll in a single day from COVID-19 worldwide.[4]

DOI: 10.4324/9781003646266-17

Anxieties about the risk of becoming infected, of not being able to find a hospital bed, oxygen or ventilator support leading to one's own death and the death of loved ones, induced a sense of panic, a desperate state; of feeling helpless against an insidious, invisible virus. This psychological state of having no agency, of being attacked and vulnerable through the very air we breathe and through that most basic of needs – human contact, may have played a role in the juggernaut-like manner and the steamrolling ease of the abrogation of old and the introduction of new legislations.

In this panic attack-like state, Indian Prime Minister, Narendra Modi, personified the 'Strong Iron Man' holding the nation together, the 'roaring lion son of Bharat Mata' as portrayed and reified on posters, who would protect Mother, Motherland and each one of us. Modi seemed the benign strong man incarnate, who is always on top of things, looks out for us and is clear and decisive as to the course of action to be followed in any situation. Freud (1921), writing in the context of the position of Christ as head of the Catholic Church, observes, 'He stands to the individual members of the group of believers in the relation of kind elder brother; he is their substitute father' (p. 94). Drawing a parallel between the members of the Catholic Church being 'brothers in Christ' with the camaraderie of being brothers-in-arms in the army with the commander-in-chief as the head, Freud (1921) posits, 'The commander-in-chief is a father who loves all soldiers equally, and for that reason they are comrades among themselves' (p. 94). Photo-ops with Prime Minister Modi clad in army fatigues meeting brave soldiers at high altitudes at the tension-ridden international border with the enemy, Pakistan, assiduously cultivate and feed into the persona. The combination of 'The Leader' with the leading idea of 'National Glory' fed by headlines proclaiming that India will be a great military power in the world has a synergistic effect.[5]

Fromm (1982), speaking of the tremendous role that transference plays in the political life of people, observes:

> One has to look only at the faces in the crowd that applaud a charismatic leader like Hitler or de Gaulle, and one sees the same expression of blind awe, adoration, affection, something in fact which transforms the face from its humdrum daily expression into that of a passionate believer.

Kakar (1982), writing of the process of becoming a Satsangi (one who prays together) in the Radha Soami sect (a Hindu spiritual religious sect headed by a 'Guru' – teacher), observes that it is akin to a process involving deprecation and depletion: 'The Satsangi renounced all claims to self-aggrandizement … and forcefully projected all the positive aspects of the self – its strength, power, knowledge, goodness, gifts, etc. – onto Maharaj-ji, who became the fount of omniscience and omnipotence.'

During the lockdown, the utter helplessness experienced by the individual in the face of an invisible invading enemy in the air, or through the touch of surfaces and human contact, was debilitating. In the midst of this miserable mental state, Modi personified the leader who decisively knew the measures needed to counter it. The intensity of faith this inspired in people seems akin to the processes described by Freud, Fromm and Kakar. If lockdowns, closure of industry and cancellation of public transport were ordered, it was for the protection of the people and the good of the nation. Viewed from the scientific perspective, it made little sense but the call by the prime minister for the beating of *thalis* (metal plates) was responded to with great enthusiasm, and to use the idiom of Fromm, 'faces transformed from feelings of helplessness into vigor and passion'.[6] The faith in Modi seems to remain unshaken by the huge number of deaths in India, the desperation induced by the lack of hospital beds, oxygen cylinders, ventilators and the waiting queues at crematoriums and cemeteries.

India's official COVID-19 death count by the end of June 2021 was 400,000. Other reports put the death toll as ranging from about 1 million to 6 million deaths overall, with central estimates varying between 3.4 million and 4.9 million deaths, with some terming it the 'worst tragedy since partition'.[7]

Lockdown and migrant workers

The COVID pandemic was a public health emergency and it would have been reasonable of citizens to expect that the instruments of governance would be geared towards amelioration of the misery and suffering unleashed by the virus and the subsequent lockdowns, then thought to be the best strategy to arrest its spread. The reality is that at four hours' notice the strictest lockdown in the world was imposed in India on 25 March 2020, causing untold misery to communities of migrant workers and the poor. Most workers were from small towns and villages scattered across India; they had migrated to big cities and metropolises like Delhi, Mumbai and Bangalore in search of work in ancillary industries or were eking out a living plying rickshaws or working as domestic servants. Many worked as agricultural labour in relatively better off states like Punjab and Haryana. With the lockdown, all industries were shut, plying of auto and cycle rickshaws was halted and agricultural operations were suspended. The workers had neither a source of income nor savings, nor a place to stay in cities where they worked. All public transport, such as trains and buses, was also halted by the government. Unable to sustain themselves in the cities, thousands of workers and their families were forced to walk hundreds of kilometres to their villages, where they could at least be sure of a roof over their heads, braving not only hunger and illness but also police violence at inter-state borders.[8]

Citizenship laws, protests and use of COVID

The sheer spectacle of thousands of people fleeing the cities evoked memories of one of the largest cross-border migrations in the world at the time of the partition of India in 1947. Just two months prior to the arrival of COVID, using the brute majority it enjoys in Parliament, the Bhartiya Janta Party (BJP) enacted the Citizenship Amendment Act, 2019 (CAA), which discriminates between citizens on the basis of religion. In tune with the ideology of the present dispensation, the amendment grants citizenship to Hindus, Parsis, Christians, Sikhs and Jains from Pakistan, Afghanistan and Bangladesh but excludes Muslims. In the present context of the rule of the Taliban in Afghanistan, the Hazaras there may be persecuted but are not to be granted citizenship in India.

The onset of the COVID pandemic was extensively used to demonise Muslims through the coinage and use of terms like 'Corona Jihad', implying the use of biological warfare by suicide bombers to cause death and destruction. At the time of the initial arrival of COVID, an international gathering of a reformist Muslim organisation called 'Tableeghi-Jamaat' was taking place in Delhi. This was extensively used by the authorities, with the media as cheerleaders, to propagate the notion that COVID was firmly linked to Islam and Muslims. The polarisation escalated communal tensions, with rumours playing a major role, at times leading to the boycott of Muslim vegetable vendors, or the refusal to accept food or other services delivered by Muslims.

The impact of the partition of the country, though more than seven decades old, continues to arouse anxieties. These fears are, in turn, used to whip up emotions and enact laws, for the first time in independent India, with regard to citizenship based on religion. The agenda of discrimination on the basis of religion was taken forward by pushing for a National Citizenship Register (NCR), which would contain the list of legal citizens of India, and a National Population Register (NPR), which would be a database of citizens. About ten detention centres have already been set up[9] while others are being developed,[10] and each district of India has been directed to set up centres for the incarceration of those deemed to be 'non-citizens'. The implementation of the NCR has led to detentions of a significant number of settled Indians in the north-eastern state of Assam in miserable conditions. Thousands of people mobilised against the amendments to the CAA, and peaceful protests were held all over the country. In an amazing development, it was the grandmothers of Shaheen Bagh in Delhi who came to the forefront and became the most recognisable face of the protests. The justification for the lockdown due to the COVID pandemic was opportunistically used by the government and coercion and criminal force deployed to break up peaceful protests, despite the fundamental right to peaceable protest under the Constitution of India.[11]

Differential impact of COVID

The COVID pandemic had a differential impact on various sections of society. In the planning of industrial areas in India, there is no provision for housing for workers. The lack of accommodation results in workers staying in one-room tenements and slums around factories. There is a lack of civic amenities in these areas. There are water shortages and constant washing of hands is not possible. The density of the population makes social distancing also impossible.

The availability of space and civic amenities like running water and electricity in the residential spaces of middle and upper classes made it possible for people to observe the precautions advised with regard to COVID like social distancing, sanitisation and repeated washing of hands. Likewise, access to computers, tablets and mobiles permitted a significant section to continue to work online and earn money. Their children could access online classes as well as explore the possibilities of learning in other areas. Adults, as well as children, took up newer interests or pursued old passions and pursuits. In sharp contrast, workers in the service and informal sectors lost their jobs and incomes. Domestic workers providing service to the middle classes were rendered jobless and their children had no access to online education. Apartment and residential colonies barred domestic workers from entering their premises. The workers in the formal sector did not fare much better as all industry was closed by executive diktat.

COVID, clinic and shared realities

In the context of the strict policy of no sharing of personal details on the part of the therapist, COVID resulted in a situation where shared realities could not be denied. The initial query 'How are you?' by many clients could not be easily sidestepped. The COVID pandemic led to many adult children returning home to live, as educational institutions and workplaces closed down. Both adult children and parents were unused to staying with each other 24/7, a situation that impacted mental health. Available treatments started online, and individuals who had no comparable experience of in-person therapy seemed comfortable with online therapy. At the height of COVID, all sessions were necessarily online. Efforts were made to reproduce, as far as possible, an in-person setting with experimentation such as switching the video off after the first few minutes akin to the client seeing the therapist as he/she enters the clinic to approximating the setting of being on a couch.

Clients who had been attending pre-COVID therapy were keen to resume physical in-person sessions, creating dilemmas for the therapist. There were clients who refused to take the vaccine due to a lack of faith in their efficacy and they still wanted to come for in-person sessions. For example: Client A had been coming for sessions for more than a decade. As a matter of faith and belief, he refused to take the vaccine but he was keen to resume in-person sessions as he felt online sessions were about 30 per cent effective compared with face-to-face sessions. Client B's take on the online–offline situation was that it was the difference between phone-sex and in-person sex. Client C believed that the vaccine was harmful and a conspiracy, and was on the brink of jeopardising their job as their employers had made vaccination mandatory for continuance at work.

These situations compelled therapists to confront and articulate their own anxieties and fears about illness and death. As cases receded in between COVID waves, and in-person sessions resumed, the issue of insisting on mask-wearing and the use of sanitisers had to be negotiated. In the pre-COVID era, it had been relatively easy to keep legal issues out of the clinic, despite my identity as a lawyer. The agony, uncertainties and unprecedented horror of the COVID pandemic made it difficult not to engage with legal issues, like the right not to take the vaccine and exclusion from public services such as travel without vaccination, in the therapy space. Client C's case was particularly poignant, as not taking the vaccine would result in loss of employment in the middle of the pandemic. My legal assessment as a lawyer was that the courts would in all likelihood uphold the requirement of mandatory vaccine requirement and Client C may not get their job back by litigation. At times, it was sorely tempting to nudge C towards taking the vaccine, rather than maintaining a value-neutral stance and letting C reach a decision.

COVID's impact on the legal system

Jurisprudentially, the Anglo-Saxon adversarial system is followed in adjudication of disputes by courts in India. Though the government issued a notification that workers were to be paid for the lockdown period, the management-owners of industrial concerns approached the Supreme Court of India against the notification. Disputes are adjudicated after giving an opportunity to the parties whose interests are impacted by the issues raised in the petition before the court. The worker-employees were the primary affected parties in the issue of wages being paid for the lockdown period and were necessary parties to the dispute. However, the management of the industrial concerns did not make the worker-employees a party to the proceedings in the petition. Instead, they sought a stay of the notification of the wages for lockdown. This non-inclusion of worker-employees in the case led to the denial of opportunity to the main affected party in the matter to be heard.

The complete shutdown of the physical functioning of courts and the introduction of online legal proceedings made it a complex and difficult task for workers to intervene in the proceedings. The offline proceedings in pre-COVID times were difficult, but had become familiar over the years. The lack of requisite skills among workers, required to negotiate online filing of petitions, increased the advantage of the management with its ready team of experts. The process of the virtual hearing of cases worked towards greater control of the court. In a physical hearing, lawyers cannot be stopped from doing their duty, articulating and presenting the arguments in the best interests of the client. The virtual hearing of cases became the domain of the control room of the court. This gave more room for the playing out of biases and prejudices. The control room had absolute power to mute or render lawyers invisible in the virtual court. In a management–labour dispute, such as in the wages for lockdown case,[12] it could well have been that the lawyers for the management had more time and opportunity to present their arguments than the counsel for the workers. The Supreme Court stayed the notification directing management to provide wages for the lockdown period. Absolving itself of responsibility, the Apex Court declared that the management and workers were free to negotiate the issue between them. The Court having stayed the notification, management did not come forward to negotiate with the workers and the issue simply died down.

Change in laws and COVID

Abrogation of social welfare legislations and new laws

In a forceful pushing of the legal regimen to tilt further towards capital, laws protecting workers' rights have been repealed from the statute books. The government seems to have opportunistically used the COVID pandemic to push its agenda. This would have been difficult in pre-COVID times, when the wholesale repealing of laws protecting the safety and security of workers would have occasioned large-scale public protests. The right to assemble and protest peacefully was effectively extinguished in the context of the public health emergency. The plenipotentiary powers under the Disaster Management Act, 2005, were exercised by the central government to curb protests. The only form of protest remaining was online webinars, but they seem to have had little impact in terms of pressure or resistance to the move to change industrial jurisprudence in India.

The government has repealed 29 labour laws protecting the welfare of workers and their rights. Laws such as the Trade Union Act, 1926; the Industrial Disputes Act, 1947; the Plantation Labour Act, 1951; the Contract Labour (Regulation & Abolition) Act, 1970; the Employees Compensation Act, 1923 and the Employees State Insurance Act, 1948 have all been abolished.

The impact of the repeal of such laws can be gauged from examining an illustrative legislation. Minimum wages are calculated keeping in mind a family of four members and taking into account the expenses of food, clothing, rent and education of children. The prescribing of minimum wages for these essential needs helps towards the formation of a stable industrial working class. The minimum wages for semi-skilled, unskilled and highly skilled work in industry were prescribed under the repealed Minimum Wages Act. The Act also provided for the wages to be paid for work in excess of the normal working hours or 'overtime' in common parlance or extra working hours put in. The non-payment of minimum wages by employers was made punishable by imprisonment and fine. Similarly, the repealed Industrial Standing Order Act, 1946, defined working time, wage rates, workmen, holidays, pay days, leave, and payment of wages, termination and misconduct. The repealed Contract Labour (Regulation and Abolition) Act, 1970, laid down that contract workers should not be employed for work that was permanent in nature.

The government has brought in four new laws called the Industrial Code, 2020; the Occupational Safety, Health and Working Conditions 2020; the Code on Social Security, 2020 and the Code on Wages, 2019 in the area of industrial relations. Law plays a role in mediating and balancing the interests of the employer and employee. The major thrust of these laws with 'pro-employee/worker' nomenclatures, rather than levelling the field, helped to tilt the law even more in favour of the employer. Under the guise of 'ease of doing business', the protection to worker-employees is eroded and the laws push for ease of doing business for employers. The legislations pave the way for a permanent cadre of insecure and temporary employees. They allow easy retrenchment and promote a 'hire and fire' regimen in industrial relations; they substantially dent the right to protest and exclude industrial concerns that employ fewer than 300 employees from the ambit of law with regard to social security provisions for worker-employees. The earlier legislations were applicable to any concern employing 100 or more workers. By increasing the number from 100 to 300 as the threshold for applicability, about 90 per cent of industrial establishments escape the ambit of the laws, and need not be under an obligation to conform to the provisions of social security.

Agricultural laws

Under the Constitution of India, subjects are classified into three lists. List 1 is the Union List of subjects on which the Centre can legislate; List 2 is the State List of subjects on which the States can legislate and List 3 is the Concurrent List, containing subjects on which both the Centre and States can legislate. Agriculture falls squarely in the domain of State Legislatures with regard to making of laws. The Centre, without holding any consultation with States, making a mockery of federalism, or having any discussion in Parliament, opportunistically used the public health emergency of the COVID pandemic to enact three major agricultural laws:

Farmers' Produce Trade and Commerce (Promotion and Facilitation) Act, 2020; Farmers (Empowerment and Protection) Agreement of Price Assurance, Farm Services Act, 2020; the Essential Commodities (Amendment) Act, 2020.

Akin to the changes in industrial law furthering the interests of employers, the thrust of the changes in agricultural law was meant to promote big agro-businesses so that gigantic seed to retail store enterprises would control the market, depress farm gate prices, raise costs and consume small farms. The push was in the direction of the farm-to-fork meat processing companies owning livestock, and farmers would be reduced to raising animals on contract. The direction was towards the abolition of the Minimum Support Price under the guise of giving the farmer more freedom to sell elsewhere at higher prices. The apparent 'freedom of contract' does not work in an equitable way amongst unequal parties, be it a small farmer and big agro-businesses or employee and employer.

The pandemic and rights

The pandemic and the invocation of the Disaster Management Act, 2005 have impacted the federal structure of the country in a major way, leading to increasing centralisation and the equating of the central government with the national interest. The ideology of the present regime – One Nation–One Leader; One Nation–One Language; One Nation–One Flag; One Nation–One Voice; One Nation–One Religion; One Nation–One Food – has led to the shrinking of space for not only dissent and democracy but also diversity and variety.

The right to life and liberty, freedom of speech and expression, and the freedom to assemble peaceably, stand deeply eroded. The equation of dissent with being anti-national has led to large-scale use of sedition and anti-terror laws. Comedians, climate change activists, civil liberty activists, even journalists have been incarcerated in prison. Simultaneously, draconian laws curtailing inter-faith marriages have been enacted.[13]

The judiciary is visualised as the protector of fundamental rights and as a check on the arbitrary exercise of power by the executive in the rule of law visualised under the Constitution of India. However, the judiciary, in present times, seems to have fallen in line and put the stamp of judicial approval on many questionable actions of the present regime. Even with no material evidence produced by the prosecution, bail has been denied to accused persons so that the process becomes the punishment. Denial of bail has put an end to the 'presumption of innocence', which is at the heart of criminal jurisprudence and leads to years of incarceration of the accused as under-trials. Perhaps the fears and anxieties, the feelings of helplessness and lack of agency against an invisible attacking presence evoked in the psyche of the individuals in the judicial chair may have played a role in judicial functioning and may provide a direction to explore towards an understanding and analysis of the role of the judiciary in present times.

The COVID pandemic has accentuated the arbitrary and discriminatory aspects of the functioning of the legal system but the fault lines lie deeply embedded in the system. In an invisible process, each of us imbibes the biases, prejudices and stereotypes of the class, community, religion, gender and caste in which each of us has been raised.[14] These play out at each stage of the legal process.

No easy way forward

The love for Mother and Motherland; the anxieties of separation and fusion; the fears of partition and dismemberment; the dread of the menacing, attacking 'terrorists'; the frisson evoked by the brave son protecting Mother/Motherland; the fear of being swamped and swallowed up by the 'enemy'; the splitting of our 'bad' parts and projecting them onto an other; making the other a 'repository' of all 'bad' feelings like lust, aggression and murderous rage are at play in all of us to varying degrees. The dramatis personae of the legal system – the drafters of law, the implementers of law, the investigators, prosecutors, lawyers and judges are all as much vulnerable to these processes impacting rule of law. The onset of COVID has accentuated and intensified intolerance and homogenisation, decreasing the space for rights, dissent, difference and diversity but, akin to the flaws in a diamond, the fault lines in society and the legal system run deeper and need to be addressed in our quest for a better tomorrow.

Notes

1　National Foundation for Infectious Diseases. (n.d.). 'Coronaviruses (COVID-19)'. https://www.nfid.org/infectious-diseases/coronaviruses/ (Retrieved 29 November 2022)

2　M. A. Andrews, Binu Areekal, K. R. Rajesh, Jijith Krishnan, R. Suryakala, Biju Krishnan, C.P. Muraly, & P.V. Santhosh. (2020, May). 'First confirmed case of COVID-19 infection in India: A case report'. National Library of Medicine, National Centre for Biotechnology Information. https://www.ncbi.nlm.nih.gov/pmc/articles/PMC7530459/#:~:text=We%20present%20here%20the%20first,rhinitis%20or%20shortness%20of%20breath (Retrieved 29 November 2022)

3　Press Information Bureau. Government of India. Prime Minister's Office. (2020, 24 March). 'PM calls for complete lockdown of entire nation for 21 days'. https://pib.gov.in/newsite/PrintRelease.aspx?relid=200658 (Retrieved 18 February 2022)

4　Mander, Harsh. (2022, 27 February). 'How many Indians actually died during the second Covid-19 wave?' Scroll.in. https://scroll.in/article/1018163/harsh-mander-how-many-indians-actually-died-during-the-second-covid-19-wave (Retrieved 18 February 2024)

5 *Times of India*. (2021, 16 October), 'Aim to make India world's biggest military power: PM Modi'. *Times of India*, https://timesofindia.indiatimes.com/india/aim-to-make-india-worlds-biggest-military-power-pm-modi/articlesho w/87051289.cms (Retrieved 18 February 2024)
6 Indian Express (2020a, 22 March). 'Watch: From clapping to beating thalis, how people responded to PM Modi's call on "janata curfew"'. *Indian Express*. https://indianexpress.com/article/coronavirus/watch-janata-curfew-claps-ri nging-bells-pm-modi-6326761/ (Retrieved 10 November 2021)
7 *India Today* (2021, 21 July). '2nd Covid wave was India's worst tragedy since Partition, saw up to 49 lakh excess deaths: Report'. *India Today*. https://www. indiatoday.in/coronavirus-outbreak/story/2nd-covid-wave-was-india-worst-tragedy-since-partition-saw-up-to-49-lakh-excess-deaths-1830894-2021-07-21 (Retrieved 18 February 2024)
8 *Indian Express*. (2020b, 25 December). 'The long walk of India's migrant workers in Covid-hit 2020'. *Indian Express*. https://indianexpress.com/article/india/the-long-walk-of-indias-migrant-workers-in-covid-hit-2020-7118809/ (Retrieved 15 February 2024); *The Guardian* (2022, 23 November). '"They are invisible": The migrant workers struggling in wake of India's Covid response'. https://www.theguardian.com/global-development/2022/nov/23/india-mig rant-workers-work-unemployment-jobs-covid-pandemic (Retrieved 15 February 2024); Dhar, Shobita (2020, 9 November). '1 in 4 migrant workers faced police brutality while going home: Study'. *Times of India*, https://timesofindia.india times.com/home/sunday-times/1-in-4-migrant-workers-faced-police-brutality -while-going-home-study/articleshow/79125333.cms?from=mdr (Retrieved 15 February 2024)
9 Singaravelu, N. (2020, 1 January). 'Where are detention centres in India?' *The Hindu*. https://www.thehindu.com/data/data-where-are-detention-centres-in-in dia/article30451564.ece (Retrieved 10 November 2021)
10 Parashar, U. (2020, 13 August). 'India's biggest detention camp nears completion'. *The Hindustan Times*. https://www.hindustantimes.com/india-news/india-s-big gest-detention-camp-nears-completion/story-nUUSAgko6WGgHPFDBbNcgN.htm l (Retrieved 18 February 2024)
11 As to the psychological factors at play with regard to the discriminatory law and protest, please see: Shukla, S. (2020, 3 March). 'Bubbling cauldron of hate–envy–fury: Playgrounds of splitting and projection'. *International Journal of Applied Psychoanalytical Studies*, 17(1): 77–83. doi:10.1002/aps.1641.
12 *Ficus Pax Private Limited versus Union of India & ors* Writ Petition (Civil) … Diary No. 10983/2020. Supreme Court of India.
13 The Uttar Pradesh Prohibition of Unlawful Conversion Act 2021. https://p rsindia.org/files/bills_acts/acts_states/uttar-pradesh/2021/Act%20No%203% 20of%202021%20UP.pdf (Retrieved 18 February 2024); The Karnataka Right to Freedom of Religion Act, 2022. https://dpal.karnataka.gov.in/storage/p df-files/25%20of%202022%20(E).pdf (Retrieved 18 February 2024)
14 For further reading: Shukla, R. (2019). Quest for justice – Psychoanalytical explorations with judges. In Montagna, P. & Harris, A. (Eds), *Law, Psychoanalysis and Society*. London and New York: Routledge.

References

Andrews, M. A., Areekal, B., Rajesh, K. R., Krishnan, J., Suryakala, R., Krishnan, B., Muraly, C. P., & Santhosh, P. V. (2020, May). *First Confirmed Case of Covid-19 Infection in India: A Case Report*. National Library of Medicine, National Centre for Biotechnology Information. https://www.ncbi.nlm.nih.gov/pmc/articles/

PMC7530459/#:~:text=We%20present%20here%20the%20first,rhinitis%20or%20
shortness%20of%20breath (Retrieved 29 November 2022).

Dhar, S. (2020, 9 November). 1 in 4 migrant workers faced police brutality while
going home: Study. *Times of India*, https://timesofindia.indiatimes.com/home/
sunday-times/1-in-4-migrant-workers-faced-police-brutality-while-going-home
-study/articleshow/79125333.cms?from=mdr (Retrieved 15 February 2024).

Freud, S. (1921). Group psychology and the analysis of the ego. In Strachey, J.
(Ed.), *The Standard Edition of the Complete Psychological Works of Sigmund Freud*,
Vol. 18. London: Hogarth Press, pp. 65–143.

Fromm, E. (1982). *Greatness and Limitations of Freud's Thought*. London: Abacus.

India Today. (2021, 21 July). 2nd Covid wave was India's worst tragedy since Partition, saw up to 49 lakh excess deaths: Report. *India Today*. https://www.indiatoda
y.in/coronavirus-outbreak/story/2nd-covid-wave-was-india-worst-tragedy-since-
partition-saw-up-to-49-lakh-excess-deaths-1830894-2021-07-21 (Retrieved 18 February 2024).

Indian Express. (2020a, 22 March). Watch: From clapping to beating thalis, how
people responded to PM Modi's call on 'janata curfew'. *Indian Express*. https://
indianexpress.com/article/coronavirus/watch-janata-curfew-claps-ringing-bell
s-pm-modi-6326761/ (Retrieved 10 November 2021).

Indian Express. (2020b, 25 December). The long walk of India's migrant workers in
Covid-hit 2020. *Indian Express*. https://indianexpress.com/article/india/the-
long-walk-of-indias-migrant-workers-in-covid-hit-2020-7118809/ (Retrieved 15
February 2024).

Kakar, S. (1982). *Shamans, Mystics and Doctors*. Oxford Indian Paperbacks.

Mander, H. (2022, 27 February). How many Indians actually died during the second
Covid-19 wave? *Scroll.in*. https://scroll.in/article/1018163/harsh-mander-how-ma
ny-indians-actually-died-during-the-second-covid-19-wave (Retrieved 18 February
2024).

National Foundation for Infectious Diseases. (n.d.). Coronaviruses (COVID-19). http
s://www.nfid.org/infectious-diseases/coronaviruses/ (Retrieved 29 November
2022)

Parashar, U. (2020, 13 August). India's biggest detention camp nears completion. *The
Hindustan Times*. https://www.hindustantimes.com/india-news/india-s-biggest-
detention-camp-nears-completion/story-nUUSAgko6WGgHPFDBbNcgN.html
(Retrieved 18 February 2024).

Press Information Bureau. Government of India. Prime Minister's Office. (2020, 24
March). PM calls for complete lockdown of entire nation for 21 days. https://pib.
gov.in/newsite/PrintReliease.aspx?relid=200658 (Retrieved 18 February 2022)

Shukla, R. (2019). Quest for justice: Psychoanalytical explorations with judges. In
Montagna, P. & Harris, A. (Eds), *Law, Psychoanalysis and Society*. London and
New York: Routledge.

Shukla, R. (2020, 3 March). Bubbling cauldron of hate-envy-fury: Playgrounds of
splitting and projection. *International Journal of Applied Psychoanalytical Studies*,
17(1): 77–83, doi:10.1002/aps.1641.

Singaravelu, N. (2020, 1 January). Where are detention centres in India? *The
Hindu*. https://www.thehindu.com/data/data-where-are-detention-centres-in-
india/article30451564.ece (Retrieved 10 November 2021).

The Guardian. (2022, 23 November). 'They are invisible': The migrant workers
struggling in wake of India's Covid response. *The Guardian* online. https://

www.theguardian.com/global-development/2022/nov/23/india-migrant-wor
kers-work-unemployment-jobs-covid-pandemic (Retrieved 15 February 2024).

The Karnataka Right to Freedom of Religion Act. (2022). https://dpal.karnataka.gov.
in/storage/pdf-files/25%20of%202022%20(E).pdf (Retrieved 18 February 2024).

The Uttar Pradesh Prohibition of Unlawful Conversion Act. (2021). https://prsin
dia.org/files/bills_acts/acts_states/uttar-pradesh/2021/Act%20No%203%20of
%202021%20UP.pdf (Retrieved 18 February 2024).

Times of India. (2021, 16 October). Aim to make India world's biggest military power:
PM Modi. *Times of India*. https://timesofindia.indiatimes.com/india/aim-to-ma
ke-india-worlds-biggest-military-power-pm-modi/articleshow/87051289.cms
(Retrieved 10 November 2021).

13 Domestic violence and pandemic
Horror and hope

Cândida Sé Holovko and Jurenice Picado Alvares

In 1915, in the middle of the First World War, Freud wrote a beautiful and poetic essay, entitled 'On Transience' ([1916]1953). In it, he reflects on the impact of the great destructions for humanity, the enormous losses and mourning that people were experiencing, and outlines the fundamental concepts of his theory contained in 'Mourning and Melancholy' (Freud, 1917). In 'On Transience', we recognise the timelessness in most of Freud's considerations that seem to be referring to the dark times of the COVID-19 pandemic that we have recently faced.

A global pandemic, such as that in which we were and still are immersed, causes uncertainty, anguish and fear of our own death. Our loved ones and people from various corners of the planet are affected by serious disease that disables and traumatises, and can be lethal. It creates situations of total isolation, in which people separated from their powerless families watch in horror the destruction caused by the deadly virus. Our Western society used to blind itself to the inexorable reality of death, but we ourselves were forced to bear witness to the millions of people carried away by the great 'Mrs Death'. In Brazil, alarmingly, the number of deaths exceeded 660,000 – a challenging historical time indeed.

How many people had to endure the loss of loved ones without the chance to perform mourning rituals that help them work through and process grief? How tragic! How many professionals lamented the destruction of what they had built over many years? Depressed teenagers, high alcohol and drug consumption, increased domestic violence, couples separating and contributing to the increase in divorce statistics were among many of the sufferings that afflicted us.

In our psychoanalytic clinic, due to the enforced isolation and the long period of traumatic time that seemed endless, we experienced an increase in psychic disorders, an explosion of psychosomatic illnesses, depressions, anxiety crises and acting outs of all kinds of violence. In fact, the mental health of individuals was invaded by another pandemic.

Overnight, and from all directions, we were faced with a threatening virus that forced us to reinvent a new way of being with our analysands in a safe way for the pairing. Thus, online services emerged as the only

DOI: 10.4324/9781003646266-18

way to provide work that could not be postponed, and in this chaotic experience a new path was opened that proved to be extremely effective and promising. In this way, many people, mainly from neglected areas and without the resources to access psychotherapy, were finally able to be assisted including by analysts who worked far from their homes.

In Brazil, before the COVID-19 pandemic, it was stated that every minute, a Brazilian woman suffers some form of sexual violence or other physical abuse in the domestic environment: a situation that became even more serious, demonstrating that the sanitary crisis is also a social disaster.

Reflecting upon domestic violence in the context of the pandemic adds to the uncertainties being faced nowadays. These are very difficult times indeed when assistance to women proves of utmost importance.

Historically, women have frequently been victims of violence in the family environment. In Brazil, the *Maria da Penha* Law (2006) created mechanisms to curb domestic violence against women by establishing measures of assistance and protection, and it is currently the main legal tool for confronting violence.

In the year 2021, when the *Maria da Penha* Law had been established for 15 years, there was an 86 per cent increase in violence against women in Brazil.[1] This exponential growth was due to the social isolation that persisted in that year, forcing women to spend longer periods of time with their aggressors in the family sphere.

Today, it is estimated that every minute 25 Brazilian women suffer domestic violence, be it psychological, physical or sexual, perpetrated by relatives or their partner/ex-partner, which is equivalent to 13.4 million Brazilian women.[2]

Given such alarming data, what can we do as psychoanalysts?

This question involving social psychoanalysis had already been raised by Freud and followers at the beginning of the twentieth century, when Freud claimed that psychoanalysis should be included in the whole healthcare social system, being a right for all individuals, rich or poor. Elizabeth Ann Danto (2020), who researched Freud's views about the social system and his action at that time, emphasises that social well-being is implicated in mental health, just as mental health is entangled in social well-being.

Project of assistance to women victims of violence

In February 2020, a project was formalised between the Brazilian Society of Psychoanalysis of São Paulo, and the Domestic Violence Against Women Court, Santo Amaro/SP branch, with the objective of offering a psychoanalytic psychotherapy approach to women in a state of vulnerability, supported by this legal institution.

The women's appointments take place online, once a week, with a maximum duration of three semesters. The project coordination holds monthly meetings with the psychoanalysts who participate in this activity in order to discuss the theoretical and clinical peculiarities of such violence.

The psychoanalytic approach emphasises the importance of attentive listening to conscious and unconscious traumatic experiences and the psychic elaboration of the consequences on women's bodies and subjectivities, as well as the role of power and cultural differences in the universe of gender violence.

Reflections upon sexual and gender violence

According to the sociologist Connell (2005; Connell & Pearse, 2015), for centuries (we could say for millennia) a patriarchal masculinity has prevailed, oriented to domination and often violence, as a hegemonic pattern that despises weakness, exalts strength, power, hypersexuality and homophobia in the man, prioritising gender relations.

This masculinity was adopted only by a minority of men but it became normative as an ideal of being and demanded that other men position themselves in relation to it and legitimise the subordination of women, who many times placed themselves as accomplices in the submission to this hierarchical system of power.

According to Connell, gender dynamics and the production of masculinities also take specific forms in colonial and post-colonial contexts such as ours, since violence played a formative role in these societies. The author associates Latin American machismo with these contexts of domination.

Referring to gender violence against the feminine, Fiorini (2019) states: 'It is neither a drive problem alone nor only of the male castration complex, but it is intertwined with strongly rooted social discourses …. It encompasses traditions, myths, shared imaginaries that express themselves in everyday life.'

Anthropologist Rita Segato (2003), in her research with male rapists, finds in contemporary times an overlapping of two social systems that underlie gender discourses: 'One that elevates women to a status of individuality and citizenship equal to men, and the other that imposes its guardianship… The latter is the rule that governs the genre and continues to demonstrate its unaltered vitality' (p. 30).

We know that contemporary domestic violence cannot be considered, even in psychoanalysis, as simply resulting from individual pathologies, as they are intersubjective acts in which other real or imaginary actors participate.

These crimes, as widely described in the scientific literature, are crossed by social, historical, religious, ethnic and legal discourses that are shared by a community and are lost in the origin of time.

According to Jessica Benjamin (2020), the denial of the boy's identifying love for his father and the non-recognition of his value and potency seem to be historically connected with the repudiation of femininity. Boys split their vulnerable aspects and project them onto girls, seen as needy, fearful and dependent. It is also a result of the fear of the primordial mother who might imprison him in a relationship of dependence, preventing alterity and constitution of his masculinity. Benjamin (2020) also proposes that the differentiation of subjects should be supported by the relationships of love and identification of parents (whatever gender they may be) with their children. She says, 'To visualise equal rights and a transformation of the relationship between the sexes, we need a redemptive vision of differentiation based on the idea of recognising the other in his/ her alterity!' (Benjamin, 2020).

In contact with abused women, we often find a reluctance to expose the situation of abuse and to denounce the abuser, which is not fully explained by the violent threats of the perpetrator. We believe that the disruptive traumatic situation produces a flood of excitations in the woman's mind, not metaphorised. This prevents the constitution of a representational chain that could account for what was experienced, true holes in the construction of representations. Getting close, remembering something that cannot be inscribed as a verbal memory but has been marked on the body, generally produces a nameless anguish that leads the victim to avoid reporting the abuser.

According to Durban (2017), people who have lived through situations of constant abuse can express anxieties analogous to paranoid schizophrenics: to dissolve, dilute, break up, lose the limits of the skin, lose the sense of orientation, the anxieties of falling into an eternal abyss; that is, anxieties that cannot be named. These archaic anxieties threaten the constitution of the ego linked to time, space and love bonds.

We also believe that guilt for what was elicited in terms of sexual arousal in the woman's body is also another source that leads to the silence of abused women. It is not uncommon for many women to repeat situations of abuse, self-harm, exposure to situations of sexual danger and serious accidents. It is common to find in a clinic for raped women, severe depression, eating disorders such as anorexia and bulimia, in addition to autoimmune diseases, among others. These pathologies are closely connected with deep experiences of invasion in the psychic and bodily envelope.

Clinical situations

Below, we write about two clinical situations – from the aforementioned project – emphasising how gender violence embraces imaginaries socially shared traditions and myths as well as some drive dynamics present in this type of intrapsychic and interpsychic pathological links. We aim to reveal the power of these psychoanalytic interventions.

Clinical situation I: Luzia and Leandro (Cândida Sé Holovko)

A young and beautiful woman from Mozambique, dreaming of professional growth and of creating a stable, united family, arrived on the outskirts of São Paulo alone. Her alcoholic father had abandoned the family when Luzia was 11 months old, returning only nine years later, totally impoverished and jobless. Her mother, a struggling woman and family breadwinner never had time for affective exchanges with her children. Luzia came to São Paulo to meet a man she had fallen in love with in her hometown, and who in a few months became her husband. After being married for a while, and with her professional life thriving, she took a technical course in administration and became a partner in a women's clothing store. She and her husband decided then to have a baby that was born prematurely after a pregnancy marked by somatisation, diabetes and high blood pressure.

At this very sensitive moment in a woman's life, when she was far from her homeland, without the due support from a social environment, with a psychic organisation marked by traumatic experiences and deficits in her egoic constitution, Luzia developed severe postpartum depression. With clear melancholic features, she expressed the cruelty of her super-ego through frequent accusations: blaming herself not only for the emergency delivery but also for interrupted breastfeeding and feeling permanently insufficient as a mother and as a woman. Here, pregnancy was experienced as yet another narcissistic wound in a framework of psychic organisation with voids of symbolisation and failures in early relationships – experiences that made it impossible to establish a structured narcissism and a subjectivity with defined contours.

Luzia said she had an abusive relationship with her husband, who drank too much, spent all his salary on gambling, was very jealous and verbally aggressive. When her daughter was one and a half years old, they separated and her husband went to live with another woman. During this period, Luzia felt very alone and very guilty about everything. She was so melancholic that she almost committed suicide. She sought psychiatric help and in this state of emotional fragility she met Leandro, who in less than a month was already assiduously visiting her house. She soon found out that Leandro was married.

Disappointed, she tried to separate from him, but he never tired of looking for her, constantly presenting her with a variety of gifts, and he swore that she was the love of his life. A few months later they began to live together again and the degree of domination that Leandro exerted in her life, and the unhealthy jealousy, became evident to the point of parking his car in front of her store every day in order to watch her.

Luzia commented that, at the time, she was passionately in love and thought that everything was wonderful, interpreting jealousy and control as care. Over time, Leandro became more and more jealous, even competing with Luzia's daughter to the point of physically attacking the girl in Luzia's absence. When Luzia found out, she rebelled and decided to break up with him permanently. Sometimes she wondered how she let it all happen. 'I was blind,' she said.

It is worth noting here that, at the beginning of her psychotherapy, during the pandemic lockdown, Luzia felt terribly worried and said she wouldn't be able to cope with supporting her daughter and the expenses at home. This was a real problem that haunted her. She suffered from fractured sleep, anguished about how to survive on the meagre government financial help. Various sessions were filled with these complaints based on reality during the lockdown period.

Luzia needed some time of intimacy in the analytical relationship, exposing situations of non-elaborated grief (the death of a very dear aunt, the departure from her motherland, the distance from her father) before being able to report the traumatic scene of the attempted femicide that she suffered from Leandro.

She then reported a dreadful experience. A week after the separation, and her continuous refusal to have any contact with Leandro, when leaving her sleeping daughter's bedroom, much to her surprise, she encountered Leandro in the middle of her living room, hooded, all in black and drunk. Taking a knife from his waist, he said, 'I'm here to kill you!' In shock she asked, 'How did you get in?' Laughing, he said he could get anywhere he wanted. At the time, she thought that if she screamed he would stab her and wake her daughter up.

She wondered if she could make use of a martial arts move she had learned in her self-defence training, but she worried that, if it didn't work, he could kill her daughter as well. Leandro, who was furious, started to pass the knife across her throat from one side to the other, saying that he would kill her because he would not accept the separation. At that moment, she thought she should comply and said: 'Dear, I'm sorry, you're completely right; wait a minute, I want to be with you. It's you I love; let's be together, let's get back together right now.'

Trying to calm him down, she said: 'See, I'm telling you the truth ... I was looking at our photos (actually, she was gathering the photos to delete them). Look what a beautiful couple we make!' Finally, he started to calm down as she tried to get him to talk. He wanted to hold her, have sex with her at all costs. She reported that she made a huge mistake when she asked how he had imagined he would kill her. At that moment, he got excited, looked like a child, and said: 'Look at this rope, I was going to tie your hands like this, I was going to stab you several times, here, here, here ... I was going to wrap your body in a cloth and throw it in the woods.'

At that point, the emotional impact of Luzia's terror overflowed and expressed itself in the body; the split as a defence was no longer effective, and Luzia went into automatic anguish. She began to tremble a lot, in panic for her and her daughter; she began to pray loudly and cry desperately. With that, Leandro was disconcerted and said he would leave. All this took many hours!

At dawn, shaken, and supported by friends, she went to a Women's Defense Against Violence Office and obtained an urgent restraining order.

This experience triggered a permanent traumatic state in Luzia (Freud, 1920), with symptoms of insomnia, anguished awakenings with shortness of breath, and sweating profusely. It was characteristic of automatic anguish without metabolisation of affection by psychic means. In addition to hypervigilance when going out, she experienced strong withdrawal symptoms, convulsive crying and frequent self-recriminations. A year after what had happened, when she found out that Leandro had been put on trial, the fear started to return because she was scared he would take revenge on her.

Throughout the sessions, the analytical work with Luzia favoured the strengthening of her ego and her life drive. She was less depressed, less somatised, excited about work and she longed for a new relationship, despite fears of repeating her pattern of bonding with men. She started to be aware of the fact that she tended to begin a relationship with a man with a high degree of idealisation and a tendency to merge with her partner in the expectation of filling her affective and representational voids. This tendency to invest in narcissistic objects contributed to her symbiotic, abusive bonds and her melancholy state.

At the present moment in the analytical process, Luzia is more aware of these tendencies. She has shown an increased capacity to think and contain her impulses and affections.

Gradually, Luzia has revealed facets of sensitivity, creativity and identification with good objects. Memories arise of a maternal aunt whom she always admired for her loveliness, sense of humour and great vitality. Eros has taken the lead over the thanatic impulses.

As for Leandro, by threatening his ex-partner with femicide, he opened wide the bonds of a 'violation mandate' that have been in place for millennia in different cultures such as ours in the West. According to Segato (2003), this refers to aggressive impulses characteristic of the 'male subject' towards those who show the signs and gestures of 'femininity' (p. 22). In his acting, Leandro intends to escape from his vulnerability, from his precarious narcissism, mortally wounded, obtaining by force the power and dominion that were threatened by the expression of autonomy of his ex-partner, Luzia.

This urgency is very often linked to the experience of psychic collapse in the abandoned partner, like a narcissistic haemorrhage that threatens his existential integrity. These experiences of loss of self with the abandonment of the partner were also present in Luzia, as evidenced at the moment of the first separation.

Signs of loss of contact with reality and poor management of impulses are evident in Leandro in the violent episode described. We can identify from his acting not only multiple determinations of the Latin American male chauvinist context but also an impulsivity that overflows and exposes the narcisistic omnipotent defence against the experience of helplessness. 'Laughing, he says that he can enter anywhere he wants!'

Estela Welldon, in her book, *Madre, Virgen, Puta* (1988), states that, in general, scenes of perversion in women involve their own bodies or their children, experienced as narcissistic extensions. On the other hand, men tend to project their violence outwards, towards the object that causes the pain of the soul.

According to Welldon, there is often a dance with death, as a border-line situation of hopelessness and terror at the dreaded black hole of melancholy.

Dancing with death alludes not only to a dangerous game between life and death, but also to a maniacal defence. In this experience with Luzia, we can state the veracity of Welldon's observations: when Luzia's husband abandons her to live with another woman, she attempts suicide, directing her aggression against herself; while Leandro, when living the abandonment, directs his aggression towards his ex-partner or, better, towards the outside, towards the object, towards Luzia.

Clinical situation II: Gabriela and Gustavo (Jurenice Picado Alvares)

Gabriela was a girl who dreamed of a happy marriage, having a home, kids and studying. Today, she is a suffering woman who just wants to survive close to her three daughters due to the threats she receives from Gustavo, her ex-partner.

As a girl, she lived with her parents and siblings. Her father was a psychically absent man, and her mother, who was demanding and strict, punished them violently. Her mother would beat her with a whip if she came back from work late in the afternoon, or if things did not conform to what she had requested.

Gabriela said that at the age of ten she took care of her younger siblings and the house; at 12 years old she also cooked for them. At that age, she was sexually abused by a 19-year-old young man, the son of a friend of her mother's. Her mother was very fond of the boy's family and encouraged his presence at their house every afternoon. This boy impregnated her at 13.

When her parents found out she was pregnant, they mistreated her a lot. Her mother did not want a 'lost daughter', as she called her; she wanted her to marry, but the boy was only ready to take on the child, not the marriage.

These memories reported in the first psychotherapy sessions were accompanied by much suffering. Gabriela cried in anguish as she relived scenes from her childhood and adolescence, when she suffered neglect from her parents and violence from the mother, who did not understand her and was distant.

During this period, Gabriela said that in adolescence she found comfort in a man who was her neighbour and in a woman who offered continence to her emotional pain. They were people who possibly occupied the roles of her parental figures, as these were negligent in her life.

At the age of 14, Gabriela met another man, approximately ten years older than her, who accepted her pregnancy and became an affectionate companion to her. Around her fourth month of pregnancy, she lost the baby.

At the age of 15, she became pregnant again with her first child. However, there was a fatality. While still on the maternity ward, she received news that a robbery had resulted in the violent death of the baby's father, whom she considered to be the first person in her life who had protected and loved her. This man became an idealised figure whom she resorted to in her thoughts, in moments of helplessness.

At the age of 22, Gabriela started dating Gustavo, a work partner, and a few months later they decided to live together. She became pregnant once again. Gabriela commented that at that time Gustavo was controlling, possessive and extremely aggressive: he monitored her cell phone use and cursed Gabriela, saying that pregnant women made him feel disgusted, and he hit her in the head. Some nights when he went out he locked her inside the house. It was a difficult pregnancy that resulted in a delivery with eclampsia.

Months after the birth of this child, she discovered that she was pregnant again with a third daughter, who was born prematurely with poor bone formation. Gustavo blamed her and assaulted her more, to the point where she received a punch that dislocated her nasal septum. Gustavo was violent with his stepdaughter as well, and threatened to set her on fire, and if Gabriela retorted he would be physically aggressive and threaten her to make her silent.

Could Gabriela's multiple pregnancies indicate an unconscious search for Eros, life drive, in a predominant scenario of death drive?

Gabriela did not mention the violence she suffered and the difficulties she experienced to her family for fear of disapproval, as she did not want any continence of her suffering.

Once Gustavo attacked Gabriela's father and sister physically, and then set fire to the neighbour's car when he came to intervene. For the first time, Gabriela called the police and Gustavo was arrested. A few months later he was released and went to meet Gabriela, telling her how repentant he was and how he was willing to change. They looked for help in the church hoping they would be fine, but the violence continued and, disillusioned, she decided to leave her partner. With her daughters, she hid in another city in an attempt to escape the violence and threats of femicide.

Gabriela, like many women who have abusive relationships, believed for a long time that her partner could change and that somehow she was to blame for the beatings. After some time, Gustavo discovered where she and daughters were hiding. He invaded the house, was arrested and released after payment of bail. At this moment, Gabriela sought legal protection, and since then she has been in a state of shock due to constant threats. She feels the need to know where he lives and where he is, otherwise she feels apprehensive and persecuted, and she is afraid that he will surprise them with some evil. She fears for her own safety and for that of her daughters.

Gustavo does not provide any support for his two daughters as determined by the court, and Gabriela is too afraid to ask for the money as she is afraid of what he might do in revenge. After attending analysis for some time, possibly due to the quality of the analytical listening and the growth of trust in the bond, she recounted the perverse aggressive acts performed by Gustavo in disputes with other men; for example, he amputated body parts such as fingers, ears, etc.

Gabriela and her daughters had protection from the Court of Domestic Violence, but Gustavo got judicial consent for accompanied visits with his daughters, which left Gabriela disappointed and distrusting of the judiciary.

Gabriela guides her teenage daughters about what they may encounter and what they should do in the case of any complications happening when they are with their father; and as protection they can use the pepper spray they carry in their bags.

Throughout the analysis process, Gabriela took possession of her hurt feelings and the resentment she felt towards her neglectful parental figures.

Joshua Durban (2017) discusses situations of neglect in the field of child abuse. He says: 'The abused child suffers an internal catastrophe where the normal limits collapse. Trust, hope, belief in continence, continuity and security are replaced by violence and despair' (p. 111).

In Gabriela's case, we observe a violence directed at herself, closely linked to the feeling of unconscious guilt, possibly related to the mistreatment experienced in her childhood and the sexual abuse suffered in adolescence. Self-aggressions expressed in melancholic self-recriminations and in the unconscious search for situations of more abuse result in her repeatedly returning to the aggressive environment.

Currently, Gabriela says that she is discovering herself and recognising her own wishes more. She feels more stable, more secure, has been promoted in her work and feels more capable of fighting for what she believes in and for the care of the daughters.

The analysis work with Gabriela has involved the opportunity for the traumatic situations to be worked through and transformed. The analyst perceived a lack of good internal objects in a melancholic relationship with constant self-recriminations.

Her relationship with the analyst provided a new experience of continence that she had not received from her relational environment and the trust in the therapeutic treatment process resulting in greater libidinal force, strengthening her life narcissism.

Gabriela has expressed more anger at the abuse she suffered and she is less afraid to face the situation with her ex-partner and to seek justice.

Recently, Gabriela contacted the Public Defender's Office, requesting two changes: the judge should cancel the paternal visits with her daughters and she should receive the parental support direct from the company Gustavo is currently working for and a formal contract should be put in place.

As for the eldest daughter, who had initially refused therapy from our project, when she noticed emotional changes in her mother, she requested analytical consultations for herself.

Regarding Gustavo's violence, he seemed to be stuck in experiences of deprivation, neglect and ill-treatment experienced since his childhood. Gabriela reported that at the age of three, Gustavo lost his father, who was stabbed in a bar he frequented. His mother, in serious mental and financial trouble, had taken her children to an orphanage.

We understand Gustavo's violence as a consequence of a life with a precarious childhood and family, in which the child grew up hating the world and attacking others. He did not recognise the limits of the law but he was also a product of cultural mandates of male violence.

Final considerations

As big as the changes in socio-cultural institutions, with respect to the rights of women, children, adolescents and LGBTQIA+ people, have been, we see an inertia of the system in the deconstruction of the hierarchical positions of male and female. It will take a long time for the behaviour to change in the individual and collective psyche.

We observed in the work with Luzia and Gabriela, the submission to the gender hierarchical positions while their partners embody these mandates of violence so present in our socio-cultural environment.

The project between DAC/SBPSP and *Vara de Família* grows gradually with the adhesion of psychoanalyst colleagues who, little by little, become sensitised in the face of this cruel reality. In theoretical-clinical discussions with colleagues, we can see the power of psychoanalytic listening for these women in highly vulnerable situations. We are hopeful that the project can expand significantly, contributing to the prevention of violence in a safer and more just society.

Finally, we remember the words of the Portuguese writer, Valter Hugo Mãe (2010), when reporting a scene of a character who attacks his wife until she almost dies, and often heard in situations of domestic violence: '*tão louco de paixão estava, tão grande amor lhe tinha*', 'so mad with passion was I, such great love I had for her'. Can we say this is love?

For us, love is what the philosopher Badiou (2009) says:

> It is in love that the subject goes beyond himself, beyond narcissism (p. 24). [...] In love there is a separation or disjunction that can be simply the difference between two people and their infinite subjectivities (p. 31).

Notes

1 Research carried out by *Instituto Data Senado*, in partnership with *Observatório da Mulher* Against Violence.
2 Research and Consultancy Intelligence – *IPEC*/March 2021 – about the year 2020. https://www.fontesegura.forumsegura.org.br

References

Badiou, A. (2009). *Éloge de L'amour* [In praise of love]. Paris: Flammarion.
Benjamin, J. (2020). Vulnerabilidad, Repudio e Violencia. A tragédia da Masculinidad [Vulnerability, repudiation and violence. The tragedy of masculinity]. Paper presented at the XIV Intergenerational Latin American Dialogue between Men and Women. Women's and Psychoanalysis Committee IPA/COWAP, 24–25 April, D. F. Mexico 'Power, Gender and Love: Contemporary Feminine Perspectives'.
Connell, R. (2005). *Masculinities*. Oakland, CA:University of California Press.
Connell, R. & Pearse, R. (2015). *Gênero: uma perspectiva global: tradução e revisão Marília Moschkovitch* [Gender: A global perspective: Translation and revision by Marília Moschkovitch]. São Paulo.
Danto, E. A. (2020). *As clínicas públicas de Freud. Psicanálise e Justiça social, 1918–1938*. São Paulo: Editora Perspectiva.
Durban, J. (2017). O complexo de vitimador [The victimiser complex]. In Holovko, C. & Cortezzi, C. (Eds), *Sexualidades e gênero: desafios da psicanálise* [Sexualities and gender: Challenges for psychoanalysis]. São Paulo: Blucher, pp. 111–140.
Fiorini, L. G. (2019). Hacia una desconstrucción de 'lo feminino': Discursos Lógicas y Poder. Implicancias teórico-clínicas [A deconstruction of 'the feminine': Logical discourses and power. Theoretical-clinical implications]. *Revista de Psicoanalisis*, 76(1): 37–51.
Freud, S. ([1916]1953). On transience. In Strachey, J. (Ed.), *The Standard Edition of the Complete Psychological Works of Sigmund Freud*, Vol. 14. London: Hogarth Press, pp. 303–307.
Freud, S. ([1917]1953). Mourning and melancholia. In Strachey, J. (Ed.), *The Standard Edition of the Complete Psychological Works of Sigmund Freud*, Vol. 14. London: Hogarth Press, pp. 237–258.
Freud, S. ([1920]1969). Além do Princípio do Prazer [Beyond the pleasure principle]. In *Standard Brasileira das Obras Psicológicas Completas de Sigmund Freud, ed. Standard Brasileira* [Complete psychological works of Sigmund Freud, Standard Brazilian edition]. Rio de Janeiro: Editora Imago.

Mãe, V. H. (2010). *O remorso de Baltazar Serapião* [Balthazar Serapion's remorse]. São Paulo: Editora 34.

Segato, R. L. (2003). *Las estruturas elementales de la violencia* [The elementary structures of violence]. Bernal: Universidad nacional de Quilmes, Buenos Aires.

Welldon, E. (1988). *Madre, Virgen, Puta* [Mother, virgin, whore]. London: Free Association Books.

14 COVID-19 and Japanese tragedies

Looking forward to our happy endings

Osamu Kitayama and Kai Ogimoto

In the first year of the pandemic, Japan's countermeasures against COVID-19 focused on the government requesting the people to implement self-restraint and self-quarantine, rather than enforcing legal control. Although the situation was unpredictable and did not allow us to relax, these measures seemed to work fairly effectively. We wish to discuss the principle that made this possible in this chapter – the mythological thought patterns of Japanese people that function in public relationships.

Japanese tragedies as seen from a dramatic point of view

We would like to begin by describing the dramatic or drama-based view of psychoanalysis. This viewpoint, which Osamu Kitayama (2009, 2013) discussed as a 'dramatic psychoanalysis' in Japan, treats a person's life as a piece of drama, and regards the mind as having an unconscious script that we repeatedly act out, irrespective of the various characters who play with us on stage. The metaphor describing life as a play appears in the writings of Shakespeare's 'As You Like It', Dante's 'La Divina Commedia' and in works by other Western and Eastern authors (Yamazaki, 1971). However, if life is to become a series of tragedies, based on this point of view, we think it would be better to read the script, interpret and revise it.

To be able to read and interpret a script that we are performing, we must distance ourselves from the stage, watch the play with someone else and think about it, rather than merely appearing in it as an actor. In other words, weaving a story from backstage rooms and rehearsal halls while looking at one's own life, together with analytical therapists or clinicians called psychoanalysts who possess this point of view. This will eventually lead to the person pulling out of the tragedy, by revising and rewriting their script.

Many patients unconsciously repeat tragic scenarios. On the other hand, classic tragedies are often written as a plot for myths and old folktales that are already shared among the people as part of their culture, or as a storyline for a popular novel. Therefore, if an analytical therapist

DOI: 10.4324/9781003646266-19

were to read these cultural materials in advance, it would give him or her opportunities to practise reading and interpreting the tragic lives of individual people. Since typical life stories are already broadly shared in a society; some people end up following an existing script without being aware of it. This understanding, too, is one of the drama-based viewpoints of psychoanalysis.

In addition, there is the question of whether or not the understanding of symbolic myths and abstract scenarios can be readily applied to gain an understanding of the actual lives of individual people. There is also a hypothesis in psychoanalysis that the tragedy of an individual is a variation on classic tragedies that are already culturally shared. Understanding Freud's Oedipus complex, based on the story of King Oedipus, is one such example. Therefore, if we were to read the story of the coronavirus pandemic from an understanding of tragedies that are known in our culture, we can identify an important repeated pattern that is featured in classic tragedies. In this chapter, we use as key references the Japanese mythology of Izanagi-Izanami and the tale of the 'Crane's Wife', which describes an intermarriage between a human and a non-human creature. On the other hand, a theme that plays a crucial role in their tragic developments is the 'Prohibition of Don't Look' (Kitayama 1985, 1991, 2010).

Japan's mythological thinking

According to the '*Kojiki*', a record of ancient matters and mythologies of Japan, compiled in the eighth century, two gods – Izanami, a maternal goddess, and Izanagi, a paternal god – descend to an island to marry. Izanami gives birth to the numerous islands of Japan. She also produces numerous deities. But when she finally bears the fire-deity, it severely burns her genitals, causing her to die. To bring his wife back to life, Izanagi follows her to the separate land of the dead and pleads with her to come back. Izanami replies: 'I will discuss my desire to return with the gods of the land of dead. Pray do not look upon me.' However, her husband impatiently breaks the prohibition and peeks inside, only to see her corpse riddled with maggots and roaring thunder deities. Stricken with awe and fear by such a dreadful sight, Izanagi flees. Enraged that he has humiliated her, Izanami dispatches ugly females and goes after him herself. Izanagi manages to escape and return home, and while crossing the pass between the land of the dead and the land of the living, he places a rock that separates the two worlds. In the end, Izanagi performs '*misogi*', or self-cleansing, to wash away with water the filth from the land of the dead that contaminated him.

Upon returning from the underworld, Izanagi talks about having gone to 'an ugly, unclean land'. The expression stems from his feeling that after seeing dirty, ugly things, he too had become dirty. The readers should know here that the Japanese word for 'ugly' is *'minikui'*, which can also mean 'difficult to see'. These 'mythological thought patterns' that follow such a scenario have become the basis on which we have come to harbor the concept of 'uncleanliness' or 'impurity'. We have ritualistically feared death, or avoided touching it, and tried to purify ourselves with water and wash away any uncleanliness. Washing one's hands with water at Japanese shrines and temples is a long-established customary practice. This 'folklore neurosis' may also appear as a disease and take the form of mysophobia. In clinical practice also, when we continue to listen to the stories that patients and clients tell us, we become aware of their commonly shared and passed-down psychology of often regarding ugly and dirty things as taboo. They try to keep dirty things at a distance, not talk about them and not call them to mind. The tragedy of Izanami-Izanagi is repeated unchanged, with people recoiling from death, illness, sex and anger, and distancing them neurotically as things that are dirty and unclean, which must be 'washed away' as much as possible. This phrase 'wash away' in Japanese can also mean 'to forgive and forget past grudges'.

This mythological thinking beautifully parallels the measures that were taken by Japanese people to combat COVID-19. People distanced others who had become 'dirty', wearing a mask to hide the self that had become 'unclean', and washed away dirt on the hands and body with water. COVID-19 itself is an infectious disease, so we were all at risk of becoming infected. Although a virus itself cannot be described as unclean, we can understand that it is mysophobia or the fear of filth that treated uncleanliness and physical contact as sinful. There was also a fear of being hurt or an obsessive fear of harming others with pathogens, filth and/or weapons, which prompted many people to exercise self-restraint.

With the 'Prohibition of Don't Look', people hold back their words and behaviours, act quietly and solemnly, and try not to cause panic. In reality, people take their shoes off at the entrance to a house, wear a mask, and keep everything very clean and virus-free. At the same time, mythological thinking, in which mysophobia predominates, also works effectively to promote infection countermeasures. A mask is used to keep people clean; the fact is, it also has the effect of hiding their faces, which chimes well with this 'shame culture'. It may also be correct to say that psychosocially the 'Prohibition of Don't Look' and hiding oneself is a 'national rule' shared by everyone.

Exclusion and childrearing

The mythological thinking of trying to keep this uncleanliness at bay, and washing and purifying the self, is transmitted intergenerationally and maintained in the context of childrearing and discipline among the Japanese. Geoffrey Gorer (1942, 1943), a British anthropologist known for his study of Japanese people during the Second World War, pointed out that the two faces that these people had – courteous and clean-loving on the one hand, but liable to become cruel and brutal on the battlefield on the other hand, as well as their neurotic tendencies of not wanting to talk about those traits – stem from the merciless and rigorous toilet-training they had received during early childhood. This view was being shown to illustrate the anal phase by Freud (1905), which claims that toilet training is linked to personality development.

It should be noted, however, that it is not only toilet training. Parents who live in a 'culture of shame' also teach their children to keep themselves clean and tidy, in general, and to live gracefully and resolutely as a process of acculturation and socialisation to make youngsters adapt to the nation's culture. In so doing, if a child were to breach this discipline, the parents intimidate him or her with the 'threat of separation', saying, 'A child like you doesn't belong in our family', 'We don't know any children like you' and 'I don't remember giving birth to you.' If such anxieties and fear of being excluded are transmitted between generations, and if the rules and discipline based on them are broadly shared and internalised, they will also function as 'mental police', not tolerating abnormalities, violations, impurities or unclean things. This can be referred to as the 'harsh superego', a term used in psychoanalysis; it may also be connected to dual personality-like tendencies possessed by many Japanese people who have been raised to become 'good little boys and girls', such as front and back, public and private, and *honne to tatemae* (what you say as opposed to what you really think).

Mythological thinking that is characterised by neurotic mysophobia is liable to lead to social discrimination and exclusion if it gets recklessly out of control. Once a person is branded with a negative 'sign' or 'mark', he or she is regarded as ugly and sinful, and becomes the target of unjustifiable attacks. Typical examples include attacks based on an excessive sense of justice, such as slanders made through social media, harassment of and discrimination against healthcare personnel and their families as well as organisations and local people who had caused clusters of coronavirus infections. Incidents were liable to occur whereby people find easy appropriate targets, make them receptacles of their sense of filthiness, gang up with others and attack them. In other words, mythological thinking had the risk of activating 'self-appointed pandemic police' within the minds of many Japanese people who were normally regarded as thoughtful, 'good' individuals, and threatened the private rights and freedoms not only of themselves but also of other people. From the same origin, namely our efforts to not become infected ourselves and to not infect other people, we shifted our focus to other people and ruthlessly drove someone into a corner. We all carry this potential within ourselves. If, during the days of confusion, in the initial stages of the pandemic, PCR tests had been actively performed, which detected infected patients, society might have treated such individuals as criminals, resulting in large-scale exclusions and discriminations. Even if PCR tests had been actively carried out at the time, there would have been people who would have chosen not to get tested for fear of being discriminated against, and excluded.

The folklore of the 'Crane Wife', in the Edo era (from the seventeenth to the nineteenth century), which we describe next, provides clues that help us to understand these developments in our culture that are based on common beliefs.

Introversion of anger in folktales

In the evening, the rhythmic sound of weaving, clackety-clack, is heard inside a room with a paper sliding door; the following morning, a beautiful cloth is ready. Like in the previous myth of the two deities, in the case of '*Yu-duru*' (English title: 'Twilight of a Crane', a drama written in 1949 based on the folklore of the 'Crane Wife'), the heroine Tsu forbids her husband Yohyo to ever look inside the weaving room. This corresponds to the pro-hibition imposed in the Izanami-Izanagi myth of 'Pray do not look upon me'. However, one evening Yohyo breaks the prohibition and peeks inside, only to find a crane weaving a cloth made by plucking out her feathers and thus wounding herself. He realises that Tsu is a crane. The crane wife, in a tale of intermarriage between a human and a non-human creature, feels deeply ashamed and flies away, leaving her husband behind.

The Japanese people's sense of shame and taboo are linked and divided into 'black impurities', relating to injury, illness and death, and 'red impurities', relating to sex and childbirth. A secret is hidden behind happiness in a drama and once the male character peeks inside, what had been hidden is exposed and sometimes perceived as something 'shameful', as a result of which the couple break up. When Izanami is seen by Izanagi, she becomes furious, saying, 'You humiliated me,' and attacks him. Generally speaking, however, these non-human wives merely feel ashamed passively, and quietly leave their male partners. Here, a significant difference is seen in the psychological developments of the story between myths that maintain an ancient form and folktales that continue to be told even today. The difference can be understood with depth psychology, that the anger that was directed and expressed towards the other person in myths is instead turned inward in folktales. Patients and clients who have been humiliated talk about their experience of feeling ashamed and wanting to disappear and/or die. Sometimes, intense anger is lurking in the background. However, instead of expres-sing it outwardly and venting their anger on the other person, they redirect it towards themselves and choose to leave the scene. They may also become angry with themselves, drive themselves into a corner and inflict self-harm or commit suicide, thinking that it would be better for everyone if they simply disappeared.

Because they cannot vent their anger on the other person, they direct it towards themselves. This is called the introversion of anger. Since it was Yohyo, the husband, who intruded despite being prohibited from looking at his wife, it was also Yohyo who made his wife weave cloth for financial gain, so he was morally responsible for her injury. Nevertheless, he is unable to find his injured wife and simply stands there, stunned, seeing a non-human creature in front of him. If we look at this man from a maternalistic perspective, he may, in a way, be regarded as infantile, innocent, even lovable. In 'The Prohibition of Don't Look' (2010), Kitayama points out the replication of the mother–child relationship in this relationship between the crane wife and the human male. The maternal wife is unable to vent her anger on the man who is selfish like a little child; she has no choice but to swallow the anger she feels and blame herself. In the end, she leaves the man, resolutely without fuss.

If considered from a dramatic point of view, because this plot is widely known in Japan, many of us end up unconsciously repeating this script in our real lives. We can see this pattern in old folktales: the heroines are unable to condemn their partners' mistakes, and instead turn it upon themselves and simply fly away. In the days when Japan was under military rule, during Japanese imperialism and colonialism, people who held different views were repeatedly excluded as being unpatriotic. Even today, this pattern is repeated in the form of bullying and discriminating against 'marked' people at school, in the workplace and in the community. In the drama of 'Yuduru', men in the village made fun of Tsu and insulted her by calling her 'Crane! Crane!'.

The female goddess Izanami was excluded by the male god, Izanagi, but Tsu, the crane wife, excluded herself. Amid the peer pressure based on group psychology shown by Yohyo and other men, in particular, we become simply helpless and passive. I believe that the mythology of exclusion of others was converted into a story of self-exclusion, of a person excluding herself/himself. Thus, to prevent repetition of the tragic ending of excluding others and the self, many people had to tackle the challenge of learning about the existence of this mythological thinking, understanding what it means, exploring happy endings and continuing to survive, even under the COVID pandemic. In the next section, I would like to examine and understand the psychology of 'dislike and repulsion' felt by Izanagi, who had experienced *'mikashikomi'*, or 'awe and fear', and by Yohyo and other men who stood petrified and stupefied.

Dealing with contamination: a sense of repulsion or self-exclusion

It appears to be a natural reflex for people to recoil from things that are dirty and ugly. But what sort of logic is at play here? If we examine this through the lens of the Izanagi-Izanami myth, the object is a rich and productive maternal deity; if we use the story of marriage between humans and non-humans, the object is a benevolent wife or a devoted maternal woman. At the same time, however, the females are wounded and on the verge of death. Persons who are regarded as almost perfect may be actually weighed down by considerable limitations; beautiful people in fact may have serious faults that are the direct opposite of beauty. If we experience contradictory situations such as discovering that good people have different, bad aspects to them, for example, we suddenly see both darkness and cheerfulness, with pluses and minuses mixed in. A feeling of unfathomable mix-up, that is 'awe and fear' in the myth, is created as a reflex culturally shared. If this becomes intolerable in the form of mental indigestion or aversion, the mechanism of encouraging the 'spitting out' or physiological exclusion of an object becomes easy to understand. If we encounter situations in which people or objects that used to be productive suddenly become unable to fly, weave cloth anymore or almost die, we cannot deal with the overall picture and become overwhelmed, stricken with an extremely strong feeling of 'awe and fear'. To prevent us from actually perceiving this feeling of an inability to swallow this undigested item or this feeling of not being able to understand 100 per cent or to try not to see it, a psychology arises, reflexively, of regarding this dirty object as a taboo and alienating it or excluding the self. This sense of unfathomable mix-up contains contrasting feelings of love and hatred, as well as likes and dislikes or, in other words, insight into the deep-seated sense of ambivalence as well as contradiction.

Needless to say, under the COVID pandemic, it was extremely difficult to protect the economy without compromising people's health. It is also important to understand that somehow dealing with the sense of revulsion that originates in this contradiction is the inevitable fate of the narratives of classic stories and folktales. In other words, Izanami died because of extensive burns to the genitals suffered when delivering a child and the crane wife became deeply hurt (symbolising postpartum hemorrhaging) as a result of being forced to overwork as a weaver by prioritising financial gain. With business and production predominating, if we engage in production activities while sacrificing the self, our way of life will literally be regarded – using a metaphor that the Japanese love dearly – as '*issho-kenmei*' (with all one's might), 'breaking one's back for work' (in Japanese: shave one's bones), and 'exerting oneself to the utmost'. At the same time, we were told to protect our health above everything else in the first year of the pandemic. If this contradiction had grown, our thoughts may sometimes have become mired in confusion and become paralysed amid mixed messages.

As I have discussed up to this point, the cleanliness and fastidiousness (self-restraint) and dislike/aversion (exclusion of others and of the self) of the protagonists in mythological thinking derive from the same source.

What the person in question fears is that he or she will be driven into a corner and succumb to paralysis of thought, which may become linked to excessive self-reproach, that 'Everything would be resolved if I simply disappeared'. And, compounded by economic hardships, if the 'beauty of leaving gracefully and resolutely', like Tsu did, is respected in the context of psychological mysophobia, the taking on of individual responsibility and suicidal tendencies may likely spread. The mythological thinking of the masses leads to large-scale tragedy, such as the ending of the folklore of 'The Little Match Girl' (1845; by Hans Christian Andersen). If thoughts become bogged down in contradictions and paralysed, as happened during the Second World War in Japan, many people end up obedient to those with authority and power, and are simply pushed around.

Conclusion: the 'I', a Japanese who lives out the conflict of 'saving people's lives or saving the economy'

Even with countermeasures to fight the novel coronavirus, we were expected to choose neither mythological thinking nor scientific views, but instead combine the two and weave them together. The perspective was required when taking part in a conflict between human lives and the economy rather than choosing between two alternatives of 'emotion or calculation, or saving human lives or saving the economy'. Here we remember that both 'I (or me)' and 'bridging (or connecting)' in the Japanese language is '*watashi*'. It's a homonym. Therefore, '*watashi*' (I) would be established by '*watashi*' (bridging or connecting the two or duality).

Needless to say, the emotion of dislike in our way of thinking, of not wanting to get dirty or not wanting to succumb to a filthy disease, must be understood. Mythological thinking such as this is rock solid since we have acquired it as an emotional way of living our lives. Because it is not easy for us to absorb scientific and rational ways of thinking, our challenge is for 'I' to continue to integrate myth and science, and emotion and intellect. If life and death suddenly become mixed up in our minds, a general sense of dislike/aversion grows as a reflex. The story of Izanami is overlapped with our circumstances and the anxiety of the premonition of our tragic ending may become sharper. But here, we – or 'I' – are being faced with the question of whether we are able to see the diseased Izanami, or the beautiful but wounded Tsu, rather than tracing the classic tragic stories and running away like Izanagi or standing there petrified like Yohyo. This also means that we are given the opportunity to rewrite a new story.

You will most likely realise that it was your sense of repulsion about the 'crane' part in you, or your anxiety about it, that made you regard other persons as 'non-human', or a 'crane'. This work entails intense pain, requires tremendous effort and is time consuming. Still, it is one of the procedures needed for releasing our thoughts that have become trapped in an internally contradictory mess. It is only after, then, that we can expect the eventual creation of new happy endings in a secure form such as 'Tsu decides to stay on instead of flying away' and 'Izanami receives treatment and revives'. The Japanese word for 'revive' is *'yomigaeru'*, which can also mean 'return from *yomi*', or 'the land of the dead'. And then 'The Little Match Girl' may well survive with the help of other people.

References

Andersen, H. C. (1845). *Den Lille Pige med Svovlstikkerne* [The little match girl]. Dansk Folkekalender for 1846.

Freud, S. ([1905]1974). Three essays on the theory of sexuality. In Strachey, J. (Ed.), *The Standard Edition of the Complete Psychological Works of Sigmund Freud*, Vol. 7. London: Hogarth Press, pp. 123–246.

Gorer, G. (1942). *Japanese Character Structure and Propaganda*. Committee on Intercultural Relations.

Gorer, G. (1943). Themes in Japanese culture. *The New York Academy of Sciences*, 5: 106–124. Reprinted in Haring, D. G. (Ed.) (1948). *Personal Character and Cultural Milieu*. New York: Syracuse University Press, pp. 273–290.

Kitayama, O. (1985). Pre-oedipal 'taboo' in Japanese folk tragedies. *International Review of Psycho-Analysis*, 12(2): 173–186.

Kitayama, O. (1991). The wounded caretaker and guilt. *International Review of Psycho-Analysis*, 18(2): 229–240.

Kitayama, O. (2009). Psychoanalysis in the 'shame culture' of Japan: a 'dramatic' point of view. In Aktar, S. (Ed.), *Freud and the Far East*. Lanham, MD: Jason Aronson, pp. 80–104.

Kitayama, O. (2010). *Prohibition of Don't Look*. Tokyo: Iwasaki Gakujutsu Shuppansha.

Kitayama, O. (2013). Psychoanalysis in the 'shame culture': A drama-based viewpoint. In Gerlach, A. (Eds), *Psychoanalysis in Asia: China, India, Japan, South Korea, Taiwan*. London: Karnac.

Yamazaki, M. (1971). *Dramatic Japanese* (Gekiteki naru Nihonjin). Shinchosha.

Part 5
Family and relationships

Introduction

In Chapter 15, 'Pandemic and Marital Relationship', Gley Costa describes in depth, based on the concepts of Freud, Aulagnier, Kaës, Maldavsky, Puget and Berenstein, how couple bonds are quite complex, and became even more so at a time when our lives were threatened by a pandemic that could kill thousands of people, generate economic difficulties and force us to bear something that compromises the couple's stability: confinement and social distancing. This is shown to heavily interfere with the marital relationship, generating a 'baseline' of anxiety that is as contagious as the coronavirus infection itself.

Arthur Leonoff, in Chapter 16, 'Disillusionment and Destructiveness in Severe High Conflict Divorce and Other Social Maladies', states that high conflict divorce, a serious public health concern, illustrates potential destructiveness in family relations not simply because of conflictive divorce but as its primary motive. It is an attack on the family ideal that the author traces to a layering of major disillusionments, destroying belief in family and undermining the capacity for family formation itself. Destructiveness is unleashed in the swirl of hopelessness and betrayal. Psychological, social and legal torments can last a decade with severe damage to all family members. This same link between destructiveness and disillusionment can be applied to other areas of conflictive human relations, including geopolitics. Countries unable to mourn their lost illusions rage at perceived betrayers and seek in war to destroy everything and everyone. In the same regard, deeply disillusioned priests too often sexually attack their parishioners, especially children. While in the mental health domain, suffering therapists can assault their patients even under the guise of enraptured love. It amounts to a strike against the family crucible, the idealised haven of safety that failed in all respects and now must be assailed without mercy or end.

Ruth Axelrod's chapter, 'The Betrayal Of Tradition: The Death of the Only Son and the Empty Nest' (Chapter 17), explains that the

DOI: 10.4324/9781003646266-20

psychodynamic work of couples is a tool that validates the possibility of simultaneous listening to a loving dyad in search of meaning, where the difficulty and achievement of love can unfold. Each couple has its own history and its own becoming, and when the psychoanalyst is invited to witness the process he or she becomes a neo-structure of it. A clinical case during the pandemic time is presented.

15 Pandemic and marital relationship

Gley P. Costa

From a psychoanalytic point of view, a fundamental function of the family organisation is the constitution of the psychism, a field in which the vincular dimension is necessarily implied, given by the presence, coexistence and interchanges between psychisms already constituted and others in the process of constitution. Besides this, the already constituted psychisms are not closed and enclosed organisations, but open and transformable, and in the constitutive process there is reciprocity: to become husband/wife, father/mother, among other places of kinship, presupposes founding milestones in the subjective becoming. Maldavsky (1991) proposes that these processes are governed by several mechanisms: some alliance mechanisms, others defensive and others projective and introjective. He emphasises that the most important factor that requires inter-individual processing is the drive, especially the sexual drive, and that erogeneity is processed by extremely different logics in the relationship with peers, including marriage. From this perspective, the several interindividual connections have as their main goal the processing of the drive, and the bonds between individuals can become more complex in function of the transformation of the drive voluptuousness into a tender bond, thanks to the renunciation of direct libidinal satisfaction.

The psychic and vincular processing of the drive provides, as one of its effects, the access to a determined identification. The identificatory processes are inextricably linked to the projective ones, and these, in turn, derive, in the constitution of psychic spatialities, from different degrees of complexity. Some projections have an interrogative character about one's own subjectivity, and their function consists in opening up to an encounter with the objects of the world, thanks to which the answers to these interrogatives will be elaborated, through an identification that allows one to take possession of the projected. From this perspective, we can analyse the value that the acts, the discourses and the desires of others acquire in the moulding of each person's ego and ideal. In this way, each type of marital structure generates, in turn, a double extra-territoriality: one towards the outside world, more extensive, with respect

DOI: 10.4324/9781003646266-21

to which diverse projects unfold; and another inside, less extensive, such as, for example, the constitution of a family which, while it has links with the outside, contains within it a couple/couple relationship and a filial bond. This in short implies an articulation between the diverse criteria for the processing of sexuality. We understand, therefore, the couple bond as a complex weave: product of transactions between desires, ideals and judgements. That is, as a formation promoted by the pulsional and desiderative impulse, and demarcated by the traditions, the conceptual demands and the restrictions of each member. In this sense, it is possible to think of the marital structure the way Freud considered the ego: as a result of the aggregation of different elements in relation, in an effort never completely achieved to obtain a synthesis. In the parallelism placed around the triple conjugal servitude, it is necessary to reiterate that the interindividual relations have as their main goal the processing of the pulsional reality and, in a secondary position, the obligation to submit oneself to the mandates of the superego and external reality.

Freud argued, in 1930, that in the origins of civilisation a change was produced that derived not only from a contextual historical action, but from an alteration in the psychism of individuals, which allowed the inhibition of certain libidinal pulsional goals in favour of productive activity. The drives of self-conservation that imposed these changes marked a path in the libidinal distribution, and one of the consequences is the installation of the superego. From the psychoanalytic perspective, this is the foundation to understand the origin of a family, a couple or a group, and the relations between its members. The destinies imposed to the drive in each of these configurations are linked to the psychic processing that is required from the individual to fit into these different contexts. The criterion that binds the members of a couple to each other is a contract, at the same time sexual, affective, economic, social and political. The psychic processes that demand inter-individual relations are ruled by a set of laws that respond to different logics, which grant more or less refinement to the distribution, inhibition and consummation of the drive. Since the family plot is heterogeneous, the relationship between spouses cannot be defined in a single sense, nor can it be understood only as a circular causality of reciprocal influx, but it must be thought with a degree of greater complexity, which contemplates that the child generates its own moulds from certain laws of psychic structuring, which also configure an exterior, for which the stimuli coming from the parents have a value and efficacy when they are rearranged as contents for its psychic apparatus according to these laws. The situations that configure the clinic of attachment reveal the fact that in certain groups the pulsional demands and/or those of reality or of the superegoic mandates to which the couple has been subjected in the scope of their inter-individual attachments have not been processed. The degree and modality of the failures in the difficulties of this multiple task will give rise to diverse disturbances in the

marital relationship, which may be linked to psychopathological cate-
gories of different characteristics and of greater or lesser severity. In any
case, overflowing affections appear in the individual and in the vindictive
plot, similarly to Freud's description of automatic anguish, with the same
characteristic: when faced with the magnitude of the pulsional and/or
mundane charges, the consciousness is flooded and its function of regis-
tering the affective nuances is harmed. The lack of psychic processing for
the drive and the consequent degradation in its modes of satisfaction can
result in a single possibility of obtaining a permanent organic enjoyment,
to finally end up in conjugal catastrophes, in which disintegrating processes of toxic or traumatic nature reign. In these cases, identifications,
projects, times and spaces that express erogeneity as language are
dissolved in the different inter-individual spheres.

It must be kept in mind, as I have emphasised above, that a couple's
bond is not only a set of desires, but their psychic processing through a
set of transactions from which derive the different manifestations that are
more or less stable, more or less achieved. In these transactions, the effi-
cient factor to promote the distribution of inter-individual positions and
identifications, resulting in reciprocities and complementarities, responsible for conjugal stability, is, without a doubt, the defence, which constitutes one of the pillars of the particular organisation built by marriage
(Freud, 1896). Each defence promotes a certain intrapsychic distribution
of the libido, but also makes it circulate in different ways in the inter-
individual bonds. The defence is a distributing factor of the positions that
the members of a couple adopt among themselves and in the bonds with
others, regardless of which erogeneities predominate in each one of them.
Furthermore, it is necessary to discriminate the positional distributions
made from one ego from those that another ego assumes, which may
have different foundations. Although in practice an interindividual commitment solution of greater or lesser fixity is reached, the particular
determinations by which the members of the bond arrive at it may be
diverse. Besides this, contextual changes may be important for a change
in the use of a defence. Several authors have worked on the concepts of
unconscious alliances in marital relationships. Puget and Berenstein
(1988), for example, position the unconscious pacts and agreements in
couples as constituents of an equally unconscious contract. They define
these concepts as a set of unconscious stipulations of which at least two
'I's' regulate the exchanges of those shareable aspects of each, for the
purpose of creating the most desired, the most profitable and the least
forbidden for each ego, in a composition with the character of a more or
less stable structure. They constitute, thus, a unit that implies and sur-
passes the mere sum of the contributions of each self, in a combinatorium
that articulates the individual object constellations. Aulagnier (1977) and
Kaës (1977) describe the narcissistic contract and the denialist pact, concepts of great use in understanding both functional and pathological

intersubjective processes. The narcissistic contract corresponds to the bonds that two or more people build in the face of a reciprocal commitment, in an attempt to sustain the very existence of the relationship and, at the same time, the subjectivity of the intervening subjects. It implies the libidinal investiture of certain common values and beliefs, as well as the reciprocal ones between the members of the couple or of the family group. The denegative pact, consists of an unconscious agreement on the unconscious that is imposed so that the bond can be organised and maintained thanks to the expulsion of those conflictive contents that could endanger its maintenance. It constitutes the necessary counterpart and complement of the narcissistic contract. It creates a non-meaningful space that keeps the subject detached from its own history. It sustains, fundamentally, the fate of repetition, and its effects can force the thought to attack itself or to try to destroy certain aspects of psychic life in others. It is that which imposes itself on the internal space of each subject to be consecrated to repression and denial, with the end of maintaining the unconscious alliance.

We know that the particular defensive fit with which each subject processes both the vicissitudes of his or her pulsional life and the demands of reality and the superego produces effects on the construction and maintenance of his or her bonds. We could say that the narcissistic contract and the denialist pact represent two ways of unfolding the concept of successful defence in terms of attachment, as is inferred from Maldavsky (2007), when dividing defences into successful and failed ones. In all these processes, the distribution of drives and intrapsychic defences is what allows us to understand the logic of the vincular exchanges. Each drive combined with some defence leads to the unfolding of specific bonds with the other. In those couples in which toxic and traumatic processes predominate, we speak of situations in which the possibility of inter-individual processing of pulsional demands and reality has failed. In other words, the inter-individual alliances fail in their anti-toxic function or in producing an anti-stimulus protective armour in a temporary or lasting way. We can conceive that, in certain occasions, when there is no family context to appeal to in the function of containment and detoxification, conditions are generated so that the libidinal stagnation lasts (becomes permanent), to the point of affecting the drives of self-preservation and promoting very severe pathologies, which put psychic and biological life at risk. In these cases, the forms of pulsional circulation in the couple's relationship may reach a type of toxic processing that corresponds to the one described by Freud (1898) in relation to the current neuroses. His hypothesis was later extended to other pictures, among which were psychosomatic disorders, addictions and family violence. Freud sustained that the toxicity of the drive derives from an impossibility of organic and psychic processing of a certain endogenous demand, and that such stagnation leads to the lack of qualification of affective states, replaced by states of sopority and apathy, sometimes interrupted by violent explosions. As for the defences developed in these bonds, a combination of denial, rejection of reality and of the paternal instance, and rejection of affection usually predominate. These defences require a support in the world; they demand intersubjectivity, since the other becomes the recipient of a vengeance, a sacrifice, falsehoods and lies, or attempts to obtain somatic pleasure and/or money. It is frequent that the disavowal unfolds in one of the members of the couple, and the repudiation of affection in another.

Finally, I consider of particular value for this general presentation of the theme of marital relations the inclusion of recent research contributions in situations in which toxic and traumatic bonds prevail. To this end, a systematic research method in psychoanalysis, the David Liberman Algorithm (ADL), integrates a set of instruments to investigate patients' discourse at the different levels at which subjectivity manifests itself (Maldavsky, 2004; Maldavsky et al., 2010, 2014). If patients describe attachment scenes in which rampant violence predominates, it is possible to warn of episodes preceding said scenes, which determine a sequence: (1) capture of a state of devitalisation in the other; (2) crisis of anguish as a reaction in the face of an identification with another's devitalisation, infiltrated in one's own body. The attack of rage is an effect of the crisis of anguish, as a failed attempt to recover from the previous identification. The devitalisation seems to be the effect of a defence against Eros, the one Freud (1920) attributes to the death drive, which consists in extinguishing all vital tension, by preventing or ruining reserve energy. This impotence to process one's own and other people's pulsional demands arouses an automatic anguish, which appears as an effect of the devitalisation register that could lead to the annihilation of the self. Violence seems to correspond to the attempt of revitalisation or tonification in order to recover and recover the other from the previous devitalisation. On occasions, the search for tonification implies explicit violence, verbal or physical; in other cases, promiscuous behaviour, consumption of alcohol or drugs, excessive eating, gambling, etc. These are two-stage solutions: in the first, the desired effect is achieved, and in the second, the paradoxical consequence observed is the increase in devitalisation due to the predominance of the pathogenic defensive process.

In this way, it is evident that marital relations are quite complex, and become much more so at a time when we find our lives threatened by a pandemic that kills thousands of people daily, generates economic difficulties and leads us to bear something that, from our point of view, is much more compromising for the stability of the couple than it appears to be and, because of this, is not duly recognised. I am referring to confinement and social distancing, which will heavily interfere in the conjugal relationship, together with the other two factors mentioned (the fear of death and financial problems) which together generate a baseline of anxiety in society as contagious as the contamination by the coronavirus itself. As we have seen, every conjugal relationship, using defences that, regardless of the number and intensity, manage to be successful. Each establishes a more or less stable pattern of coexistence, and it is this pattern that I would like to focus on in the context of the pandemic. We must also recognise that it inevitably offers a considerable burden to any relationship, however good it may be, resulting in many cases in the separation of the couple, as evidenced by statistics.

Didactically, I divide the conjugal relationships which, within the established defensive arrangements, could be considered as 'stable', independent of their quality, into three models. I will describe these with their eventual consequences, motivated by the confinement and social distancing prescribed by the health authorities to limit the contamination.

Model 1

The model 1 of marital relationship is characterised by little contact between the spouses, each maintaining a life in which the other participates very little. In this model, the confinement and social distancing generate great difficulty for the couple, who are used to keeping a regulatory distance, both physical and social, propitiated by intense professional activities and the company of other couples, to go out to dinner, travel or do any other kind of programme. In these couples' relationships, the children often play the role of friends, which is to prevent the spouses from being alone for too long or getting involved in each other's lives beyond a certain limit. Apparently, these are the couples that are separating the most, even because the bond that existed before the pandemic was very tenuous, sustained precisely by the poor relationship between spouses and by the presence of friends and children, now physically distant due to the pandemic.

Clinical example: Jardel and Luana, both in their sixties, married for about 30 years, with two children studying in universities abroad, who, due to the pandemic, have not visited them for over a year. Luana is a clothing store owner. Jardel comes from a country town, where he created and developed a large automotive industry. He used to spend most of the week in the interior and on weekends, although at home, he spent little time with his wife, who was always very involved with her business. The company of friends at home or when she went out with her husband was almost a constant. The couple used to travel very often, for business or pleasure, sometimes together, sometimes apart. The couple's sexual relations were infrequent and decreased even more when Luana entered menopause. From the emotional point of view, apparently, Luana is more stable, while Jardel, according to his wife, has a 'dual personality'. At home he is taciturn, moody and keeps himself isolated most of the time. On business trips, on the other hand, he usually meets up with friends and goes out with women, although he tells his wife that these occasional meetings mean nothing to him affectively, they are just to pass the time. It is interesting to note that just as Luana complains that Jardel has 'lovers', which he peremptorily denies, justifying his refusal to have sex when he wants to, Jardel complains that Luana gives more importance to her friends than to him. Because of the pandemic, the couple greatly reduced their professional activities and mainly their trips, remaining most of the time together at home. This situation started a succession of frictions that led them to live separately in the same house. However, after a while, through a shared rationalisation (professional issues), they decided to leave the house and each went to live in an apart-hotel. From that moment on, they re-established a reasonably friendly communication through WhatsApp and eventual meetings. This way, apparently, they avoided a separation that was beginning to appear due to the pandemic, which by keeping them together longer broke a successful pact of coexistence that they had established and maintained for 30 years of marriage.

Model 2

Model 2 is characterised by a marital relationship in which the couple maintains a fully satisfying sex life with many common interests but flexible enough for both to maintain a life of their own, as well as to retain previous, possibly individualised, activities and friendships. It is the flexibility of these relationships that allows one or both spouses to better cope with difficult situations, as is the case with the pandemic. In these cases, maintaining a closer relationship or for a longer time does not offer the fear of being engulfed by the other, because both cherish their individuality, which is why it is rescued periodically. Because of this, couples united according to this model tolerated the pandemic better and, in many cases, even related better, with more affection and dedication.

Clinical example: Rafael and Marina, 34 and 33 years old, respectively, had in mind the possibility of working from a home office, despite the decrease in earnings, as a way to protect themselves from being infected by the coronavirus. They decided to move to a small farm they owned in the countryside where, until then, they had only spent occasional weekends. However, in order to serve as a residence, the couple decided to dedicate a daily amount of time to housekeeping, doing everything, as they said, 'with their own hands'. After a few months, they were surprised and delighted with the work they had done together, including the creation of a garden that they jokingly called 'Jardin des Tuileries' because it encircled the small house. It was a remembrance of the years when, on account of a scholarship, they lived in Paris, where they met and married. They did not intend to live there for the rest of their lives as they both had plans in their professional areas that they aspired to realise, but they considered that this experience revealed a personal creative capacity that they did not know they had. They enjoyed the pleasure provided by the shared activity, which was quite rare until then, as 'each one was busy with their computer'. This is likely due to the fact that the spouses came from simple families in the countryside and from a very early age they lived alone and took care of their own lives. Besides, of course, they both had a pleasurable sexual relationship, which contributed to the good understanding the couple had.

Model 3

Model 3 is characterised by a closed and undifferentiated relationship, which, with even greater isolation and social distance, becomes extremely toxic for the couple. There is a tendency towards emotional outbursts often accompanied by physical aggression. Social isolation does not constitute a change in the life of these marriages, nor does confinement. But the excessive growth of the latter, added to the fears of getting sick and dying, worsens the marital pathology that existed before the pandemic. Despite this, these couples do not usually separate because one needs the other to discharge their tensions that, with the pandemic, became even greater. As a consequence, what we see in this model of conjugal bonding, besides mutual aggressions, is an exacerbated alcoholic consumption aimed at numbing and calming the violence in the relationship. Eventually, one or both members of the couple may get worse from existing organic diseases or present organic diseases that did not exist before.

Clinical example: Augusto and Marilia, both in their fifties and with law degrees, maintain a successful law office together. Despite their particularities, Augusto and Marilia have several points in common, with a predominantly adhesive and undifferentiated functioning. The way the libido circulates is paradoxical in the couple's relationships, since it is characterised by an excessive attachment on the one hand, and by a total affective disconnection on the other. Maldavsky (1995) called this form of bond between two individuals 'disconnected attachment', which operates in the manner of a suction cup or a leech: the bodies adhere to each other by a monotonous sensoriality that captures the intrasomatic processes of others; the result of perception without awareness and the disinvestment of attention. This way of attaching to the other is maintained at the expense of a disconnection from the sensitive universe. As Maldavsky (1995) points out, disconnection implies endowing the ego's sensitive surface with a viscous cover, in which sensory impression is ineffective. When a stimulus manages to get through this layer of indifference, it is not perceived as a qualifying excitation but as an intrusion, a blow to which the individual responds with hostility. This contact criterion is possible to detect in Augusto and Marilia, in whom for lack of qualification of affections the sensitive universe remains misty and undifferentiated. The attention is only aroused by inciting stimulus and not by a libidinal movement directed to the outside world. This functioning becomes quite evident when, in a session, Marilia in a fit of rage, insulted Augusto, screaming and making him leave the lethargic state he was in and connect with the environment. He achieved this in part because he was indifferent to the accusations, starting a description of his childhood experiences. Despite the marked worsening of the relationship, and the accusations from both sides during the sessions over the course of a year of the pandemic, at no time did the couple vent the possibility of separation. However, Augusto presented a considerable worsening of his arterial hypertension.

Conclusion

As we have seen, according to these three stable relationship models, confinement and social distancing in two of them (1 and 3) interferes markedly. In the first one, a need to distance oneself is generated to avoid marital catástrofe. In the second one, there is greater toxicity, offering risks of serious illness, but without any idea of separation as one depends on the other to release non-elaborated traumatic excesses. In both cases, it is evident that defences that were successful until then fail in the face of new demands imposing on the couple new internal and relational defensive combinations, not always possible to obtain. From the therapeutic point of view, model 1, as in the example described, even at the expense of rationalisation, was able to avoid a divorce that was on the agenda of the couple's therapy that had begun about six months before. During the treatment, personal problems of a family nature were brought to the sessions by the spouses, enabling the analyst to help them become aware of the links between these conflicts and the couple's relationship. This resulted in better integration, each one assuming their own responsibility for the conjugal conflict. After both received the first dose of the COVID-19 vaccine, they were less anxious, friendlier and planned to spend time with their children together after the second dose.

The case cited in model 3 offers the analyst a situation of much greater difficulty due to the regressive level of the defences predominant in the relationship of the couple. They did not seek to obtain through therapy an understanding of the conflict but a relief of internal tensions not infrequently abandoning the treatment for failing in this goal. A typical defence that is observed in these couples is habituation, consisting of defensive sleeping in the face of excessive inducements. This sleeping as a refuge from worldly stimulus is tense and does not have to do with energetic recovery. It leads us to wonder about the means to which Eros initially resorts to neutralise the death drive when the motor performances that involve some kind of sadism are not yet active. Apparently, for some reason, those individuals didn't manage to appeal early to that resource and present a pathology of reflective attention – the one that, according to Freud (1895), is commanded from the object that remains uninvestigated since the pulsional life. Therefore, the perceptual world has no differential significance, it is not worth as a quality but as a frequency. We must keep in mind that the passage from the formalisation of the sensory world, in terms of frequencies to its organisation as a universe of qualities, requires an investiture from the erogenous life. It requires an intermediate step that everything seems to be missing in these conjugal couples, the opening of the erogenous zones, a process that corresponds to the time in which the language of the primary oral eroticism is developed. In other words, it is the passage from a psychic apparatus that functions in terms of tension-discharge relief to a more developed one that functions in terms of pleasure-pleasure.

The difficult work to be developed must have as its goal the construction of the experiences that are not felt so that they can have meaning in the conjugal relationship. In other words, to go from the calmness of the death drive to the vitality of the life drive in order to feel, perceive and think. In many cases, it is fundamental to help the couple to progress in the development of a self-observing function that allows them to begin to maintain a careful attitude towards themselves. This deficit is related to the failure of the psychic alarms that sustain the drives of self-preservation as a result of the denial of attribution judgement regarding what benefits and what harms the individual. With this end in mind, the attitude of the analyst, different from the traditional technique, should be predominantly facilitating, reanimating, explanatory, discriminating and inter-relational, always keeping in mind in the transferencial relationship the difference between intersubjectivity and trans-subjectivity, as a way of avoiding a narcissistic crossing. It implies fusionist and adhesive investments giving rise to the formation of a continent of undifferentiated contents in the analyst–couple relationship. In the field of countertransference, the greatest risk that the analyst runs is to allow him- or herself to be contaminated by the apathy of the couple or, on the contrary, to enter into a state of impatience or growing anger in the eagerness to get them out of their passivity. In truth, the difficult success of therapy in these cases depends on the permanent and active vitality of the analyst, without losing the indispensable neutrality demanded in any analytic treatment.

The relationships that fit into model 2, by adapting to the restrictions imposed by the pandemic, do not usually seek treatment, although many of these couples have had individual or joint therapies before. Rafael and Marina, in the case cited, for example, had already undergone a couple's analysis when, after almost a year apart, they returned to Brazil to finish their master's degrees. During the pandemic, established in their country house, they made an appointment with the analyst for a few sessions over the Internet. This was to let him know how they were doing, to resume some of the more critical points they had dealt with in the analysis and to examine with him their plans for the future.

References

Aulagnier, P. (1977). *La violência de la interpretación* [The violence of interpretation]. Buenos Aires: Amorrortu.

Freud, S. ([1895]1977). Projeto para uma psicologia científica [Project for a scientific psychology]. *Obras completas psicológicas de Sigmund Freud* [Complete psychological works of Sigmund Freud], Vol. 1. Rio de Janeiro: Imago.

Freud, S. ([1896]1976). Novos comentários sobre as psiconeuroses de defesa [New comments on defence psychoneuroses]. *Obras psicológicas completas de Sigmund Freud* [Complete psychological works of Sigmund Freud], Vol. 3. Rio de Janeiro: Imago.

Freud, S. ([1898]1976). A sexualidade na etiologia das neuroses [Sexuality in the aetiology of the neuroses]. *Obras psicológicas completas de Sigmund Freud* [Complete psychological works of Sigmund Freud], Vol. 3. Rio de Janeiro: Imago.

Freud, S. ([1920]2017). Além do princípio do prazer [Beyond the pleasure principle]. *Sigmund Freud: obras completes* [Sigmund Freud: Complete works], Vol. 14. São Paulo: Companhia das Letras.

Freud, S. ([1930]2016). O mal-estar na civilização [Civilisation and its discontents]. *Sigmund Freud: obras completas.* [Sigmund Freud: Complete works], Vol. 18. São Paulo: Companhia das Letras.

Kaës, R. (1977). *El aparato psíquico grupal* [The group psychic apparatus]. Barcelona: Gedisa.

Maldavsky, D. (1991). *Procesos y estructuras vinculares: mecanismo, erogeinedad y lógicas* [Linking processes and structures: Mechanism, erogeneity and logic]. Buenos Aires: Nueva Visión.

Maldavsky, D. (1995). *Pesadillas en vigília: sobre neuroses tóxicas y traumáticas* [Nightmares while awake: About toxic and traumatic neuroses]. Buenos Aires: Amorrortu.

Maldavsky, D. (2004). *La investigación psicoanalitica del lenguaje* [The psychoanalytic investigation of language]. Buenos Aires: Lugar Editorial.

Maldavsky, D. (2007). *La intersubjetividade en la clínica psicoanalítica* [Intersubjectivity in the psychoanalytic clinic]. Buenos Aires: Lugar Editorial.

Maldavsky, D. (2010). Sobre la investigación de los processos subjetivos e intersubjetivos en psicoterapia de pareja [On the investigation of subjective and intersubjective processes in couple psychotherapy]. *Revista subjetividad y processos cognitivos*, 14.

Maldavsky, D. (2014). La desvitalización y la economia pulsional vincular [Devitalisation and the linked drive economy]. *Revista subjetividad y processos cognitivos*, 18.

Puget, J. & Berenstein, I. (1988). *Psicoanálisis de la pareja matrimonial* [Psychoanalysis of the matrimonial couple]. Buenos Aires: Paidós.

16 Disillusionment and destructiveness in severe high-conflict divorce and other social maladies

Arthur Leonoff

Intimate partner violence and coercive control, two bellwether indicators of domestic violence, worsened during the depth of the coronavirus pandemic. The online respected news source, *Mother Jones*, reported on its sharp rise in the United States as stay-at-home orders took effect (Pauly & Lurie, 2020). The authors reviewed data from 13 American cities that recorded marked increases in calls to emergency services and hotlines. The pandemic was a petri dish for how violence and conflict can escalate in family relationships.

Partner violence, however, is only one form of intra-familial aggression. It is certainly a major societal problem on its own terms, never to be underestimated, but the prevailing literature tends to focus on one-sided causation, usually male aggressors oppressing female victims. This perspective minimises the role of family systems, and stresses personality characteristics as compared with relationship factors (Giordano et al., 2022). When information is provided about both members of a couple then it can be possible to discern important dyadic contributions that contribute to intra-familial aggression (Fritz, Slep, & O'Leary, 2012; Herrera, Wiersma, & Cleveland, 2008).

Additionally, in prevailing narratives, power and control are conceptualised as a constant force with one person exerting subjugating violence over another. This ignores the dynamic and shifting power gradient within dyadic relationships. Although some power and control abuse occurs to subdue opposition, most family aggression arises after a period of escalating verbal conflict (Winsock & Smadar-Dror, 2021). Often, there is contest around an issue and the tensions escalate until one might lash out physically, throw things, storm out of the house or summon the police, among a myriad of possibilities of enactment. In other words, to better appreciate the complexity of intra-familial aggression, it should not be reduced to a fixed gender dynamic, one that invariably sees the man as abuser overpowering his weaker female partner.

The context in which violence occurs is also important. It is often situational and linked to relationship conflict. Much of it can be minor from a physical standpoint while being cataclysmic from an emotional

DOI: 10.4324/9781003646266-22

perspective (Jaffe et al., 2008). Where violence occurs in a single episode, it tends to happen in the process of breaking up. The acting out arises at a time of emotional upheaval and represents a toxic aggregate of helplessness, grief, fury and fear.

Of course, the refrain that it takes two to tango can be used as cover by violent, controlling men to rationalise their intimate terrorism and avoid accountability (Stark, 2009). Indeed, coercive control in the recently separated is a higher predictor of serious outcome, including femicide, than a history of previous violence (Glass, Manganello, & Campbell, 2004). At the same time, focusing solely on violent men misses so much of what happens in families and how power and control factors wend their way through family relationships. It is ultimately a human field in which couple interaction and conflict occur.

High-conflict divorce

High-conflict divorce is a much graver problem than what the nondescript term implies. It can lead to years of intractable misery and almost certain psychological harm to children and adults alike (Wallerstein & Kelly, 1980; Schoppe-Sullivan, Schermerhorn, & Cummings, 2007). Yet, why certain individuals and ex-couples regress into socio-legal mayhem post-separation can be hard to discern. It implicates only a minority of divorces, but these cases consume at least half of total family court time (Johnson, 2017). They tend to spill over into child protection services at a high rate and are especially challenging because of the degree of acrimony, manipulation and expectation that the agency will hold the other parent accountable and advance the respective parent's legal case (Houston, Bala, & Saini, 2017).

Some sufferers are personality disordered, but most are not. The response to the breakup in the high-conflict group is deeply traumatic, with a counter-impulse to attack the ex-partner, including a child who sides with the ex-spouse's cause or a parent's relationship with a child. There is an unmistakable destructiveness that permeates the family system and infects the psycho-legal mechanisms employed to manage and resolve such conflicts.

This discussion is an attempt to explain this phenomenon within a psychoanalytic framework. My premise is that two major ingredients underly this profound relationship dysfunction. First, they are narcissistically fragile individuals who experience the breakup as a profound betrayal. Second, they will have suffered from a layering of major, upending disillusionments in their lives, culminating in the breakup of the marriage, that compromise their belief in family and capacity for family formation.

Thus, there are two elements to this explanation for divorce destructiveness: disillusionment and capacity for family formation. The word 'disillusionment' carries a very different meaning from its companion term, 'disappointment' (Lafarge, 2015). Whereas disappointment refers to unfulfilled wishes, disillusionment charts a sense of a false promise that threatens the very basis of wishing and hope. It is often experienced as permanent and, thus, deeply threatening to one's capacity to orient in the world. It bears the risk of emotional despair because it implies that what was believed was false.

I am using the term 'family formation' to describe an integrating psychic act leading to an internal representation of a family envelope (Houzel, 1996). It would seem to be an extension of the good breast or its idealised form. In the high-conflict population, however, this introjected family envelope is eroded through narcissistic injury and disillusionment. Where there has been no stable, heuristic process guaranteeing family as a safe harbour for subjectivity, this must be constructed *de novo*, in real time by the partnering adult. It is often cobbled together from flimsy idealisations of the other that are themselves at serious risk of disillusionment.

The result is a fragile family alliance based solely on agreeing and always getting along. These individuals have a weak rapport with each other and a meagre capacity to communicate. When tested, the couple alliance ruptures with paranoid thinking emerging. It is my premise that family itself, not just the partner, is viewed as having profoundly failed the subject. The attacks that ensue are as much aimed at family as false promise as at the now ex-spouse. In this subgroup, divorce is not a solution. It is the experience of two adversaries chained interminably together by the eternity of shared offspring. Children are often psychologically damaged due to incessant interparental conflict, preoccupied and poorly attuned parents. Family resources, including financial and emotional, become drained.

Optimally, when marriages end, families are reframed but are sufficiently resilient to continue to raise children in a cooperative system. Family is differentiated from marriage in the minds and values of the protagonists. Step-parents can be added, leading to blended families. These adjustments are challenging, but a healthy capacity for family formation is essential to post-divorce adjustment. In the severe high-conflict group, in contrast, the family envelope often does not survive. When the union fails, so does the family. It rips apart as destructive forces take hold. It is in this context that children may resist or refuse to visit one of their parents and internecine war prevails.

Family as developmental achievement

There is a universal longing for family, as an ideal of safety and identity. It likely evolves from the ideal parental imago, itself constructed on the ideal breast. It is a source of endless nostalgia in song, film and Hallmark cards, which reveals its illusory appeal. A good enough experience ably contributes to a capacity for family formation that includes an ability to foster partnerships with others and to resolve conflicts and reach consensus.

I view this capacity as a developmental achievement that reflects a sufficient degree of recognition (Benjamin, 2004), reciprocity and third-ness to allow the individual to form close, intimate bonds with another that can include children as well. Thirdness, in this regard, can take several forms within a family matrix such as a relational third with the other adult, but also a differentiating third between the rhythm of adult relationships and that with children. It also suggests a belief in family, sufficient to sustain hope in the face of difficulties and challenges in the willingness of others to achieve family goals. This core representation of a family ideal must survive inevitable disappointments, even disillusionments, to remain as a symbol of sanctuary and site for love and protection that can be actualised in one's life.

Individuals most at risk of severe high-conflict divorce are those whose capacity for family formation is weak or degraded by prior disillusionments. Relationships are established often on idealised, illusory terms that carry the entire load of hope for a future. There is little proven capacity to successfully deal with problems through consensus and conflict management. When problems arise, acute disillusionment occurs, and there is an air of catastrophe, experienced in terms of betrayal and persecution. Conflict escalates and hope is the first casualty.

Family and society

In the post-war era, the nuclear family was promoted as the ideal. It is a model that has survived for the well-off who can still afford a home in a neighbourhood of houses. It is not the case for the majority, however, who live in various combinations of fragmented and single-parent or divorced scenarios. As *New York Times* columnist David Brooks concluded, these permutations of the nuclear family lack the 'shock absorbers' to handle the breakups and disruptions that often occur (Brooks, 2020). This was less an issue when multi-generations lived in communal settings in which family was more widely defined and could buffer such fractures and disruptions.

Psychoanalysis has been an urban discipline and, thus, was indirectly aligned with the transition from multi-generational extended families that served agriculture and rural family enterprises to nuclear families in the cities. Freud's psychology was premised on this nuclear family model. His Oedipus concept was based on triangular relations as the first emanation of family, a heteronormative structure through which love, hate and sexuality pulse and are organised. It is a microcosm of the world.

From a contemporary perspective, the Oedipus complex, mother–father–child, seems a quaint and idealised notion in comparison with many variations of what constitutes family in today's world. Of course, the Oedipus is a structure for meaning, specifically sexual, not just family relations tied to one or another socio-historical model. It features a para-digm-changing thirdness that resonates with possibilities. There is the capacity to accept exclusion, but the other important attribute is the capacity to form broader alliances that allow for group relations and not just a series of narrow dyads. Thirdness is a window to the world at large. It imagines something beyond any one relationship.

As societal change has led to smaller and more fragile and transitory family units, the psychic capacity for family formation, the ability to make broader alliances, has taken on greater importance. Those with inadequate capacity tend to create unstable bonds that shatter when tested by interpersonal conflict, life stresses or both. These very brittle unions then lack the internal capacity to absorb and adjust to dis-appointments and, worse, disillusionments. In fractured, isolated units, often of a single parent and child, there is no buffer to life crises as could be mobilised by the collection of kin that was once commonplace and could fill in the gap and help stabilise adults and children during crises.

This brief overview helps identify the importance of thirdness in the capacity for family formation when understood as the ability to foster a caring, holding affiliative structure that supports the identity and coex-istence of its members. As such, it is a developmental achievement and, truly, a microcosm of the world.

High-conflict mayhem

Conflict suffuses interaction between the separated or divorced pair, and no issue is too small to remain uncontested. Children are curiously invi-sible to their parents in the process that is supposed to be about their care. Extreme states of mind prevail in the sufferer, but this description does not do justice to the destructiveness that occurs. Attacks, in what-ever form, are often directed at the reputation, relationships and legal or family entitlements of the former partner. Examples are legion but include: poisoning a relationship between the other parent and a child, false reports to police and child protection agencies, following, blocking and threatening the ex-partner with an automobile, creating trouble with tax authorities, financial manipulation to deprive the other of support, using aggressive attorneys to propagate endless litigation as way of depleting the other of funds and energy, creating hostile and threatening scenes at transitions despite the children being present, poisoning the atmosphere at children's activities and using social media to disparage the other's reputation in the hope of causing irreparable harm. It is com-monplace as well for this toxic high-conflict group to attack the reputa-tion of health and social service professionals who are perceived to be identified with the ex-spouse or their cause.

Sean and Maria

Maria and Sean had been separated for several years when the court ordered a family assessment. It was the children's behaviour that was especially worrisome. There were three children: two teenage boys and a pubescent girl. One son had brandished a kitchen knife at his mother during an argument and the daughter was becoming increasingly hostile with her father and refusing to visit. The situation was volatile with no middle ground or neutral space between the two tense households. At a school theatre event in which one of the children had a lead part, the parents openly feuded backstage before the performance. The school sent each letters setting boundaries for the future. A grandparent who attended the event suffered chest pain, necessitating a 911 call.

At some point in the nine-year saga, Maria accused Sean of trying to run her down with his car and this resulted in a report to the police. Sean blamed Maria for alienating their daughter and sided with the son who had threatened his mother with a knife. Murder was in the air.

It was fair to say that Maria and Sean hated each other but what they were experiencing could not be reduced to affect alone. They had created a family through childbirth but, apart from a self-suffering commitment, they were never an effective unit. Separation was no solution either and the conflict intensified.

The legal case curiously mirrored the relationship, featuring hostile lawyers who attempted to expose the other party as fully responsible for the destructiveness while suppressing, minimising or negating their client's contribution. This led to a psychotic degree of splitting. When Sean chased his daughter out of the home on one occasion, in what must have been a very frightening experience for the child, he blamed Maria when the girl refused to return. At another time, Maria had forcibly held down this same daughter, who had decided to see her father; an incident that Maria framed as an 'escape', as it occurred in the context of an altercation. The child protection agency raised the possibility of foster care, but never followed through with this threat.

Sean's career was mediocre, a fact of which Maria had often reminded him during their rocky marriage. His father was a prominent physician and Sean was expected to achieve at the same high level but, though his academic credentials were impressive, his career had struggled. He was regularly passed over for promotions.

Sean had always had a reactive, volatile side to his personality, and this was an issue in childhood. Yet, he was a good student, and this was all that seemed to matter to his parents. His temper episodes were overlooked, and he was protected from consequences. He had little insight or willingness to reflect on the issue of his anger and its management. He did relate one incident, however, in which his parents had hired a math tutor in his senior year, even though his grades were good. This tutor had substituted during the schoolyear for his regular math teacher who was dealing with an ongoing health issue. According to Sean, his parents were confident that this tutor would have inside information about exam questions. He felt that they were bribing the tutor to ensure his good grades. Sean was sure that his parents had limited confidence in him, and that Maria 'never' gave him support either or suggested that she believed in him.

Maria worked as a research scientist and was well regarded and successful. Her usual composure and style, however, hid her deep enmity for Sean. Hers was not open, noisy hostility as much as silent fury. She was also deeply contemptuous, and one could not sense any vestige of affection in her attitude towards him. It was as if he had never been her partner. There were the three children, but it was hard to imagine any scene in which Maria ever cared for Sean.

Maria described herself as having been an odd child born to a very odd mother who treated her daughter as her twin. On the one hand, her mother's lack of psychological boundaries made it difficult for Maria to emancipate from her mother's grip. Her mother dressed her in clothes that accentuated this oneness theme. On the other hand, her mother was an accomplished community college teacher, and she encouraged Maria academically. Maria did exceedingly well at school. As an older adolescent, she separated somewhat dramatically from her mother, and this led to almost a decade of strained contact. She continued to be wary of her mother as an adult and resentful that her mother had enforced this peculiar twinship on her for her own reasons.

Maria had a better relationship with her father, who was much older than her mother and died when Maria was in her early twenties. She loved her father, but the age gap made it hard for him to understand her or for her to fully appreciate him. This added to the dominance of her eccentric mother in her life and made her more vulnerable to her mother's merger needs, which Maria found discomfiting, if not threatening. She was an only child to her parents, and it was only later that Maria learned of a sibling born to her parents who lived a few days after birth. She wondered whether this had played a part. She was also aware that her mother had lost her own mother as a teenager and that this loss almost certainly played a part in her mother's behaviour.

During the marriage, Sean was full of blame and took little responsibility for what was occurring between them. After explosive episodes, he would become very childlike and docile, but this was short-lived. Having children made it worse between them. Sean was not particularly helpful, and he held a constant resentment as if too much were being asked of him. The marriage imploded after a vacation incident when Maria could not take his infantile behaviour any longer. When they returned home, she insisted that he live elsewhere for a reprieve, but then her attitude hardened, and she demanded separation. It was not received well.

Two years later, Sean's bitterness was toxic, and Maria's fury was no less. They seemed locked in a terrible struggle that sealed them off from everyone else, including their children. It was very high conflict that lasted for almost a decade and only really ended because their children became old enough to make their own decisions. Their respective families became involved and thousands of dollars in family financial resources were spent on lawyers, assessors, mediators, therapists and family court. It was a bizarre spectacle that left their children neglected and damaged.

Some years later, the middle child, a son, consulted me due to increasing depression after being accepted and beginning dental school. He had to withdraw to seek treatment. This was the child who, on the surface, had seemed most durable during his parents' chronic divorce war. Underlying his depression was a profound resentment of his parents, who had destroyed his childhood and still expected him to take his place as a normal, healthy adult, as did the rest of the world. His parents, he thought, did not deserve a successful child and part of him savoured the idea of scuttling his life to get back at them. It was a theme to which he often returned: the price his siblings and he paid for the war of attrition that dominated their parents' priorities.

This son was able to resume dental school a year later and completed his studies, although he still required psychotherapy over the ensuing years. He often felt lost and his capacity for relationships was hampered by reminiscences of his own childhood but also states of psychic emptiness. In the noise of his parents' divorce chaos, there was a troubling void that reflected a profound de-cathexis of the children, which had certainly imprinted itself on this young man's mind as a gap or blank spot in his own identity. His revenge fantasies, omnipotent in a way, mirrored his parents' cruelty and attacks on one another. The destructiveness had momentum.

Disillusionment and destructiveness: geopolitics and other boundary violations

Besides current fixations with narcissism and narcissistic personalities that saturate the Internet and self-help books when it comes to high-conflict divorce (see, for example, Eddy, 2018), we are more likely to identify destructiveness in other domains such as world politics where diabolical leaders get hold of nations and wreak havoc. The link between disillusionment and destructiveness is important in this regard.

As the Ukrainian war is ongoing as I write, it is useful to consider destructiveness from the mindset of Russia's president, Vladimir Putin. One might hypothesise, for example, that Putin loves Ukraine, which has been separated from Russia for at least four decades. He wants to draw it close again but cannot handle the disdain and rejection he has received to the westward looking country. In other words, he is a misguided and spurned lover who is wreaking havoc in response. He sounds like an omnipotent narcissist who cannot imagine that Ukraine would want anything else but to join Mother Russia considering the towering greatness of the country and its destiny.

From this perspective, destructiveness is framed as a consequence and not a cause. It characterises Putin as a troubled and misguided family man, peddling a delusional family romance. This formulation would require us to focus on personality pathology rather than on profound destructiveness as the fundamental motivation itself.

There is another version, however, that seems more to the point of destructiveness. Here, Putin can be said to hate Ukraine for putting a lie to his faded empire dreams (the family ideal in nationalistic terms equated with a mythologically glorious Soviet Union) and, thus, in a rage is attacking and destroying Ukraine one person and building at a time, despite the staggering outcome for Ukraine, of course, but also Russia. Here, he is not a lover but a hater, full of retaliatory vitriol. Putin can be seen as an interminable mourner for a lost Soviet paradise that never existed. His rage is palpable. He wants to destroy what he cannot attain, which is not Ukraine so much as a mythical Soviet or czarist glory. This severe disillusionment feeds an inner destructiveness that seems unquenchable. It is what makes Putin so dangerous, a deeply disillusioned, destructive leader with a big army, impermeable to the human and societal cost of his actions. He is a boundary violator on a grand scale attacking the family symbol of a failed dream.

Wherever major disillusionment arises in human experience, destructiveness can ignite. There is an attack directed at the family ideal or some symbol of it, as the bearer of ultimate trust. The 6 January 2021 insurrectionist attack on the Capitol building in the United States would be a case in point. The Capitol represented to the mainly white male attackers a family home harbouring liars and stealers who betrayed the American people and needed to be overthrown if not hung.

Boundary violations

Psychoanalysts are more familiar with the destructiveness borne of boundary violations (Gabbard & Lester, 1995; Gabbard, 2017). Although often portrayed as misguided love, this can mask the analyst's severe disillusionment, hopelessness and deep resentment. Gabbard (2017, p. 154), though, observed the relationship between sexual boundary violations, disillusionment and destructiveness:

> Over time I have noted that analysts who have become sexually involved with a patient have often become disillusioned, bitter, and resentful about their analytic training, their analytic organization or the analytic field in general. There is also a deep narcissistic wound

in such analysts who think that they have not been treated in the way that they deserve to be treated by their analytic colleagues. They may have been denied a promotion as a training analyst or an administrative position. They also may feel bitter about their training analysis itself.

What is a boundary violation if it is not an attack on the family crucible, represented by the intimate ethics of the analytic encounter? Most sexual boundary violators claim to be rescuing while they are destroying. It is the perverse logic that equates harm with protection. Gabbard (2017, p. 154) reminds his readers, alluding to Steiner's work, that analysts apparently hate analysis as well as loving it. I am not sure of this conclusion, but it rightly underscores that love and hate both course through families, even the analytic one.

Sexual boundary violations amount to an assault on the patient's right to exist as a protected other, free of the narcissistic and bodily appropriation of the analyst. The abuse is akin to 'incest', again revealing its family origins in which the analyst/therapist enacts a distressing part of their own history. The profession shudders from the blow at the hands of the offending analyst who might appear to be love-sick and even naïve. Colleagues, however, reel from the destructivity of the violation. In the contrecoup, there is silence concerning the offender, as if the betrayal of the 'family' is too great to process.

In this regard, Celenza describes a clergy man who used the alter for sexual abuse of parishioners and characterised his actions as a way of 'fucking God and the church at the same time' (2007, p. 44). It is an attack on the family ideal fuelled by disillusionment.

Whether it is the priest ('father') that attacks the parishioner, the physician that victimises the patient or the analyst that appropriates the analysand, we should not underestimate the destructive motive at the core of the behaviour. Of course, some are paedophiles and predator psychopaths, but most are not. The priesthood and health professions mirror the level of trust that should exist in families, an ethical structure that demands protection and a deep responsibility of care. The violator, however, radically rejects this ethical demand, even when it is framed as true love. The target might seem to be the victim but, in my view, the deeper aim is to attack the family ideal, destroy the sacred and ignore protective boundaries.

Boundary violation and high-conflict divorce

This brief charting of the link between disillusionment, destructiveness and boundary violation is intended to clarify that the destructive behaviour observed in divorce pathology is not a unique phenomenon (Leonoff, 2021). The metaphor of boundary violation emphasises the notion of crossing a barrier as the offending act. It would be more accurate, though, to view it as one of destroying an ethical space marked by incalculable responsibility for the other. The notion of crossing seems tame relative to the consequences. It is more akin to the destruction of ethics, which is why it is so damaging.

In cases of severe high conflict, the crime of boundary violation amounts to a destruction of family ethics. The wish to vanquish over the ex-partner displaces any concern for that person, someone presumably once loved, and there is a profound disregard for what this means for the children. The ex-partner can be deemed so repugnant that it is assumed that the children will benefit from marginalisation of this parent's role and presence in their lives.

Indeed, the other is reduced to a bundle of projections that eliminate boundaries. As an example, if a parent had some struggles with addiction, then they are deemed a dire threat to the children and should only have parenting time under severely limiting conditions of supervision until the children are teenagers. If there was some scuffle at the cusp of marital separation, then the individual is portrayed as a criminal abuser who should be jailed and kept out of the children's lives. Attempts may well be made to achieve these ends.

The attack on the 'third' seems important in this context, with the third representing the family envelope as an ethical structure that exists apart from two adult participants and which frames their duty to care.

Returning briefly to our example case, in a prescient moment, Maria acknowledged, 'I have a major disappointment disorder.' This underscored the depth of despair, helplessness and sense of betrayal and disillusionment that she had experienced throughout her life, culminating in her union with Sean. She had retained a capacity for reflective thinking, unlike Sean, whose concreteness and lack of reflective capacity were significant. Nonetheless, she was locked in a struggle, and knew that she was, but had no means to step back for the sake of her family. The Rubicon had been crossed, and destructiveness had taken over. It was a land where resolution and destruction were the same.

This is precisely the dilemma in high-conflict divorce. Something was destroyed and, to make matters worse, is constantly being destroyed in the myriad of interactions between the ex-couple. The promise of family as a safe harbour, an ideal and ethical container for the self, fails to survive, if it existed at all.

Conclusion

'All pain comes from living,' states Hanna Segal (1993, p. 55), but it is the rupture of illusion, the sense of being deceived and left with nothing that seems to be at the core of much of human suffering. Layers of disillusionment leave a void that destructiveness can fill, attacking the source of betrayal and deceit, which can be another person but also the ideal of family itself. This is precisely what occurs in severe high-conflict divorce, although it is apparent in other societal domains, wherever there is sacred trust and the promise of family fealty and protection. The attack is on the family crucible or whatever stands for it. In high-conflict divorce, the destructivity is blistering, relentless and seemingly without concern for self-preservation. Scorched earth is observed in this context and elsewhere in the human enterprise when destruction is more important than life itself.

References

Benjamin, J. (2004). Beyond doer and done to: An intersubjective view of thirdness. *The Psychoanalytic Quarterly*, 73(1): 5–46. doi:10.1002/j.2167-4086.2004.tb00151.x

Brooks, D. (2020). The nuclear family was a mistake. *The Atlantic*, March. Retrieved from: https://www.theatlantic.com/magazine/archive/2020/03/the-nuclear-family-was-a-mistake/605536/

Celenza, A. (2007). *Sexual Boundary Violations: Therapeutic, Academic, and Supervisory Contexts*. New York: Jason Aronson.

Eddy, B. (2018). *5 Types of People Who Can Ruin Your Life: Identifying and Dealing with Narcissists, Sociopaths, and Other High-Conflict Personalities*. New York: Tarcher Perigee/Penguin.

Fritz, P. T., Slep, A., & O'Leary, K. (2012). Couple-level analysis of the relation between family-of-origin aggression and intimate partner violence. *Psychology of Violence*, 2(2): 139–153.

Gabbard, G. (2017). Sexual boundary violations in psychoanalysis: A 30-year retrospective. *Psychoanalytic Psychology*, 34: 151–156.

Gabbard, G. & Lester, E. (1995). *Boundaries and Boundary Violations in Psychoanalysis*. New York: Basic Books.

Giordano, P., Mackenzie, M., Longmore, M., & Manning, W. (2022). Micro-cultures of conflict: Couple level perspectives on reasons for and causes of intimate partner violence in young adulthood. *Journal of Marriage and Family*, 84 (4): 1062–1080.

Glass, N., Manganello, J., & Campbell, J. (2004). Risk for intimate partner femicide in violent relationships. *DV Report*, 9(2): 1, 2, 30–33.

Herrera, V., Wiersma, J., & Cleveland, H. H. (2008). The influence of individual and partner characteristics on the perpetration of intimate partner violence in young adult relationships. *Journal of Youth & Adolescence*, 37(3): 284–296.

Houston, C., Bala, N., & Saini, M. (2017). Crossover cases of high-conflict families involving child protection services: Ontario research findings and suggestions for good practices. *Family Court Review*, 55: 362–374.

Houzel, D. (1996). The family envelope and what happens when it is torn. *International Journal of Psychoanalysis*, 77: 901–912.

Jaffe, P., Johnston, J., Crooks, C., & Bala, N. (2008). Custody disputes involving allegations of domestic violence: Towards a differentiated approach to parenting plans. *Family Court Review*, 46(3): 500–522.

Johnson, J. (2017). Commentary on the entrenched post separation parenting disputes: the role of interparental hatred. *Family Court Review*, 55(3): 424–429.

Lafarge, L. (2015). The fog of disappointment, the cliffs of disillusionment, the abyss of despair. *Journal of the American Psychoanalytic Association*, 63: 1225–1239.

Leonoff, A. (2021). *When Divorces Fail: Disillusionment, Destructivity and High Conflict Divorce*. New York: Rowman & Littlefield.

Pauly, M. & Lurie, J. (2020, 31 March). Domestic violence 911 calls are increasing. Coronavirus is likely to blame. *Mother Jones*. Retrieved from: https://www.motherjones.com/crime-justice/2020/03/domestic-violence-abuse-coronavrius/

Schoppe-Sullivan, S., Schermerhorn, A., & Cummings, E. (2007). Marital conflict and children's adjustment: Evaluation of the process model. *Journal of Marriage and Family*, 69: 1118–1134.

Segal, H. (1993). On the clinical usefulness of the concept of the death instinct. *International Journal of Psychoanalysis*, 74: 55–61.

Stark, E. (2009). Rethinking custody evaluation in cases involving domestic violence. *Child Custody*, 6: 287–321.

Wallerstein, J. & Kelly, J. (1980). *Surviving the Breakup: How Children and Parents Cope with Divorce*. New York: Basic Books.

Winsock, Z. & Smadar-Dror, R. (2021). Gender, escalatory tendencies, and verbal aggression in intimate relationships. *Journal of Interpersonal Violence*, 36(11–12): 5383–5400.

17 The betrayal of tradition

The death of the only son and the empty nest

Ruth Axelrod

The psychodynamic work of couples is a tool that validates the possibility of simultaneous listening to a loving dyad in search of meaning, where the difficulty and achievement of love can unfold. Each couple has its own history and its own becoming, and when the psychoanalyst is invited to witness the process, he or she becomes a neo-structure of it.

Berenstein (Berenstein & Puget, 1997; Berenstein, 1976, 1990) clarifies that the analysis of the couple and the family, which began as an application of psychoanalysis, has allowed investigation and treatment of the family bond, introducing an innovation and a change of technique that implied a new practice and, in turn, allowed us to develop theoretical productions that modified some aspects of the understanding of individual analysis. Just as we should not confuse the 'inner child' with the child under analysis, neither should we confuse the world of internal objects that constitute an inner family with the family bond observed and treated as such. This is a 'linking reform'. The instrument of this practice is the interpretation of the symptomatic productions of the bond as well as of the subject structure produced by that specific relation. This field presents another of the extensions of psychoanalysis.

Freud (1926) described resistance to treatment and challenges in unveiling the unconscious. Berenstein (2001) takes it up by saying that 'the resistance lies in the difficulty of identifying what has been inscribed or incorporated into a significant bond as alien that which is not easy to identify and which nevertheless marks it as the subject of that relationship'. They can be the parents, the other in the love relationship, as well as the analyst in the therapeutic relationship, being that the other inevitably alters narcissism no matter how much the ego declares itself inaccessible. It defends itself with a resistance that would work in opposition to alienity and bonding in order to re-establish individuality and similarity. It is not the *Verleugnung* (denial) that denies what comes from the sense of reality where the ego denies an absence, that of the penis in the girl, and affirms an imaginary presence attributed to an infantile explanation. In the resistance to bonding, it is opposed to giving rise to a presence indicated by the alienity of the other. Their rejection is not of the

DOI: 10.4324/9781003646266-23

order of repression with disinvestment and the possibility of counter-investiture. It is not a return to a previous representation but an opposition to a new inscription of the other. The psychic apparatus refuses to accept that the other is there, whether visible or invisible. However, the marks of archaic linking leave traces that the psychoanalyst can circumvent.

Freud (1917) argues that although love is originally narcissistic, the subject in loving tries to incorporate and psychically devour the other, even if it is dangerous. In this place where love and narcissism are intertwined, the dominance of the ego and the traumatic aetiology of 'intropressure' (internal pressure) defined by Ferenczi (1912): 'Man loves only himself, loving another is equivalent to integrating the other into his own' as a constitutive and defensive psychic movement, dynamic of love life and transference.

The challenges of listening work with couples, both face-to-face and virtual, include empathic listening, neutrality, non-judgement to establish a therapeutic alliance, as well as a rigorous analysis of counter-transference (Velasco et al., 2006). This makes it possible to examine the roles that patients project on the analyst, which will be of great help in understanding what the history of their love bonds has been. There will always be the provocation to empathise more with one person than another, a provocation to choose a favourite that it will be important not to participate in. Framing with couples has its own style and requires being very attentive to the concept of psychodynamic betrayal in order to carry out the work with the whole team and not exclude any participant (Axelrod, 2017).

Treason will be defined as the breaking of a covenant, between two or more people over their ideas; something said or unsaid that breaks an agreement. The rupture, surprises, that which breaks the law, that which alters an established order, a structure that can range from the biological to the psychic and the social. For Akhtar (2013) it is an integral component of psychic trauma. Couples psychotherapy requires a lot of attention to pacts and their modifications.

Montagna considers it important to consider the value of the law within psychoanalytic work, a space that integrates multiple inter-disciplinary fields of juxtaposition of the different areas of knowledge that require dialogue in individual and couple work (Montagna & Branco-Vicente).

Love in the time of …

Times are dynamic and humanity adapted to the encounters of evolution, especially in times of the COVID-19 pandemic. The world transitioned to confinement, and psychoanalysts to virtual work, to attend to couples online, to listen to the multiple losses. From the concrete spatial, as Casillas

(2022, p. 17) says, we learned to listen to follow a common thread with different directions of the novel, the fantasised, the desired, the feared, the historical and all the speeches of nameless terror of each dyad. The loss of old illusions, along with the enigmas that haunted the daily life of a couple confined in a pandemic.

The enigma of the sphinx together with the prayer of the Oracle gave the continuity, 'They are two brothers, one begets the other and the other begets the first', as a possible search for the origin of Oedipus. Giving an interpretation, he answers: 'Like two brothers, day and night, one begets the other, and the other begets the first.' The only thing that interrupts is death.

Care to survive was our manic defence to believe in fantasies of omnipotence or protection, to avoid 'the new melancholia' (Recalcati, 2019). Death knocked and entered every home with force and left spaces without bodies with impossible mourning, inadmissible smells and anguish of collapse in all homes.

Without borders, without limits, without law, we heard how the contiguous suffering traumatised the collective. Virtuality distanced us, although it protected us, it also allowed us another form of emotional bond with our patients. There was room in the minds of analysts trained to listen to the pain of others from families in distress.

Catz (2022) considers that the pandemic has left fathers in an overwhelming spectrum of complexity due to the fall in the symbolic efficacy of the paternal law. During the plague of this century, he emphasises, there were states of psychic orphanhood that generated fragility in the roles of upbringing. These incapacities confronted the death that denounces everything.

Parents who lost children, children who lost parents. Questioning the unmanageability of the traumas of destiny. And of grief, whether healthy or pathological. Deaths of all kinds, some manageable, some not. The death of a child is an event that is named as irreplaceable (Roitman et al., 2002).

Freud (1929, p. 431), in his letter to Binswanger following the death of his son, says: 'We know that the acute grief we feel after such a loss will come to an end, but we shall remain inconsolable and never find a substitute.' In this letter, he states that grief will not end up finding a replacement; he recognises that loss is irreplaceable. He had previously said, 'We know that grief, as painful as it may be, expires spontaneously ….
Then our libido is again free to … replace lost objects with new ones that are, as far as possible, as appreciable, or more appreciable.' These two views on the possible substitution or not of the object, once the mourning is over, show a contradiction in Freud. The possibility of investing new objects will only be possible after accepting that the one that has been lost is irreplaceable. Allouch (1996) argues that the paradigm of grief is no longer that of the father as formulated by Freud, saying that 'it was the

most terrible loss in a man's life', but that the paradigm of grief is that of the death of a child. This paradigm shift is one of the main features of Allouch's version of grief. 'The father is someone who has left traces, and even someone who at the time of his death has stopped producing news, as if his account was complete.' Then, from those traces, the work of mourning could be done. 'With a child, the loss is more radical, you lose not only a loved one, or a common past, but what a child could potentially have provided if he has lived. The measure of the horror of the mourner is a function of the measure of the non-fulfillment of the life of the dead.'

The son represents that transgenerational bond that justifies one's own existence, is the repository of primary identification and the organiser of his mother's narcissistic equilibrium. The dead son is not Green's (1980) dead mother, it is not the white depression in life. It is the dark depression, and it is more than a void, the black hole that does not contain the psyche.

It is that place of the terrifying gain of preconception ambivalence, giving way to the death drive, alive and incandescent. It is here that we find the betrayal of tradition marked by the expectation that it is the children who bury their parents, and not that it is in any other order; that it is a disorder. When the law surprises, betrayal attacks the ego, the whole self that, devastated, has to accept this unexpected becoming.

Clinical approach

Once upon a time there was a desire, in a game of two that merged to become one gestating in a third, which would continue with the known ideas and fears, a new generation with philia and inheritance, with the trans-generational and its unnameable traumas, and then …

Carlo (Dr Co) and Carla (Dr Ca) met, fell in love, got married, got pregnant and had a child, a boy who became the compass of their desires and expenses. D was born as a happy baby but his internal constitution was defective, a change had to be requested 'alluding to the guarantee of buying and selling', for which a urethral surgery helped him during his second year of life, although he suffered from physical limitations due to kidney diseases.

His mother devoted herself to the care of the little boy, but D evidently grew up wanting, and suffering his ailments. She questioned whether this defect was her responsibility, and with that doubt she preferred not to conceive again. With dedication but guilt for these genetics, Dr Ca took care of her offspring every day.

In his childhood years, there were some games and sports that D could not play because of his limitations. Being the son of two PhDs of science, it was easy for him to become a good student. He entered medical school, happy and with a girlfriend. In his third semester, he was already participating in the support team of a hospital and it is where he received the news and the rules to navigate the current pandemic. As an apprentice doctor, he was unconditional and very committed.

His mother-in-law fell ill with COVID-19, his girlfriend also, from which they recovered and it was he who took care of them. Subsequently, D fell ill with COVID-19 and following the protocol he stayed at home and isolated himself. At first, because he was an aspiring doctor, he thought he knew how to get out of the mess. He continuously measured his oxygenation. He received food at his door, he did not approach his caregivers – who turned out to be his parents – and who, although specialists in basic biological science, were a little scared. However, his symptoms became complicated and one night he was unable to breathe normally. His parents managed to get him admitted to a hospital far from home because as the epidemic was in full swing there was no room in the nearby hospitals.

Despite all the care and high costs, he never got out of the surgical bubble in which he was isolated; he could not win the war against that invisible viral presence, incomprehensible, unusual, treacherous and vile. His distraught parents received the news of his passing 18 days later.

Without words, without a name, without known traditions, without announced farewells, without deadly rituals, experiencing the ominous and nameless terror, death embraced this monophilic family, which entered a morass due to the visit of the undesirable 'Catrina' (Mexican folklore woman skeleton for death).

The body of their 'baby' was offered to them in a container of ashes, no longer in the vital but in the mortal of absence, where the negative presence resonates. Two weeks after this horror event, I received the phone call from Dr Co requesting a virtual appointment for him and his wife.

The first virtual scene began with both of them onscreen, shedding unstoppable tears. They talked about the whole story, about her constant struggle with death, and about her desire to die with her son. We committed to a virtual framing once a week. At that moment, I doubted if it was enough. I told them that we would evaluate it as we went along.

The first impression in the first session is always a decisive beginning in the pre-conceptual fantasies of psychoanalytic work with couples. There are endless questions about what can be achieved psychodynamically with what one has and what one does not have.

The mind of the patient and/or the analyst remains in the line of fire, which ceased to be a saying to take me to a complex and painful virtual reality, a challenge that went beyond the orthodox technique: the fire of absence–presence in clinical work in a pandemic; that, without being able to know this couple who were in pain physically, we had already been meeting for 18 months.

Was the healthy mourning of the only child possible?

Psychiatric consultation was necessary for both parents, despite the logistical nightmare for the analyst. Dr Ca is a sensitive mother, who questions everything and feels directionless. She has six siblings and three are very close to her. With the news, they have become very close to the couple and accompany them on the weekends. With the work of historicization, we have been able to discover that she presents primary melancholic nuclei, that her childhood was complex and she was the youngest of her clan.

Dr Co is a little more organised than his wife. He accompanies her so that she ends up every night in the marital bed and they can sleep together, although very scared. During the pandemic, two of his father's brothers also lost their lives. It is a family that has accumulated many losses, and this makes them feel very vulnerable. The couple is very concerned about their genetic predisposition to the virus, so they learned to work from home.

The psychotherapeutic process brought us together every week. She was included after 12 months in a virtual self-help group, simultaneous to the online psychoanalytic work, and commented, 'I realise that I'm not that special, that there are other people who have also lost their children and who share their losses, but I have a narcissistic attack because I don't want to share anything about the loss of my only son yet.'

Being scientists, they have little approach to spiritual spaces and their explanations about and after death can only be rational, precepts that throw them into the psychic void constantly. They have put the ashes in the middle of the living room of their house; their son's room remains closed. The sessions were full of thanatic content, complaints, anger, revenge, questioning, with insufficient answers; 'less Plato and more Prozac' to be able to get through the first months of this unexpected empty nest encounter. The psychiatric management has changed several times because she developed a tolerance to the medications, improved for a few weeks and at the same time presented very extreme mood swings, from not wanting to bathe or eat, to staying in bed for days. The frightening topic of the absence of their son, in order to work in session, was very sporadic; they preferred to comment on other matters than on the enormous pain they had to go through. After 18 months of the constant analytic process, something led us to a new psychic spectre and they began to talk again about death, about death displaced to their place of work.

Now their scientific investigations are directed to the pursuit of cell development, and I hear this shift from the angst of life to micro experimentation; a place controlled by them.

He says: 'I work so that the cells that I use in my laboratory are happy, that they have life and light of their own, that every cell eats deliciously and can reproduce, and it is then that we can kill them so that they do not reproduce anymore. We have to know how to treat the cells, we use the cells obtained from a tumour ovary to understand histochemical death. At the microscopy level, death does not occur in a moment, it occurs little by little. Even though the cell seems already in its last stage of life it follows a programmed and organised death, the cell has the responsibility to die silently, a cell dies slowly ...'

I answer: 'It is impressive, what do we do with this knowledge? We can find a way to include it in us.'

Something of this was left in another place and now we can talk about death without pain; it is even possible to go from a passive position to an active one where they endorse killing. A scientific sublimation? A form of revenge? A discourse of science endorsing the sadism that distances them from masochism? Ovarian cancer cells have viruses? Anything related to a death wish for the agent who killed their son?

The next virtual session, I observed them sitting together and more serene. They continued with the discourse of their professional work and their encounter with symbolisations in order to talk about their emotions. Dr Co worked this week on the topic of his science research project and explained certain difficulties about the cell population he works with. He mentioned what he understood as cellular corruption.

I asked: 'How are cellular functions compromised? How do they get corrupted? The cells can be corrupted?'

With didactic intentions, he told me: 'A toxic environment is required, which is the main element that alters cells, because it breaks with the normal patterns of behaviour that can affect and alter them. A corrupt, malignant cell no longer conforms to the social programmes of its tissue organisation. This is also what happens to us humans. There is competition to stand out among them. Everyone has their role and some do it altruistically because they are not waiting for any recognition. But if they do not do their function properly, they can become corrupted. If the cell is corrupted, it takes away the food from the others, and not only does not fulfil the function it should do, but it reproduces continuously and becomes an ever growing parasite, developing a disease until the death of the subject.'

Dr Ca laughs and says that she finds it very interesting how Dr Co explains the pedagogy of biology and the role of corruption in social balance or imbalance including death. She mentions: 'We were taught to see and to observe the invisible, metaphorising is a way in which we can approach cellular violence, to understand biological and social phenomena.'

I asked: 'And how did you teach all this to your son, may he rest in peace?'

Dr Co calmly told me, for the first time, that her son was different and a very intelligent boy. He explained in a detailed way how he taught him the concepts of the origin of life, of vertebrates and invertebrates and of the origin of planets. He added: 'He was very good at mathematics, he knew how to program very well, and he liked robotics. It started with wanting to go into engineering. One night he designed a program, but when it was finished he didn't feel satisfied, since then he definitely preferred medicine.'

He was a very good student, he had an average of 9.4; he was very self-taught, if he didn't understand a concept, he researched it. He liked to speak languages like English or Japanese and he was even learning Chinese. He wanted to be a neurosurgeon. Dr Ca jokes by saying: 'I told him that a career in medicine required many years of study, and with so much work, when are you going to support me?' She laughs again.

Before closing the session, I pointed out that this was the first time we could talk calmly about their deceased son, that we commented about what he liked and what he didn't like. In this session, the screen was in the living room of the house where, for the first time, I noticed that there were three decorative figures hanging on the wall, grey and making a spatial game.

I asked them about this new element in the session, that of the three figures. Dr Co replied that he liked them very much because there were three of them and three of them are still there today. The work of mourning allowed them to remember the lost object with less affection and less pain. There is authorisation for the liberated self to laugh and to think deeply about the childhood and youth of a child, and the social corruption that ends in death.

The law looms everywhere, the law of the universe, the law of human limits and the corruption of them. Whose power is it? The themes are based on corruption, death, the biological law that also includes that of the human social group.

I can say that they are better, calmer, reinserted in their work and already in an active routine of acceptance of their new reality. They come to their virtual session grateful for accompaniment and offering material from their internal world to continue learning to live in their current conditions. I asked them for permission to write about this psychodynamic process of couples and they agreed to my request.

I accuse Alizade (1996) of confirming the idea that the life drive triumphs decisively when the subject operates intrapsychically, the transformation movement of narcissism that gives access to a certain amount of wisdom and to stay positive in life by taking into consideration one's fellow man. Otherness becomes relevant within the framework of an ethic. Existence is inserted in the primacy of the principle of relativity and the destruction drive manages to be tamed (Freud, 1937). To this transformation of narcissism, a place of importance must be dedicated.

Finally, the work of the analytic field has the capacity to sustain the psychic apparatus in moments of collapse, and in the analysts the capacity to accompany the re-symbolisation of each traumatic experience of the patient who requests it.

I close with a metaphor. Gotlieb (2021) suggests that happiness should be classified as a psychiatric disorder and included in the main diagnostic manuals under a new name – major affective disorder of the pleasurable type. A review of the relevant literature shows that happiness is statistically abnormal, consists of a discrete group of symptoms, is associated with a number of cognitive abnormalities and in all likelihood reflects irregular functioning of the central nervous system.

Is happiness a perversion? Or is it part of the law?

References

Akhtar, S. (2013). *Betrayal, Developmental Literary and Clinical Realms*. London: Karnac Books.

Alizade, M. (1996). *Clinic with Death*. Buenos Aires: Biebel.

Allouch, J. (1996). *Erotics of Mourning in the Time of Dry Death*. Buenos Aires: Eldep.

Axelrod, R. (2017). Psychodynamics of betrayal. In *The Body of Psychoanalysis and the Psychoanalysis of the Body*. Mexico: APM, pp. 75–88.

Berenstein, I. (1976). *Family and Mental Illness*. Buenos Aires: Paidós.

Berenstein, I. (1990). *Psychoanalyze a family*. Buenos Aires: Paidós.

Berenstein, I. (2001). *The Bond and the Other, Psychoanalysis: Method and Applications*. Buenos Aires: Revista de la Asociación Psicoanalitica, pp. 9–22.

Berenstein, I., & Puget, J. (1997). *Link it. Psychoanalytic Clinic and Technique*. Buenos Aires: Paidós.

Casillas, J. (2022). *The Mental Pandemic, Dangers and Consequences of an Endless Story*. Buenos Aires: Vergara.

Catz, H. (2022). *Mourning a Lost World. The Mental Pandemic, Dangers and Consequences of an Endless Story*. Buenos Aires: Vergara, pp. 49–58.

Ferenczi, S. (1912–2001). *Full Freud-Ferenczi Correspondence*. Madrid: Síntesis.

Freud, S. (1917). Lecture 26, the theory of libido and narcissism. *Obras Completas* [Complete works], Vol. 16. Buenos Aires: Amorrortu.

Freud, S. (1926). Inhibition, symptom and distress. *Obras Completas* [Complete works], Vol. 20. Buenos Aires: Amorrortu.

Freud, S. ([1929]1962). Letter to Binswanger (of 12 April 1929), in Freud, E. (Ed.), *Epistolario 1873–1939*. Madrid: Biblioteca Nueva.

Freud, S. (1937). Construcciones en análisis [Constructions under analysis]. *Obras Completas* [Complete works], Vol. 22. Buenos Aires: Amorrortu.

Gotlieb, L. (2021). *You Should Talk to Someone*. Mexico: Uranus.

Green, A. (1980). The dead mother. In *Narcissimo de vida, narcissimo de muerte* [Narcissism of life, narcissism of death]. Buenos Aires: Amorrortu, pp. 209–238.

Montagna, P. & Branco-Vicente, L. (2019). The context of socio-affective parenting. In Montagna, P. & Harris, A. (Eds), *Psychoanalysis, Law and Society*, ch. 10. London: Routledge.

Recalcati, M. (2019). *The New Melancholy. Destinies of Desire in Hypermodern Times*. Milan: Raffaello Cortina.

Roitman, A. (2002). Mourning the death of a son, Aperturas. *International Journal of Psychoanalysis*, 12.

Velasco, F. (2006). About love, the couple and its complications. In *The Lovers and Their Discontents*. Mexico: Lumen.

Index

For Product Safety Concerns and Information please contact our EU
representative GPSR@taylorandfrancis.com
Taylor & Francis Verlag GmbH, Kaufingerstraße 24, 80331 München, Germany

www.ingramcontent.com/pod-product-compliance
Lightning Source LLC
Chambersburg PA
CBHW070327270326
41926CB00017B/3786

9 7 8 1 0 4 1 0 8 6 1 3 0